C000173309

THE YOUNG NELSON
IN THE AMERICAS

by the same author

NELSON AND HIS WORLD

CHELSEA REACH
The Brutal Friendship of
Whistler and Walter Greaves

FIGHTING GENERAL
The Public & Private Campaigns
of General Sir Walter Walker

REMEMBER NELSON
The Life of Captain Sir William Hoste

Travel
LONDON WALKS

THE YOUNG NELSON
IN
THE AMERICAS

Tom Pocock

COLLINS
St James's Place, London
1980

William Collins Sons & Co Ltd
London . Glasgow . Sydney . Auckland
Toronto . Johannesburg

First published 1980
Tom Pocock 1980
ISBN 0 00 216562-7
Set in Garamond
Made and Printed in Great Britain by
William Collins Sons & Co Ltd Glasgow

For Hannah

CONTENTS

ILLUSTRATIONS

MAPS

INTRODUCTION

The canoe rounded a bend in the San Juan river and the great trees of the Nicaraguan jungle parted like curtains in a theatre to display a view that was both beautiful and dramatic. At the head of a sparkling, sun-lit reach and above the wild, white water of rapids, a black castle stood upon a green conical hill. There was something malignant about the fortress and its domination of the charming landscape; something sepulchral about its damp-darkened walls that sloped like the sacrificial pyramids of Central America.

This was almost exactly the view that Captain Horatio Nelson — and his friend Captain Edward Despard — had seen almost two centuries before, although those walls had then been white and the flag of Spain had flown from the keep. For the traveller in the canoe there was satisfaction in the thought that he was now probably the only one of Nelson's biographers to have visited all the important scenes of his subject's life and one of the very few of his countrymen to have visited what he himself remembered with horror and pride as 'St. John's castle'. It was then and there on the Rio San Juan that I determined to write this book.

Two principal aspects of Nelson emerged from the mass of unpublished manuscripts that I was to find during my subsequent research. One was that his professional worth had been fully recognised when he was a mere frigate captain of twenty-one and that this flair, displayed on the expedition into Nicaragua, came within reach of changing the history of the Americas and, perhaps, the world. The other, that his capacity for friendship, which was at the heart of his future success as a commander, emerged from his relationships with those others involved. Indeed, the complexity of his own character was reflected in the variety of his friends.

The preparation of this book involved much travel in the

Caribbean and North as well as Central America and I am indebted to many who helped with this and with documentary research. I could never have reached the castle of San Juan in 1978, when the civil war was beginning in Nicaragua, without the help and generosity of Mr. and Mrs. Kenneth Matheson of Managua, who obtained the necessary permission and organised the charter of light aircraft and canoes. On the river itself, I was told much about its ecology by Mr. Joe Almond of Tarpon Camp and, without the skill of his Nicaraguan boatmen – not least in shooting the rapids of El Castillo – I could never have followed in Nelson's wake. For making the introductions that made my expedition possible, I must thank Mr. and Mrs. John G. McCarthy, to whom students of Nelson owe so much, and Mr. K. Hamylton Jones, then H.M. Ambassador to Costa Rica.

In the Caribbean, I visited several of the islands where these events took place. In Jamaica, I was helped by Mr. Clinton V. Black, the Government Archivist, at Spanish Town; Mr. Tony Aaron, the Director of Archeology at Port Royal; Miss Hope Sealy, then of the Jamaica Government Tourist Office; and Mr. H. P. Jacobs of Kingston. In Antigua, Mr. E. C. Stevens, the Supervisor of Nelson's Dockyard, showed me English Harbour and Shirley Heights. In Nevis, thanks to introductions from Mrs Hester Marsden-Smedley, Mr. Spencer Byron of Montpelier gave me the freedom of the garden where Nelson conducted his courtship and Mr. Robert D. Abrahams of the Morning Star estate allowed me to explore his collection of Nelsoniana.

On my visit to Canada, I was given valuable guidance by Mrs. N. M. Gallimore, Librarian to the Canadian High Commission in London; and Mr. C. E. Thomas of the Public Archives in Halifax, Nova Scotia, shed new light on Nelson's adventures in Boston Bay and on his friendship with the ebullient soldier, Captain Bulkeley.

For help with long-distance air travel I am grateful to Mr. David Hunter, then of British Airways. My work as Travel Editor of the London *Evening Standard* enabled me to visit Canada and the West Indies, so taking me most of the way to Nicaragua, and, for this, I am indebted to two editors, Mr. Charles Wintour and Mr. Simon Jenkins.

In England, the full story of Nelson's American years

emerged with the help of the librarians and archivists of the Public Record Office, the British Library (including its Manuscript and Newspaper Departments), the National Maritime Museum, the National Army Museum, and the Wellcome Institute of the History of Medicine. I am particularly grateful to Mr. Keith Kissack and Mr. Andrew Helme, successive Curators of the Nelson Collection in the Monmouth Museum; Mr. A. R. B. Fuller, Librarian to St. Paul's Cathedral; Mr. H. L. Blackmore, Deputy Master of the Armouries at H.M. Tower of London; Lady Chapman, Archivist to Madame Tussaud's; Mr. Frank Sayer, the Norfolk County Archivist; Mr. William Serjeant, the Suffolk County Archivist; Miss Janet Smith of the Liverpool Record Office; Miss Nicola Fraser of the Royal Naval Museum, Portsmouth; the staff of the Bath Local Studies Library; and Major B. T. S. Clarke of the Royal Hospital, Chelsea. Mr. Hercules Ross and Mr. M. H. Despard kindly gave me access to their family papers; Dr. Gordon Ostlere (Richard Gordon) advised on tropical diseases and medicine and Mr. E. P. Thompson was a valuable guide to the radical politics of the eighteenth century.

In the search for suitable illustrations, Miss Elspeth Evans and Mr. R. J. B. Walker of the National Portrait Gallery, Mr. E. H. H. Archibald and Mr. P. T. van der Merwe of the National Maritime Museum, Mr. Hugh Leggatt of Leggatt Bros., and Mr. John Herbert of Christie's, gave useful help.

I was again lucky to have the historian's wisdom and publisher's shrewdness of Mr. Richard Ollard to guide the development of the book; and my wife, Penny, to make constructive comment upon it and compile the index.

For the spur that urged the journey into Nicaragua I must look further back to the many naval officers and historians with whom I have discussed the abiding fascination of Nelson; foremost among the latter was my father, the late Guy Pocock, from whom 'The Immortal Memory' was inherited.

Tom Pocock
Chelsea, London

PROLOGUE

On the chill and foggy night of 5th November, 1805, news reached London that was to throw Great Britain into a state of emotion that, in immediacy, intensity and composition, its people had never felt before and have not experienced since. The news, brought to Whitehall by a naval officer from the Atlantic, was of the Battle of the Trafalgar, and triumphant joy erupted with a choking grief. The price of the most decisive of victories was expressed in the heavy black type of a poster announcing simply, 'Britons! Your Nelson is dead!'

Their grief was not occasioned primarily by the poignance of the death in action of Vice-Admiral Viscount Nelson at the moment of his destruction of the combined fleets of France and Spain. It was the loss of the man himself that hurt. In a dozen years, he had emerged from the obscurity of semi-retirement in a Norfolk village to dazzle the world with a display of dash and courage as a fighting sailor and of tactical and strategic brilliance as a commander; he had also won the hearts of the nation by humanity and humour, made vivid by the public knowledge of his human weaknesses. Horatio Nelson had become not just the national hero, but everybody's friend.

Even before the British made their formal farewell at a vast and sombre funeral in St. Paul's Cathedral, their grief was being given expression in commemoration on a gigantic scale, as if the constant repetition of his name might drag the fallen hero back from the shades. First came the obituaries, the ballads and the hastily-engraved portraits and allegorical cartoons; then, the monuments — one of the earliest being in the Canadian city of Montreal — and the paintings, from miniatures to gilt-framed canvases; finally, a great out-pouring of popular art and artifact in his memory: statuettes and medallions, tankards and snuff-boxes, teapots and horse-brasses, mourning rings and door-knockers. Nelson became a place-name on new maps of the world and an inspiration to generations of writers, composers, artists, playwrights and historians. He became fixed at the forefront of his countrymen's imagination as only mythological heroes had been enshrined before.

Amongst the earliest and most popular means of maintaining what the Royal Navy has ever since called, without further explanation being necessary, 'The Immortal Memory,' was a visit to Madame Tussaud's celebrated collection of waxwork figures, 'modelled from life.' Her touring exhibition – 'The Grand European Cabinet of Figures' – displayed the images of King George III and Queen Charlotte, their former enemies, Napoleon Bonaparte and George Washington, and a rogues' gallery of the most blood-stained leaders of the French Revolution. But there were two names – one at the top of the exhibition's advertising poster, one at the bottom – that attracted the most immediate attention because, not only had their two lives ended in circumstances as different as could be imagined, but, it was known, the two had formerly been friends. The names of the wax figures were Admiral Lord Nelson and Colonel Despard.

Perhaps a few middle-aged or elderly men who had known both in the days of their friendship, a quarter of a century before, would muse on the chance, fate, or ambition that caused them to share such success but follow such divergent paths. Perhaps, they remembered, too, the risks and rewards of those past years and what life in the Americas could give and what it could take away.

CHAPTER ONE

Theatre of Action

American waters made Horatio Nelson the man he became. There he learned to handle, navigate and command a ship; to fight a battle; to lead men and love women; to gamble for the highest prizes of fame and fortune with his own future as the stake. From the Gulf of St. Lawrence to the Bay of Honduras, the fogs of Boston Bay to the heat haze of the Mosquito Shore, from New York to Port Royal he was to face the dangers of the sea and the violence of the enemy.

These American waters between the Arctic Circle and the Equator were to dominate the first thirty years of his life. Even in early childhood there was an awareness that the cold, grey North Sea that broke on Norfolk sands near his home in the isolated village of Burnham Thorpe, was the same salt water that, warm and brilliant, was called the Caribbean. In 1759, a year after his birth, his maternal uncle, Maurice Suckling, a captain in the Royal Navy, had fought a gallant action against the French in those waters and its anniversary, 21st October, was remembered with an annual celebration by the Nelson family. It was that same sea that the young Horatio Nelson was to call, from his own experience, 'The Grand Theatre of Actions.'

Himself the son of a gentle, scholarly parson, young Horatio admired this uncle extravagantly, as brave, intelligent and urbane; akin to those flattering portraits of famous naval officers posed before heavy velvet curtains slightly parted to reveal a distant battle scene. From his early boyhood there was a longing to part them further and take part in the fiery actions

[17]

beyond. So when the captain's sister, Catherine Nelson, died, leaving her husband, Edmund, to bring up eight children on his modest stipend, the hero-worship and day-dreaming were turned to practical account in the enthusiasm with which Horatio sought to emulate his uncle and go to sea at the age of twelve. Any doubts his father may have had about delivering the child into the rough embrace of the Royal Navy were lessened by the knowledge that he would be going on board his brother-in-law's own ship.

From the day Horatio joined the *Raisonable* – a third-rate captured from the French – at Sheerness in March, 1771, Maurice Suckling guided his development with a deft hand. It was peacetime, but the captain saw to it that his nephew's early years were filled with interest and experience. When he took the boy with him to the *Triumph*, then moored as a guardship in the Thames, he arranged for him to make a voyage to the West Indies in a merchant ship commanded by a friend. During the months that followed he not only saw the great parade of green islands curving from the Florida keys to Venezuela but got to know the ordinary sailor, an understanding that was to prove as valuable to him as any.

Back in the *Triumph*, the fourteen-year-old midshipman was put to boatwork, sailing up the Thames to London and coming to consider himself a skilled pilot among shoals, sandbanks and swift tidal currents such as he remembered in the creek at Burnham Overy Staithe, the little seaport a mile or so from his Norfolk home. Then, hearing that the Royal Society was fitting out a scientific expedition to be carried to the Arctic in two warships, the boy found that his uncle could have the age limit waived in his case and arrange for him to join one of them, the *Carcass*, a heavily-built bomb-vessel chosen for the task because her hull should be able to withstand collision and crushing in polar ice.

Scientifically, the expedition of 1773 was a failure and the two ships narrowly escaped being trapped in the ice, but, for the boy, it was a magical experience. He returned with memories of hardship and some danger, of a strange white and ice-blue world lit by a pale sun at midnight, in extraordinary contrast to the vivid colours of the Caribbean he had left a few months before.

Now, it seemed to Captain Suckling, it was time for something even more demanding: experience of life at sea in a 'taut ship', an operational frigate commanded by a disciplinarian. This was to be the *Seahorse*, of twenty-guns, bound for the Indian Ocean and the Bay of Bengal. Now he faced what was for many young officers of gentle upbringing, like himself the normal realities of life in a King's ship. On an average of three times a week, he had to attend the brief and savage ceremony of a flogging and, for the first time, heard guns fired in anger when the *Seahorse* attacked and took an armed vessel belonging to Hyder Ali, the Francophile Indian potentate whose ambitions in Mysore had become troublesome to the East India Company.

He also had to face the realities of disease which swept away far more young officers and men than did enemy shot. At seventeen, Horatio was short but sturdy and his countryman's constitution, tempered by active years at sea, probably saved his life when he was struck down by malaria, the 'ague', or 'intermittent fever', that was then beyond medical understanding and often fatal. He was shipped home in another frigate, the *Dolphin*, 'almost a skeleton' and not expected to survive the voyage.

He grew as emotionally depressed as he was physically weak, doubting even his uncle's bounty. Then came a sudden upsurge of delirious optimism which seemed to focus on 'a radiant orb'. He later described how 'a sudden glow of patriotism kindled within me, and presented my King and Country as my patron. My mind exulted in the idea. "Well, then," I exclaimed, "I will be a hero, and confiding in Providence, I will brave every danger." This confidence stayed with him, but the help of his uncle proved to be of even greater value than hitherto when the *Dolphin* reached England in September, 1776.

Captain Suckling had always been an officer of influence through being distantly related to the politically-powerful Walpole family in Norfolk as the great-nephew of Sir Robert Walpole, who had been Prime Minister for more than two decades earlier in the century. During Nelson's absence he had

[19]

been appointed Comptroller of the Navy, the senior of the four administrative officers making up the Navy Board, and he was now preparing to become Member of Parliament for Portsmouth. To his nephew, he had long been admired as the beau ideal of the naval officer so, with his elevation to the Admiralty, sophistication was added to this. The youth was particularly impressed by his ownership of a smart town house in Mayfair, as well as a country seat in Norfolk, and this became part of his own ambition.

On his return, Horatio was sufficiently recovered to take advantage of the increased power of this patronage, joining the third-rate *Worcester* as an acting-lieutenant. The ship was engaged in escorting convoys between the Channel and Gibraltar, necessitated by another great change that had taken place during Nelson's absence and which would continue to mount in scale and intensity.

While he had been away, the most shocking of all conflicts had broken out; for the armed revolt of the American colonists amounted, in the context of an expanding British empire, to civil war.

The increasing independence of the colonial Americans and their growing estrangement from the Crown and rule from London had come to a head in the spring of the preceding year with armed clashes between local militia and the British Army. In June, George Washington had been appointed Commander-in-Chief of the gathering rebel forces and, despite a British victory at Bunker's Hill near Boston that same month, the conflict rapidly hardened into full-scale war. By the summer of 1776, both sides could claim successes, the British having been forced to evacuate Boston and the Americans driven from Canada, but aid was now beginning to reach the rebels from France. It seemed that the insurrection might evolve into something far more dangerous.

When on 4th July of that year, the rebels published their Declaration of Independence attitudes were sharply divided. In Norfolk, for example, there was much sympathy for the insurgents, led by the Whig landowners, among them the Nelsons' neighbour Thomas Coke, the great agriculturalist, who drank to the health of George Washington each evening as 'the greatest man on earth'. The Nelsons, on the other hand, were Tories and so supported the suppression of the revolt, Horatio himself considering the rebels traitors to the King he now regarded as his personal patron.

With the possibility that a domestic conflict might develop into international war, Nelson's newly-found self-confidence was timely. Convoy duty in the Bay of Biscay, where the weather seemed continually rough, was arduous but he took pride in his efficiency as a watch-keeping officer, claiming that his captain used to say that 'he felt as easy when I was upon deck, as any officer in the ship.'

The following year, he was to take his examination for promotion to lieutenant and, on 9th April, 1777, he presented himself at the Admiralty in London, bringing with him a certificate claiming that he was over the age of twenty, although he was not yet nineteen. The chairman of the interviewing board was the Comptroller himself but he made elaborate play with a pretence of not knowing his nephew, although it is unlikely that many of those present were deceived. The young man having been accepted for promotion, Captain Suckling proudly announced their relationship, saying that he had not wanted the youngster to be favoured.

Nelson gave the news to his brother William, an under-graduate at Cambridge, with a touch of the whimsical humour they had from their father, writing, 'I passed my Degree as Master of Arts on the 9th instant.' Next day, he was appointed second lieutenant of the frigate *Lowestoft*, of thirty-two guns, commanded by Captain William Locker, and now fitting out at Sheerness for service on the Jamaica station.

Of all the professional introductions affected by Captain Suckling none was to be more rewarding than this. For William Locker was far more than a fine seaman and a seasoned veteran of the Seven Years War, who had served under the great Admiral Hawke. He was a man of education as well as action; a tactician as well as sea-dog; a son of the middle class, motivated by professional ambition and patriotism as well as prize-money.

Now aged thirty-six, Locker was a strongly-built man with a slight limp from an old wound suffered when boarding a French privateer in the Mediterranean. He had a wide, generous face – accentuated by thinning hair – and shrewd, humorous eyes. The liking between captain and lieutenant was immediate and, before the summer was out, the latter was writing a letter to the former, not as 'Dear Sir', but 'My most worthy friend.' It was Locker who urged Nelson to visit the London studio of the painter John Rigaud, a Royal Academician, to have his portrait painted.

Nelson had come up the river with a party from his ship's company that was to be quartered near the Tower of London on impressment duty, manning a rendezvous – probably a tavern – where volunteers could enlist, convicted prisoners, who had opted for sea-service instead of prison, to be collected and from which the press gang could raid the waterfront to round up unwilling recruits. It was unpleasant duty and, as a result of cold nocturnal forays through the damp alleys along the Thames, he suffered a recurrence of malaria and returned to his ship, leaving Rigaud's canvas unfinished.

Yet the portrait that the artist had to put aside, in the hope that his sitter might eventually return, already showed a remarkable young man. It was of three-quarter length, so flattering the slight figure that stood short of five and a half feet; the face was sensitive yet resolute; the blue uniform coat, clean but worn with negligence – a lapel hanging across the white waistcoat – in a manner that was to seem characteristic to his friends.

The expression and the stance in the portrait seemed to show a young officer able to command obedience and to show kindness. Indeed, a story illustrating both generosity and a sense of duty may well come from this time.

He was spending an evening, it is said, with the family of a hosier and, as he usually spent his time in London either at Captain Suckling's house near Hyde Park, or with another uncle in Kentish Town, it is possible that this was a few hours' relaxation from impressment duty in the City. While there, his host entered laughing from the street to tell of a practical joke he had just seen played. A market-woman had, he said, set up her apple stall beside the roadway and a passer-by had, while pretending to admire the fruit, tied one end of a cord to a leg of the stall and the other to the back of a halted hackney carriage.

Then the coach had moved away, the stall had collapsed and the fruit had cascaded into the mud. At the recollection of it, the hosier laughed immoderately.

But his guest did not join the general laughter. Instead, he at once left the house and walked down the street until he found the victim of the prank collecting her muddy apples and pressed some money into her hand.

On the last day of April, the *Lowestoft* sailed and, for the first time, Nelson found himself on active war service. The long peace which, however uneasy, had lasted since the Treaty of Paris had closed the Seven Years War in 1763, seemed to have ended, although the formalities of a declaration of war were yet to be made. The fighting in America had increased in scale and almost one-third of the fighting strength of the Royal Navy was now based on New York under the command of Vice-Admiral Lord Howe. There was, as yet, no rebel navy to fight on the seas but there had been a hard-fought contest between rival squadrons during the preceeding year on Lake Champlain, which commanded the waterway between the St. Lawrence valley and that of the Hudson river. The British were also conducting amphibious operations on a large scale in the disposing of their land forces. But American privateers were already a problem, ranging far beyond their own coastal waters and reaching the vulnerable Caribbean islands.

While this was enough to keep ships of the Royal Navy alert on both sides of the Atlantic, the most ominous threat came from France, which had declared its support for the rebels. So the convoy system had been introduced and one such collection of merchant ships was to be shepherded across the Atlantic by the *Lowestoft*.

It first made for Madeira and arrived in Carlisle Bay, Barbados, on 3rd July. Then the frigate sailed north, past the French islands of St. Lucia and Martinique, then Antigua, where the Royal Navy could shelter in English Harbour to cover the long spread of the Leeward Islands. Now she steered westward, passing the peaks of Hispaniola, and, on the 19th, sighted on the western horizon the shadowy shape that might have been cloud but slowly resolved into the green hills of Jamaica.

Morant Point, the westerly headland, was passed and the hills behind heaved higher into the lilac-shadowed ridges of the Blue Mountains to the north of Kingston Bay. Sailing along the nine miles of the Palisadoes spit that linked them with Port Royal, the *Lowestoft* brought to and awaited the pilot-boat. A thicket of masts and yards stood above the distant dockyard and amongst them could be distinguished the white flag of Vice-Admiral Clark Gayton. So, as the ship glided through the narrows, the reports of her thirteen-gun salute thumped and echoed against the steep slopes of the Hellshire Hills. The batteries of Fort Charles slid by to starboard and, to port, the hill-top platform that had been named Rodney's Lookout after one of Admiral Gayton's recent predecessors. As they swung round Gallows Point, a magnificent panorama spread before them.

Sheltered by the long arm of the Palisadoes lay a natural harbour in which every ship of the Royal Navy could have anchored with room to spare. At the landward end of the spit, could be seen two forts, Castile and Rock Fort, steep hills rising behind them, the sun-scorched foothills of the Blue Mountains. Westward, a green, wooded plain stretched from the waterfront to these heights and there lay the town of Kingston. Behind the jumble of jetties, wharves, warehouses and moored ships, straight streets ran inland, crossing others at right angles, to the white spire of the parish church in the town's centre.

Kingston was the commercial capital of Jamaica; the political capital, Spanish Town, where the Governor had his seat and where the Assembly met, lay fourteen miles to the north-west in lovely, rolling country that would have delighted the eye of an English landscape-painter. On a fine day such as this, it was a scene of pastoral tranquillity as conjured up by such toasts as were proposed at dinner parties, like 'Success to Trade' and 'Peace and Plenty.'

Above the trees rose an occasional plume of smoke from sugar-mills to remind that this was the most important of the 'sugar islands' upon which the British felt their prosperity depended. This was an exaggeration, but then everything about Jamaica lent itself to high-flown hopes, fears and excitement. It was a tropical island where fortunes could be founded, as was to

[24]

be seen by the extravagance of sugar-planters returning to England to take the medicinal waters of Bath, and by the ostentation of the mansions they built there when they retired. Yet it was also a paradise cursed by mysterious and lethal diseases that seemed to delight in fastening upon the young and the strong.

On passage to Jamaica, the officers of the *Lowestoft* probably raised their glasses in the traditional naval toast to, 'A sickly season and a bloody war' that would offer rapid promotion. It was now the relatively healthy dry season between the rains of May and June and those of September and October. But when the hurricanes of August swept in the rain clouds from the Atlantic, they would notice that along the sand and shingle of the Palisadoes yellow flowers would begin to bloom and might hear that these were known to the local people as 'Kill Bakra' – *bakra* being their word for European. The sickly season would have begun.

It would then be the white-skinned people who would sicken and die, particularly the men and especially the newly-arrived. But the bulk of the population would be immune to the worst of the fevers for they came from stock bred in the tropics. They were the slaves upon whose labour the prosperity of the 'sugar islands' depended. Jamaica, an oval island of thickly wooded hills about one hundred and fifty miles long by fifty miles wide, had a population of nearly a quarter of a million. But, of these, some two hundred thousand were Negro slaves shipped from Africa, or descended from those imported during the past century and more. About thirteen thousand were of European stock, varying in social status from prosperous planters owning vast sugar estates, their overseers and clerks, merchants and shopkeepers, soldiers and sailors down to the 'poor whites'. These included 'indentured servants', often Irish, who worked under long-term contracts that had earned them a single payment when originally signed. In addition there was a like number of mulattoes, creoles and quadroons of mixed racial ancestry – usually the descendants of slaves and slave-masters – and free Negro slaves. Seldom can a society have been so stratified and divided.

There was, in consequence, a constant fear of rebellion. In

recent years there had been several insurrections, including an attempt, just forestalled, to burn Kingston. These were attended by atrocities: the rebels, having the advantage of surprise, slaughtering European families with enraged savagery; then the avenging white men putting down the revolt with torture and executions in the hope of discouraging another.

But now the fear of slave rebellion was combined with that of invasion by rival European empires. France was openly supporting the rebels in thirteen colonies in North America and French privateers, flying the rebels' flag, were already preying upon British shipping in the Caribbean. Where France led, Spain might follow to shore up its over-stretched empire on mainland America, the 'Spanish Main'. When this took place, bloody war and sickly season would combine to give surviving naval officers all the chances of quick promotion they could want.

The realities of life, and death, in Jamaica became apparent to Nelson and his brother-officers during the following three weeks when their ship lay at Port Royal preparing for her first operational cruise. The rich planters ashore were known for their hospitality and the lavish dinner parties and routs at their great plantation houses and there was never lack of invitations for naval officers. But on such excursions a disturbing factor in the current crisis would have become apparent to new arrivals from England, who looked upon the American rebels as traitors. This was that there was so much sympathy for the rebels among the Jamaican planters that, but for the presence of British ships and battalions, they might well give them open support.

This added tension to the frequent divergence of interests and attitudes between the planters and merchants, whose capital was Kingston, and the Governor, representing the King at Spanish Town. It was Nelson's good fortune to meet in these early days a Jamaican of high standing, who was able to keep a foot in both camps, commanding respect in each. It was Captain Locker who introduced Nelson to Hercules Ross, whose great house and sugar-mills – or 'pen' – he was often to visit. Ross was what his contemporaries would describe as 'a man of bottom', as successful socially as commercially and taking as much delight in dinner-table conversation as in field-sports. His

[26]

company was particularly interesting to naval officers, for, as well as being involved in the raising and training of the militia in the island, he owned and operated a small squadron of privateers against the King's enemies at sea.

When the time came for the *Lowestoft* to sail, during the second week in August, and face the first storms of the hurricane season as well as the American – and, possibly, French – enemy, her captain had to be left ashore. Locker suffered recurrent bouts of malaria and this one aroused fears for his life.

On her first cruise the *Lowestoft* captured a small American merchantman with a cargo of rice. For her second, Locker was well enough to resume command. She sailed from Port Royal on 6th November and, before the end of the month, had taken another prize in an encounter which gave Nelson the satisfaction of showing off his zeal under his captain's approving eye.

An American ship had been chased and stopped in heavy seas and Locker had ordered his first lieutenant to board her. This officer at once disappeared to his cabin on the excuse of having mislaid his sword. The frigate's boat had already been launched and was being thrown about so violently that there was danger of her being swamped, or stove in against the ship's side. Also, the American seemed to be in danger of foundering.

At the first lieutenant's prolonged delay below, Locker, bracing himself on the heaving quarterdeck, became increasingly impatient, finally shouting, 'Have I no officer in the ship who can board the prize?' Nelson hesitated in his anxiety not to offend the first lieutenant, but, hearing the master – the ship's non-commissioned navigating officer – volunteer, he reached the ship's side first and jumped into the plunging boat alongside, calling out to him, 'It's my turn now and, if I come back, it's yours!'

Pulling across to the American, Nelson found her waterlogged after shipping so many green seas during her flight from the *Lowestoft*. As she wallowed into a trough, the approaching boat was lifted by a crest and swept over her gunwale on to her deck for a moment before being lifted off again as the ship took another sea. Finally, Nelson scrambled aboard and signalled to Locker that the prize was his. But the danger was not over and, as the ship disappeared from view beneath towering crests, or in flurries of gale-blown spray, she was more than once given up for lost.

The storm abated and, for the second time, the frigate returned to Port Royal with the prospect of prize-money. Such chases became routine, day or night, and a typtical entry in Locker's log was that for a Saturday night and Sunday morning in January of 1778.

'Fresh breezes and fair,' he noted. 'At 10 p.m. saw two sail to windward and gave chase. Fired one 12 pdr. shotted at Ditto, she returning the same. Fired two 12 pdrs. with round and grape shot with a volley of small arms, upon which they brought to and proved to be from Philadelphia bound to Jamaica, three weeks out. At 9 a.m., tacked ship. Punished Thomas Dodd with one dozen lashes for Neglect of Duty. At 12 performed Divine Service.'

Such a prize was likely to lead to complications and claims for prize money might take months, or years, to progress through the prize-court. This ship claimed to come from Philadelphia, which the British had occupied nearly four months before, and might well be carrying a legitimate cargo. But Jamaican merchants were known to be trying to continue their profitable trading with the rebellious colonies, so was it possible that the ship's papers had been falsified and her cargo thus contraband?

During their third cruise, which was mostly in the open seas between Hispaniola and the Bahamas, Locker took as prize a schooner that he decided would make a useful cruising consort for his ship. He named her after his six-year-old daughter, the *Little Lucy*, and gave her command to Lieutenant Nelson, who had become increasingly restive, so that, as he put it, 'even a frigate was not sufficiently active for my mind.'

This was his first command that was more than a ship's boat and he revelled in the new-found independence. When the *Lowestoft* returned to Port Royal to have her bottom sheathed with copper for protection against the wood-boring teredo worm, barnacles and weed that proliferated in these warm waters, the *Little Lucy* remained at sea. Her cruising-ground was mostly among the islands along the north coast of Hispaniola and Nelson noted that he made himself 'a complete pilot' of those waters with the same satisfaction he had shown in his mastery of the Thames.

On 9th February, he made his first capture as captain of his own ship, reporting this to Locker by letter on the same day, 'I am happy of having an opportunity of writing by Mr. Ellis, who comes down in the *Abigail* schooner from François bound to Nantucket. We took her this morning at four o'clock, after a chase of eight hours.' Nelson, like most British naval officers, regarded the insurgent colonists as enemies, but, when he came to meet them, his manner was courteous, as when he asked this prisoner to be kind enough to take his letter, instead of giving it to a member of his own prize-crew.

This was due in part to self-confidence. There was no doubt among British naval officers but that the Royal Navy's command of American waters would enable it to impose a blockade and transport armies at will, so eventually bringing about the collapse of the rebellion. Yet, three days before the capture of the *Abigail*, the next step towards a major international conflict had been taken by France.

This move had been prompted by the bungling of land operations in America by an over-confident British command. General Burgoyne, having initially scattered the rebels before him, was advancing south from Lake Champlain to the Hudson river and New York, when he found his force of some three thousand men, surrounded by three times that number of rebels and running short of supplies. A relieving force from New York, led by General Clinton, had been unable to reach him and, on 17th October, 1777, he had surrendered. Encouraged by this, the French government increased its support for the rebels and, on 6th February, signed a treaty of trade and friendship with them.

But the French felt able to delay open hostilities until the summer because their fleet, which was almost equal to the British in numbers, was not yet ready for sea. Yet the lengths to which they were already prepared to go became apparent to Nelson when, on 6th May, he took the *Little Lucy* out of Port Royal in the wake of the *Lowestoft* on another cruise.

On the 27th, when their ships were still in company, they

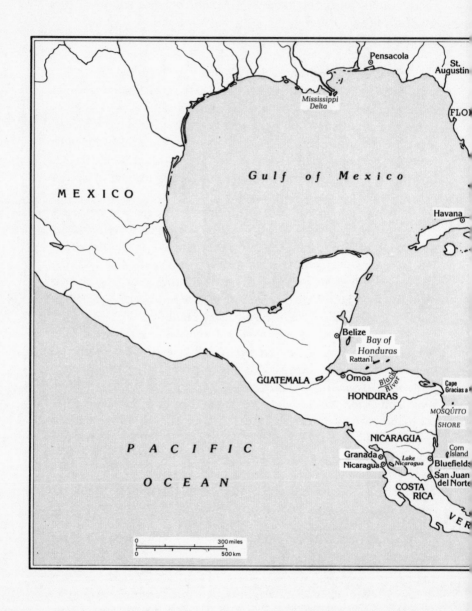

Pensacola

St.
Augustin

Mississippi
Delta

FLO

Gulf of Mexico

MEXICO

Havana

Belize
Bay of
Honduras
Rattan I.

GUATEMALA
Omoa
Black
River
HONDURAS

Cape
Gracias a

MOSQUITO

SHORE

NICARAGUA

Corn
Island

Granada
Lake
Nicaragua
Nicaragua

Bluefields

PACIFIC

San Juan
del Norte

OCEAN

COSTA
RICA

VER

| 0 | | | 300 miles |
| 0 | | | 500 km |

CENTRAL AMERICA

B A H A M A   I S L A N D S

A T L A N T I C

O C E A N

B A

tego Bay

Windward Passage

HISPANIOLA

S. DOMINGO

PORTO RICO

AMAICA   Kingston

St. Kitts
Nevis
Monserrat

Antigua
Guadeloupe

Leeward Is.

Dominica

Martinique

St. Lucia

C A R I B B E A N   S E A

St. Vincent
Windward Is.

Grenada

Barbados

Tobago

Trinidad

Curacoa

Cartagena

NEW
GRANADA

V E N E Z U E L A

R. Orinoco

DARIEN
Panama

sighted two strange sail in the Windward Passage between Cuba and Hispaniola. These proved to be an American schooner escorted by a French frigate, the *Inconstant*, commanded by the Chevalier de Cuverville. Determined to board and search the schooner, Nelson stood ahead of Locker and was almost alongside the American, which was lying under the muzzles of the *Inconstant*'s guns. As he was about to board, musket fire crackled from the frigate's upper deck and Locker, watching anxiously, at once made the signal for Nelson to haul away and come under his own stern.

To have hesitated would have been fatal, as the French might next have fired grape-shot. So, having retreated out of range, Nelson hoisted out his boat and was pulled across to the *Lowestoft*. Locker he found still determined to examine the schooner, whatever the outcome. So he suggested that, as a duel between the British and French frigates seemed unavoidable, he should bring the *Little Lucy*'s crew on board to help fight the ship. But de Cuverville had no wish to become involved in open warfare and, seeing the British frigate preparing for action, allowed his bluff to be called. The schooner was duly searched, found to be ostensibly of French ownership and allowed to proceed.

During June, Nelson resumed his former duties in the *Lowestoft* as Locker was again sickening and it seemed probable that he would have to give up his command. But before the captain went ashore at Port Royal and resigned himself to being invalided home, he had a last service to perform for his ambitious lieutenant.

In March, Admiral Gayton had been succeeded as Commander-in-Chief on the Jamaica Station by Rear-Admiral Sir Peter Parker, who had come down from North American waters. Like Locker, he had fought in the Seven Years War. For the past two years, he had been fighting the Americans, learning a bloody lesson when his ship, the fifty-gun *Bristol*, joined the disastrous attempt to force the entrance to Charleston harbour in South Carolina. Unpredicted tidal currents thwarted the attacking squadron, three of which ran aground. The two surviving fourth-rates, one of them the *Bristol*, finally hauled away after engaging shore batteries for ten hours and losing nearly two hundred men killed and wounded.

Subsequently, Parker had served under Howe at New York, and taken part in the capture of Long Island. He had then sailed north for the landing on Rhode Island, that commanded the magnificent natural harbour of Narragansett Bay, and remained there for several months as senior naval officer. Tough and opinionated, he came from a naval family that had little to learn of the ways and means of promotion through patronage. So, when his old friend Captain Locker recommended a Lieutenant Nelson to his attention he was well aware that he was a nephew of the Comptroller of the Navy and what the eventual rewards of a little generosity might be.

At the end of June, Nelson was appointed third lieutenant of the flagship. Sir Peter was pleased to find that the well-connected young officer was also able and, by September, when the flagship led the squadron on an offensive sweep past Cap François, had promoted him first lieutenant. Whatever part the power of distant patronage played in this promotion, there was a touch of irony to the sad news that reached the squadron when it returned to Port Royal at the end of October. Captain Maurice Suckling had died in July, but his patronage had now been resurrected in the Commander-in-Chief of the Jamaica Station. For Nelson himself there was a sentimental coincidence, for the cruise, on which the squadron had just taken seventeen prizes, had been across the very stretch of water where his uncle had fought the action that his family still remembered with such pride.

The prizes had been French ships bound to or from Hispaniola because, on 10th July, the French, confident that their fleet was ready for sea and battle, made the formal declaration of war. Indeed, their ships were already at war stations, the Toulon fleet of a dozen sail of the line under the Comte d'Estaing having crossed the Atlantic and started cruising in American waters before the declaration, arriving off New York twelve days after it.

This was disastrous for the British. Committed to supply and support their armies in North America, the Royal Navy had also to defend their possessions in the Caribbean and their trade with India and the Far East. There was also the hitherto

[33]

unthinkable possibility of an invasion of the British Isles once the heavy squadrons were far distant.

With France at war, it was probable that Spain would follow, if only to wrest Gibraltar from the British, and then, possibly, the Dutch. There was no European ally to whom the British could look and there was even a strong body of opinion amongst themselves that openly sympathised with the American rebels. Just as disheartening was the failure of British counter-measures to contain the rampaging French squadrons. Bad weather thwarted Howe's attempts to bring d'Estaing to battle off Rhode Island and scattered Admiral Byron's fleet that had pursued him from Europe, while Admiral Keppel had failed to force a decisive engagement when he intercepted the Comte d'Orvilliers on a sortie from Brest.

Having shaken off Howe and Byron, d'Estaing steered south to the Caribbean, avoiding Parker's squadron and reaching the Leeward Islands. There he took the British island of Dominica without difficulty, so starting a sequence of raids and counter-raids as one side or the other was able to concentrate a preponderence of naval power.

Just as the British took their turn early in December, when Rear-Admiral Samuel Barrington captured the French island of St Lucia with his Leeward Islands squadron, Nelson was promoted commander and left the flagship to become captain of the brig *Badger*.

His departure from the *Bristol* was marked by a pleasant coincidence. Five years before, he had briefly met a midshipman aged twenty-five; ten years his senior. A worthy but undistinguished family in Newcastle-upon-Tyne had been unable to find any patronage for Cuthbert Collingwood. He had become an accomplished seaman, but lack of humour and a tendency to worry over decisions, had not attracted a senior officer's attention sufficiently to win him promotion. But eventually this had happened when, at the engagement with the rebels on Bunker's Hill, Midshipman Collingwood had been in charge of a party of seamen carrying ammunition up to the troops. He had behaved with calmness and courage and, in reward, was promoted to acting-lieutenant on the battlefield, this being confirmed by the Admiralty in due course.

Even so, lack of patronage continued to plague him and a long spell in an unhappy ship under a tyrannical captain finally ended with his appointment as second lieutenant of the *Lowestoft* in succession to Lieutenant Nelson. At their second meeting the two men – so different in looks and temperament: the one tall and morose, the other slight and vivid – had liked one another. So it was particularly agreeable that, when the younger, more successful man left the flagship, he should again be succeeded by the older, but junior, lieutenant. An abiding friendship had begun between opposites, each complementing the other and noting the differences in each other's behaviour and attitudes with affectionate humour.

As commander – or junior and unconfirmed captain in command of a small ship – Nelson joined the *Badger* on the last day of 1778. His task was, in addition to the hunting of privateers and taking of prizes, to watch for Spanish moves in the waters between Jamaica and Central America and along the coast known as the Mosquito Shore. This was the eastern seaboard that linked Mexico with South America – including the Spanish colonial provinces of Guatemala, Honduras, Nicaragua, Costa Rica and Veragua – and had been named after the Mosquito Indians who lived in its coastal villages. Although under Spanish rule, settlements of British planters and wood-cutters had been tolerated in the Bay of Honduras – particularly at the mouth of the Black River (the Rio Negro), and relations between them and their Spanish neighbours were taken as a barometer of those between their respective governments.

Nelson cruised on this coast and visited the nearby island of Rattan and Omoa, paying calls on the British settlements there. Ostensibly under the control of a Superintendent-General, appointed by the Governor of Jamaica, the settlers – many of them Scottish – were not, in practice, subject to the laws of Britain or Spain, except on the rare occasions when the government in London ordered a brief tightening of the reins. They were notoriously unruly, even under so light a governing hand, but had a tendency to make much of any visitor of importance on the chance that he might further their interests.

So it was with Nelson. Having been sent 'to protect the

Mosquito Shore and the Bay of Honduras from the depredations of the American privateers' he reported that he had 'gained so much the affections of the settlers that they unanimously voted me their thanks and expressed their regret on leaving them.' In return they asked him to stress their vulnerability in the event of war with Spain when he reported to Admiral Parker. This seemed a natural request but, behind it, lay their hopes that the arrival of British troops on the Spanish Main might lead to the annexation of territory and their transformation from settlers to colonists.

Otherwise his cruises were uneventful, enlivened by the stopping and searching of ships and the taking of an eighty-ton French coaster, *La Prudente*, which he identified as such only after a search of two days for her papers that were eventually found hidden in an old shoe. The one major excitement came towards the end of his last cruise in the *Badger* when, on 1st June, he entered the anchorage in Montego Bay on the north-west coast of Jamaica. He noted in his log, 'At ½ past 3 p.m. came in a sail of the London Fleet under convoy of H.M.S. *Glasgow*, which anchored at about the same time. At 6 p.m., saw the Alarm of Fire on board the *Glasgow*. Sent out boats and the boats belonging to the merchantmen with bucketts and men to their assistance.'

To Locker he described the scene in a letter: 'It was a most shocking sight; and had it happened half an hour later, in all probability a great many people would have been lost. She anchored at half-past three; and at six she was in flames, owing to the steward's attempt to steal rum out of the after-hold.' The thief had been breaking open the hatch by the light of a naked flame.

As Nelson's boats pulled over to the blazing frigate, he shouted to those of her crew who had not already jumped over her side to throw as much gunpowder as possible into the sea and, as some of her guns were loaded, to train them to their maximum elevation so that, when the flames exploded their charges, the shot would be less likely to damage other ships in the bay. The survivors were hauled into the boats and brought across to the *Badger*; thanks to Nelson's prompt action only one life was lost when the *Glasgow*'s master died from burns the following morning. After burning for more than two hours, the ship was cut adrift, towed out to sea and abandoned, blazing in the night. She blew up at midnight.

The *Badger* then sailed round the island to Kingston Bay to join the dozen ships of Parker's squadron off Port Royal. It was then that he learned of his promotion to post-captain and of his appointment to command the frigate *Hinchinbroke*. His last formal act on board the brig on Sunday, 20th June, was to make a final entry in her log to record another pleasant coincidence: 'at noon Cuthbert Collingwood Esq. superseded me in command. Horatio Nelson.'

Now his future was secure. If he kept his health and committed no serious breach of discipline, his promotion would be automatic and his place in the hierarchy inviolable until he became an admiral.

But the *Hinchinbroke* was still at sea and so long overdue that there were fears she might have been taken by the French, of whom wild and contradictory reports kept reaching Jamaica. When reliable news of the war – but not of the frigate – did arrive, it was as sombre as could have been expected. On 18th June, d'Estaing had taken the island of St. Vincent; then Grenada at the beginning of July. On 16th June, Spain had at last declared war on Britain, which now faced both her most formidable rivals and the American rebels without a single European ally. Would it be Jamaica's turn next?

While awaiting news of d'Estaing's next move and of his own ship, Nelson stayed at Port Royal, his admiral's anxiety for the *Hinchinbroke* reaching the point where he considered sending him out in the *Lowestoft* to search for her. Meanwhile the impatient captain lived in an officers' mess ashore, where he made friends with a jolly, red-faced captain of thirty-six, the Honourable William Cornwallis, son of Earl Cornwallis and known to his sailors as 'Billy Blue.' Like Locker, who had sailed for England, Cornwallis liked to pronounce little maxims for the ambitious naval officer, such as 'You can always beat a Frenchman if you fight him long enough', and 'The difficulty of getting at them is sometimes more fancy than fact.'

There was no lack of hospitality, particularly since Captain Nelson was on the Governor's guest-list at the King's House in

Spanish Town. A regular feature of official entertaining there was the inviting of groups of naval officers from newly-arrived ships at Port Royal to dinner parties, or even to a formal breakfast, and during the social seasons to dance in the galleried ballroom. Nelson had presumably been invited to the King's House when first lieutenant of the flagship, if not before, but now he had more time to get to know his host, Major-General John Dalling, Governor of Jamaica.

For the first time he was moving in the world of politics and mixing with men whose decisions commanded obedience even from god-like admirals. John Dalling, now aged forty-eight, was a handsome, soldierly man running to fat through lack of exercise due to lameness from gout and an old wound in the foot, suffered when fighting the French at Quebec. But when he entertained in his new residence across the piazza from the Assembly building in Spanish Town, he was a kindly, ebullient host, who enjoyed the company of intelligent young officers.

To talk with a man who had fought at Louisbourg and scaled the Heights of Abraham to command the light infantry at Quebec, when he himself had been only one year old, was enthralling enough. But to meet a friend of General Wolfe's, whom he had long admired as a brilliantly unconventional soldier, was a rare experience.

Nelson and Dalling were both enthusiasts, delighting in ideas and action. There was also a particular bond between them in the discovery that they were both East Anglians. Dalling came from Bungay in north Suffolk a few miles from the home of Nelson's late uncle at Woodton in south Norfolk. There was also the more subtle bond in that, while both men were connected with the landowning aristrocracy their own status was middle-class, this proving a spur to ambition. For Nelson, the contrast between the mansions of his distant cousins, the Walpoles, and his father's parsonage was piquant, particularly so when one of his brothers, Suckling, was keeping the village shop at nearby North Elmham and a sister, Susannah, working as a milliner's shop assistant in Bath.

Dalling was also related to the East Anglian gentry through his mother, who belonged to the Windham family, neighbours of the Walpoles. She had married the middle-class John Dalling of Bungay in Suffolk but, on her death in 1738, her son had been cared for by her father, Colonel William Windham, who was comptroller of the Duke of Cumberland's household. So maternal relationships helped his career, too; the Duke arranging a commission in the Army for the boy and taking him as a junior aide-de-camp on his campaign against the Scottish rebels in 1745.

As a loyal 'Williamite' – the so-named Duke now being Commander-in-Chief of the British Army – young Dalling's prospects were limitless. Posted to North America early in the Seven Years War, he fought under Wolfe at Quebec and accompanied his regiment to Jamaica, where he was given the command of Fort Charles at the mouth of Kingston harbour. He married Elizabeth Pinnock, daughter of a rich planter, Philip Pinnock, who was also Chief Justice and Speaker of the Assembly, so ensuring himself a secure and rising social and political place in the island's hierarchy. She had died in 1768, but he was by then so firmly established that he was chosen as Lieutenant-Governor of the colony.

As deputy to Sir Edward Trelawny, an able naval captain and a popular Governor at a time of prosperity, he had proved an efficient temporary successor for more than a year following his death at the end of 1772. So when the new Governor, Sir Basil Keith – another naval officer – himself died after three years in office, Dalling was appointed Governor.

Political peace was matched by domestic contentment. Two years after the death of his first wife, he had married Louisa Lawford, a well-connected girl from Surrey, and she bore him a large family. But, as so often, the tropics took their toll, so that eventually Dalling's heir was his fifth son.

Fear that this satisfactory state of calm might not long continue was prompted by more than the mounting pressures of the war. Dalling's first father-in-law had died early in 1778 and with him was lost his soothing influence on the sometimes volatile Assembly. It was ominous that his successor was one Jasper Hall, known for his tendency to question decisions made at the King's House, or in London.

The Governor's military and family background had given

him neither an aptitude, nor a temperament, suitable to a politician. Whereas the social uncertainties in Nelson's background had bred self-reliance and a trust in Providence — this helped, perhaps, by being related to no less than fifteen clergymen who were, he may have imagined, privileged in matters of divine will — Dalling's had resulted in a tendency towards resentment and distruct.

Yet such traits are unlikely to have emerged in the relaxed gatherings at the King's House. The vitality, enthusiasm and the occasional readiness to take violent action that Dalling and Nelson recognised in each other were illustrated by stories that each could tell.

Nelson recalled one of them many years later in a letter to an Army friend, writing, 'Perhaps you did not know General Dalling, therefore I will give you an anecdote of him. After the Rebellion in 1745, when he was Aide de Camp, I believe, to the Duke of Cumberland, he was in company and a gentleman gave *Sentiments*, as was the fashion. *"May the seed of the Thistle extirpate the seed of the Turnip."* It was drank, and Dalling begged to give a Sentiment. *"May there never want a Williamite to kick the arse of a Jacobite"* — and he put his sentiment instantly into execution.'

A somewhat similar story was told in Dalling's family about Nelson's grandfather, Dr. Maurice Suckling, a parson who had the living of Woodton near Bungay and was known to the Windhams and Dallings. Dr. Suckling, it was said, had also once taken such action and this had been described by Horace Walpole, whose own family lived nearby: 'Dr. Suckling, who married a niece of my father, quarrelled with a country squire, who said, "Doctor, your gown is your protection." "Is it so?" replied the parson: "but, by God, it shall not be yours!"; pulled it off and thrashed him — I was going to say damnably, but, at least, *divinely*.'

While awaiting his ship, Nelson was fortunate in having such hospitable friends ashore, as life in Jamaica could be demoralising for a young officer. Army officers suffered from boredom, often took to drink — rum, as a product of the sugar plantations, was plentiful and cheap — and frequently acquired black mistresses. The hospitality at the plantation houses was often *louche* and involved what was known as 'creoleing', both men and women dressed in the coolest and loosest of clothes lounging on the verandahs, perhaps with their feet on chair or table, drinking and smoking cigars. When a young officer took to drink, he was said to be doomed in the next sickly season; alcohol was thought to prepare the way for the mysterious vapours exhaled by the damp tropics that brought on deadly fevers.

One of the few young Army officers who was busily employed at this time, and who also caught the eye of the Governor, was Lieutenant Edward Despard. On arrival in Jamaica with the 50th Regiment of Foot, he had shown an aptitude for engineering – particularly in the design and siting of batteries and fortifications – and the threat of invasion presented many opportunities for this. Indeed, Lieutenant Despard's enthusiasm and efficiency in preparing defences to be manned by the militia, had earned him a vote of thanks both from the Assembly and the smaller Council which directly advised the Governor. It may be that the first meeting of Captain Nelson and Lieutenant Despard was at this time.

Edward Marcus Despard was a strikingly handsome man of twenty-eight. Strongly-built, he had the high-mettled looks and scornful lip of the hard-riding country blade that he would have been had he remained in Ireland. Of French Huguenot and Irish blood, he was one of six brothers, of whom the eldest inherited the family seat at Donore, near Mountrath in what was then called Queen's County to the south-west of Dublin, while the others took commissions in the Army. Theirs was a socially well-connected family with a tradition of military service and their prospects were good.

Edward had joined the 50th Regiment of Foot as an ensign at the age of sixteen and was promoted lieutenant six years later when in Jamaica. He had transferred to the 36th Regiment and then, back in England, in 1778, was seconded to the 79th, which was being raised in Liverpool, and which his younger brother, Thomas, was about to join as an ensign. When the regiment sailed for North America – and, later, Jamaica – there would be three Despards in that theatre of operations; an elder brother, John, was already fighting the rebels as a major in the

Loyal Americans.

That August Jamaica was in turmoil. As reports arrived of the Comte d'Estaing assembling an invasion fleet off Cap François, Dalling mobilised his defences, moving regular troops and militia into the coastal fortifications covering Kingston and camps nearby, and having warships warped into positions from which their guns could command the likely inshore channels of approach.

Hercules Ross put his privateers at the disposal of Admiral Parker and sent his slaves to work on the building of batteries, supervised by Lieutenant Despard. To Nelson, the Governor entrusted the keystone of the island's defences, Fort Charles. Built of limestone blocks and red brick in the time of King Charles II to command the entrance to Kingston harbour, it had been strengthened by Sir Henry Morgan, when the old buccaneer had been appointed Deputy Governor of the island, and it had survived the great earthquake of 1692. The old, ruffianly town of Port Royal and five of its six defending forts had then subsided beneath sea and sand, but Fort Charles still stood on the tip of the nine-mile spit of limestone and coral sand that ended within a mile of the steep, green shoulders of the Hellshire Hills, its guns commanding the harbour mouth between.

It was crumbling now but could still mount more than a hundred guns in two tiers of batteries. When on the wooden platform behind the upper embrasures, seeing blue water beyond the gun-muzzles and scanning the rim of the horizon for sails, Nelson could have imagined himself on the deck of a great, moored ship of the line. He was as proud of his command as if it had been such, writing later, 'I was both Admiral and General . . . As this place was the key to the whole naval force, the town of Kingston and Spanish Town, the defence of it was the most important post in the whole island.'

The defences of Jamaica might have seemed strong. Nelson could see a dozen British warships moored before Kingston, but four of them were third-rate and fourth-rate ships of the line, the remainder frigates and anything able to mount a dozen guns or so. He knew that some seven thousand soldiers had been mustered ashore – five thousand camped outside Kingston, a thousand in Fort Augusta across the bay, three hundred manning, the Apostles' Battery on the far side of the harbour mouth, and he himself had been promised five hundred at Fort Charles – but the bulk of them were from the part-time militia and so more comical than warlike.

They might have to face formidable odds, for it had been reported that the French might attack with a hundred and twenty-five ships, including nearly thirty sail of the line, and twenty-five thousand soldiers – most of them trained regulars – in the transports. So Nelson was not sanguine, writing to Locker, wryly, 'I leave you in England to judge what stand we shall make . . . I think you must not be surprised to hear of my learning to speak French.'

Then, at the end of the month, the sails of the *Hinchinbroke* came up over the rim of the horizon – safe after all – and, soon after, came news that d'Estaing had finally sailed, but was not heading for Jamaica. In response to urgent appeals for help from the American rebels' leader, General George Washington, he was steering north with twenty sail of the line and five thousand troops towards the scene of action on the coast of Georgia. With mixed relief and disappointment, Admiral Parker wrote to Lord Sandwich, the First Lord of the Admiralty, 'It seems strange that Comte d'Estaing should let slip so favourable an opportunity of attacking this island.'

But, by then, Captain Nelson had already returned to the absorbing and intricate procedure of taking over a new command and preparing her for sea. On 1st September, he made his first entry in the log of the *Hinchinbroke*, 'Moderate breezes and clear weather. Took command of the ship and read my commission to the ship's company.'

When, after re-rigging, repairing and re-supplying the ship with water, stores and ammunition, he took her out of Port Royal on 5th October, he felt the heave of a deck again after more than three months. The frigate's bowsprit pointed to the open sea and the Blue Mountains of Jamaica faded in the haze.

CHAPTER TWO

A Trip to the South Sea

Danger of invasion had passed this time. Captain Nelson had taken his frigate to patrol off the Spanish Main and Lieutenant Despard had returned to regimental duties. In the King's House at Spanish Town, General Dalling spent an increasing amount of time with a large atlas open before him on a polished mahogany table.

This was *The West Indies Atlas*, published four years before in London, in which the maps of the late Thomas Jefferys, Geographer to the King, had been beautifully printed, complete with annotations of the latest settlements and decorated with little ships sailing its seas. The atlas showed the sea-route from England to the Caribbean, the mainland and islands from Florida to Venezuela and westward, beyond the isthmus of Central America, to the Pacific, or, as it was then called, the South Sea.

For Dalling, whose mind had now turned from the tactics of defending Jamaican beaches to the broad strategy of the war, the atlas was incomplete. The Comte d'Estaing had already sailed beyond its scope on what proved to be his abortive attempt to drive the British from their newly-won foothold at Savannah on the coast of Georgia. Indeed, it was now more clear than ever that the theatre of war had come to cover all American waters between the mouths of the St. Lawrence and the Amazon. The French had been able to switch their main fleet quickly from threatening Jamaica to attacking Georgia, and, although this had failed, it had had a valuable consequence. The commander-in-chief of British land forces in

North America had been so alarmed that he had ordered the evacuation of Rhode Island and its anchorage in Narragansett Bay and ordered the withdrawal of its garrison to New York, so giving the French as great a prize as any that d'Estaing could have won in battle.

Yet the maps did stretch as far north as the farthest shore of the Gulf of Mexico and so encompassed the range of strategic possibilities that concerned Dalling himself. In the secret letters that regularly arrived from London, Lord George Germain, the Colonial Secretary in Lord North's administration, had warned him of the imminence of war with Spain and stressed that this would present both threats and opportunities. Spanish America – or 'New Spain' – was sparsely defended, Germain had pointed out, and so vulnerable to British raids, which would keep their land forces away from the main conflict in North America. Both men had fought in the Seven Years War and needed no reminding of the brilliant success of British strategy in using sea power and seaborne armies to concentrate upon the distant possessions of France and Spain; so routing the former in Canada and India, and the latter in Cuba and the Philippines.

Dalling might care to cast a soldier's eye, Germain had suggested, on the Mosquito Shore, or even as far north as the former French colonial capital of New Orleans on the Gulf of Mexico, which might be taken if he could send an expeditionary force to join the British garrison at Pensacola in north-west Florida. It was stimulating to think in such terms but also daunting because of the lack of necessary forces. The garrison of Jamaica consisted of little more than two regiments of regular soldiers – the 60th, which was accustomed to the tropics, and the 79th, which was not – together with several thousand volunteers and conscripted militiamen and the possibility of rounding up some hundreds of sailors, slaves, foreigners, prisoners and 'freebooters' into formations for which 'irregular' would almost be an expression of flattery.

Yet the Governor realised that, while such offensive action would gratify the politicians in London – and his own martial ambition – it would alienate his Assembly, who were complaining with increasing vehemence of the paucity of their defence and the consequent risks to trade. More troops in the

British Isles were said to be preparing for West Indian service but, until their arrival, any reduction in the garrison of Jamaica to mount an expedition would meet with widespread opposition induced by fear.

But while Dalling pondered such possibilities, the Spanish command was doing likewise and they were the first to take a decision and to act. While the British general at Pensacola in Florida was still ignorant of Spain's declaration of war, news reached him that Spanish troops had crossed the Mississippi and taken four hundred and fifty British prisoners in the forward posts along the east bank of the river.

At dawn on 15th September, the British settlers at St. George's Key, on the coast of Honduras near Belize, were surprised by a Spanish raid. A squadron of warships had sailed close inshore during the night, landing parties burning the settlement and rounding up those settlers unable to escape. Loading the plunder and the prisoners into their ships, the Spaniards sailed for Havana while the anguished survivors surveyed the charred and smoking ruins of their homes and crops and decided, as they often had before, to demand protection from the Governor of Jamaica.

When the news reached Dalling, he was sunk in depression for which musing on strategic contingencies was a relief. He was being widely blamed for the poor state of the island's defences during the fears of invasion and the Assembly was getting restive. On the 12th, in one of the bouts of despairing self-doubt to which he was prone, and which alternated with an equally manic insistence in refusing to reconsider wrong decisions, he wrote to the Colonial Secretary, 'What with the crookedness of the Assembly, the little choice of men for a better, the discontents among the Militia, ill-intentioned people blowing the coals and my own ill health from the gout . . . both Men and Things appear now in so many points of view, and all so complicated, that they puzzle and perplex me exceedingly and give birth to so many difficulties that I know not which way to turn . . . and I am obliged to profess myself in every respect, saving the Military line, unequal to the task.'

The news of the Spanish attacks galvanised Dalling into action. An energetic and unconventional officer of the Loyal

Irish Corps, Major William Dalrymple, was dispatched to re-capture St. George's Key with his own men, a company of the 79th and whatever irregulars he could collect on the way. Imagining the settlement to be strongly held by the Spaniards, he decided the task was beyond him, but meeting three British warships from the Leeward Islands squadron – one of them, the *Lowestoft* – at sea, under the command of Commodore John Luttrell, the two decided upon a more promising objective. This was to be the Spanish port of Omoa in the Gulf of Honduras, where Guatemalan gold was stored for shipment to Havana.

Omoa was defended by the strongly-manned fort of San Fernando with cannon mounted on walls eighteen feet thick, but it was caught as unawares as St. George's Key had been. Dalrymple's raiding party of one hundred and fifty soldiers, sailors, marines, Mosquito Indians and Negroes were landed well away from the town on the night of 19th October. Scouts had found trails through the jungle and the raiders followed them, giving the password 'Bayonet' to the advance party and being given the countersign, 'Britons strike home.'

The assault was launched at four in the morning with skill and dash. Only two of the startled garrison were wounded before the remainder, who outnumbered the assailants by more than two to one, surrendered. Dalrymple was delighted by the spirit of his men and, in his formal report of the action to Dalling, wrote, 'Your Excellency will pardon my mentioning an instance of an Elevated Mind in a British Tar which amazed the Spaniards and must have given them a very high idea of English Valor. Jack, not contented with one cutlass, had scrambled up the walls with two and, meeting a Spanish officer without arms, who had been roused from his sleep, had the generosity not to take any advantage but, presenting him with one of his cutlasses, told him you are now on a footing with me.'

In the attack, a midshipman, three sailors and a private of the Loyal Irish had been killed but the capture was far greater than had been expected. Cargoes and bullion worth three million dollars was collected and taken aboard Luttrell's ships before the little expeditionary force sailed away to the island of Rattan, leaving a small garrison in Fort San Fernando. This, in turn, would have no choice but surrender when a Spanish relieving force arrived at Omoa a month later.

Had Nelson remained in the *Lowestoft* he would have earned a handsome share of prize money but, as it was, his lonely cruise in the *Hinchinbroke* brought him some success, with prizes taken eventually bringing about £800. After patrolling from the mouth of the San Juan river, which marked the boundary between the provinces of Nicaragua and Costa Rica, to the island of Curaçoa, he returned to Jamaican waters, cruising along the north shore and spending nearly a fortnight at anchor off Port Antonio. Usually the ship was alone but, in late November, there were some happy days spent operating in company with the *Badger* and a chance to meet Cuthbert Collingwood again.

It was the familiar routine of sighting and chasing strange sails, stopping and boarding ships and, more often than not, finding them to be neutrals or friendly privateers. December began with violent gales and when Nelson took his ship into Port Royal on the 12th, it was to repair storm damage as well as to replenish and take on water at Rock Fort.

He found that the mood of the place had changed. Instead of the suppressed panic that had been about during the threat of invasion, there was an excitement and an air of resolution. Dalling had appointed Hercules Ross to be his Agent-General with wide powers to buy, hire and requisition on behalf of the military. Since there now seemed no imminent danger of attack, this could only mean that an expeditionary force was being prepared.

Talk of the Spanish Main and Guatemalan gold turned thoughts to fortune-making. To naval and military officers, most of whom had chosen their profession with hopes of financial or social advance, Jamaica was a place to stimulate such dreams. Most of the great houses at which they were entertained had been built from fortunes made within the past century and the elaborate marble monuments, commissioned in England and shipped to the churches of Spanish Town, Kingston and Port Royal, commemorated the *nouveaux riches*. Even the soldiers and sailors could live in hope, excited by exaggerated legends of Port Royal's orgiastic past in the time of the buccaneers. Occasionally, a privateer put in with a rich prize to demonstrate that there was money still to be made.

Dalling's eye was on Guatemala. Yet to make a landing and establish a lodgement, it would clearly be an advantage to make use of the coast already largely under British control farther south on the Mosquito Shore of Honduras and Nicaragua. The settlers there had long been pestering him for British troops. If he could now grant their wish – on condition that they themselves raised a force of irregulars – there might be enough men to undertake an expedition to Guatemala, overland or by way of the rivers.

The Governor knew little of the Mosquito Shore and less of its hinterland; indeed, geographically and politically, it was something of a mystery even to those who lived there. Ostensibly part of New Spain, it had never been fully colonised by the *Conquistadores*, so that, forty years before, British, and, particularly, Scottish, settlers had found its riches ripe for harvesting. The territory ran some three hundred miles down the coast of the two provinces and about a hundred miles inland to the mountains. Its coastal waters were rich in fish and, in spring, with green turtles; the estuaries of its rivers, with the strange manatee 'sea cow.' Ashore, the coastal savannahs, forests and wooded uplands were alive with game, and promised good farmland. What was also to be had for the taking was timber; particularly mahogany and cedar that was so much in demand for furniture-making in Europe and logwood, from which came the basis of dyes for textiles.

The indigenous inhabitants were Mosquito Indians, who had been joined by 'Samboes', the descendants of two cargoes of Negro slaves, who had survived shipwreck on the coast of Nicaragua and intermarried with them. These had been joined by British adventurers, who had prospered, and the then Governor of Jamaica had sent a small detachment of troops for their protection. When this provoked no Spanish action, the British Government, in 1749, authorised the Governor to set up a loose civil administration there under a Superintendent General responsible to himself. The first of these was Robert Hodgson, a captain in the Jamaica Regiment, and, on the death of himself and his successor, the office had passed to his son, also named Robert.

From time to time, the Spaniards had made half-hearted attempts — military and political — to rid themselves of the British settlers. But they were resilient, with a reputation for being the roughest of merchant-adventurers; a sea-captain, making a complaint against them in a Jamaican court of law, referred to them just as 'those Scotch buggers'. But they took care to maintain the friendliest relations with the Mosquito Indians, whose leaders they invested with British military, naval or noble rank and names. Amongst the names of Indian chiefs frequently mentioned were 'General Tempest', 'the Duke of York' and 'Prince Eugene.'

The most dangerous conflicts were among the settlers themselves. The tendency of Jamaican planters to oppose their Governor as the representative of London, was echoed in the resentment of the farmers and wood-cutters of the Mosquito Shore against their Superintendent as representing Spanish Town.

Hodgson was an able man but probably demanded too high a standard of morality and so was accused of tyranny. The discontented settlers found a champion in Captain James Lawrie, a Scottish adventurer and a new arrival on the Shore, and together they intrigued against the Superintendent, Sir Basil Keith, then Governor at Spanish Town, was aware of the weakness of British colonial claims to the Shore and considering it a tiresome irrelevance. He and the Colonial Secretary in London were both wearied and worried by the constant wrangling between Hodgson and Lawrie and finally, in 1776, decided to recall the former to London for an enquiry.

Taking his family with him, Hodgson set out, but the sloop in which they sailed was unseaworthy and the voyage to England lasted more than two months longer than expected. When he finally arrived in London the following year and presented himself at the Colonial Office, he was met with shattering news. Lawrie, too, had sailed for England and, arriving after a swift passage, had engaged the services of a sharp-witted solicitor, Robert White, as the settlers' agent. Together they had presented their case against the absent Hodgson to the appropriate minister, Lord George Germain, and done so with such conviction that he had assumed the Superintendent's unexplained absence to be an admission of guilt. As result, James Lawrie had returned to the Mosquito Shore as its new Superintendent-General.

So it was to Lawrie that Dalling now sent an urgent request for his opinion of the various military options open in Central America. The Superintendent was, of course, delighted to comply because a military presence would increase the chances of a formal annexation of the territory and the establishment of colonial rule. In that event, he would be the natural choice for governor and would be able to take his pick of the newly-available farmland and stands of timber.

When Lawrie's report arrived, Dalling studied it with Jeffery's atlas at his side. It was a seductive document, describing in voluptuous detail the aspiring colonist's dream of a rich, beautiful, almost untenanted country, awaiting his plough and axe. He concentrated upon the principal British settlements – from north to south – and the rivers that led into the interior and were the easiest means of transport inland. First, was the largest settlement, at Black River, on the southern shore of the Gulf of Honduras, which ran down from mountains that here stood closer than usual to the coast. Then came Cape Graçias a Dios, where the easterly lie of the coast turned sharply south and Wank's River – named after a Dutch buccaneer called Vanke – ran into the forests towards the distant mountains.

Finally, he moved from Honduras to Nicaragua. Here the settlements were in the north at Pearl Key and Bluefields – named after a Dutch trader, Blauvelt – and its river flowing into the fine anchorage sheltered by the headland of Bluefields Bluff. Farther south along a low, wooded shore and beaches of dark volcanic sand, lay San Juan del Norte, otherwise known as Greytown, or St. John's. Here there was no settlement but a small and ramshackle town inhabited by Indians, some Samboes, passing traders and sailors from the few ships using its meagre anchorage within a treacherous sand-bar that came close to sealing the mouth of the San Juan river.

Each place that Lawrie described had its own enticements. Sea and rivers teemed with fish and he wrote of forests of valuable hardwoods and groves of fruit-bearing palms that 'abound in the highest degree with game'. There was ground suitable for the growing of rice, cocoa and maize. At the Cape was 'a savannah abounding with excellent pasture and capable of maintaining vast herds of cattle — the beef I have killed there would not disgrace Leadenhall Market.'

But this account became of more interest to a strategist than to an agriculturalist when it reached the Rio San Juan. For this river did not just meander into jungle and mountains. It ran wide and, apparently, deep to the inland sea of Lake Nicaragua, the far shore of which lay, it seemed, within about a dozen miles of the Pacific Ocean, the South Sea.

Dalling read Lawrie's words with care: 'The River St. John . . . forms a commodious harbour where ships of the largest size may lie. Above thirty miles above its mouth stands the Castle of St. John's. The River is pretty broad and, in high floods, navigable for flat-bottomed schooners of small burden. . . Near the Castle are several violent runs or falls, particularly opposite to it. The channel for small vessels is close by the walls. It is easy to get behind this Castle as was done during the Spanish War in 1741 by a party of a few whites and Mosquitomen, who fired their muskets against the Castle and would have taken it had they been possessed of a single piece of cannon.

'From the Castle to Granada, situated on the further bank of the Lake of Nicaragua towards the South Sea, is navigated by flat-bottomed schooners.'

Granada was the largest city in Nicaragua, although Leon was the capital of a country that was 'open and dry, full of towns and villages and abounding with necessities of every kind. . . The militia consists of a body of ill-disciplined Horse, and worse Foot.'

In the last century, buccaneers had ascended the San Juan, crossed the lake and sacked Granada; indeed, Lawrie claimed to have met the light-skinned grandchild of a buccaneer when travelling in the interior of Nicaragua.

He had already touched upon the feasibility of a raid into Guatemala, or the Spanish provinces in the far south, but, when he had completed his description of the San Juan river, he made the suggestion that fired Dalling's imagination. He wrote, 'The river and the Lake of Nicaragua present an easy channel for distressing them in some of their richest provinces; there is nothing to interrupt the passage of the Troops but the Castle of St. John, which would be easily attacked and carried from the land side.'

He turned again to the atlas and saw that the map seemed to confirm Lawrie's optimism. Although the Rio San Juan was marked with the ominous words 'Full of cataracts', there was so much evidence that it was navigable and it led directly to the vast lake that appeared to measure about one hundred miles by forty. This lake gave directly on to the central plains of Nicaragua and, being on the far side of the mountains that marked the western borders of the Mosquito Shore, offered a sure route to Guatemala, outflanking its natural defences.

The text of Jeffery's atlas also supported Lawrie. It confirmed the agricultural wealth of Nicaragua in cattle, timber, grain, fruit, sugar cane, cotton, cocoa, hemp and tar. But he also noted a testy passage in which the cartographer criticised a predecessor for inaccurancy in showing a canal connecting Lake Nicaragua with the Pacific Ocean. 'If such a communication had existed,' he wrote, 'it would produce a new order of things in the government, trade and navigation of the West Indies.'

These were words to set ideas racing. It was one thing to plan a raid on a Spanish settlement but quite another to cross the continent from one ocean to the other. If the river could be ascended — as it apparently could — then the lake could be sailed by a squadron such as the Royal Navy had launched upon Lake Champlain in North America to fight the rebels three years before. From the ships, armies could be landed at any point of their choosing to dominate the isthmus. Then, one day, it might be possible to dig such a canal as the King's Geographer had mocked and cut the Americas in two.

Even in the first stage of acting upon such heady speculation, there were advantages and dangers for Dalling. An immediate advantage would be that such a display of initiative would offset his impulsive confession of incompetence to the Colonial Secretary. Lord George Germain was a soldier and an aristocrat as well as a politician and, by all accounts, not the man to welcome emotional confidences from a subordinate.

Germain, who had changed his name from Sackville to meet the terms of a will, had himself undergone professional tribulation, having been harshly treated in a court-martial resulting from confusion over orders at the Battle of Minden in 1758. But with unruffled self-assurance, he embarked upon a successful political career and, in 1775, had been appointed Colonial Secretary, and Lord Commissioner for Trade and the Plantations, by Lord North. Now aged sixty-three, he was a formidable figure; often arrogant in public, charming in private and with haughty good looks marked by determination and intelligence. He had been implacable in his efforts to put down the American rebellion and could be expected to welcome any plans for aggressive operations. Indeed, when warning Dalling of the imminence of war with Spain, he had urged him to take independent action against the new enemy.

The danger was that the sending of any regular trooops from the colony would provoke the Assembly to greater hostility to himself and sympathy for the Americans. Jamaica was so volatile a place and so fraught with risks that the maintenance of tranquility within was as important a duty of the Governor's as efforts to guard against threats from without.

But Dalling was an enthusiast and unable to resist the temptation to play the conqueror. The possible consequences of bold action seemed increasingly melodramatic. Much of New Spain was said to be on the brink of revolt and needing only the spark that he could supply. If this was so, might not all New Spain collapse before his advance? With the British Army commanding the countries that linked North with South America and the Royal Navy, the oceans to east and west, anything would be possible. Even if the thirteen American colonies were lost for a time, they could be replaced by new colonies taken from Spain. In his excitement, Dalling could imagine all South America at his mercy.

'I see hardly a possibility of not succeeding in whole or in part,' he declared.

When Dalling's proposal reached Germain, the concept came as no surprise because, soon after war had broken out with Spain, a similar suggestion had been made to him by Hodgson in 'a paper containing a digested view of the manner to obtain a South Sea Port by way of the Lake of Nicaragua.' Both plans met with the Colonial Secretary's approval.

So, with the support of Hercules Ross, Dalling began the detailed planning. The natural choice for commander – or Captain-General – of the expedition would be Dalrymple, .the victor of Omoa, and he at once wrote, telling him of his appointment and that the enterprise might be launched in the first weeks of 1780.

Regular troops for the expedition could be drawn from two regiments stationed at Kingston. The most experienced of these was the 60th Foot, also known as the Royal American Regiment, since it was largely recruited from loyal colonists. Before coming to Jamaica, the 1st Battalion had been stationed in South Carolina and Quebec and, unaccustomed to the tropics, had, on arrival, suffered heavily from malaria 'and an epidemic of yellow fever.

But, while the 60th was now 'seasoned' to the tropics, the other line regiment was still suffering the miseries of acclimatisation and vulnerability to infection. This was the 79th Foot, the Royal Liverpool Volunteers, nicknamed 'the Liverpool Blues' because of the preponderance of blue in the colours of their uniform coats. They had been raised in the spring of 1778 and financed by public subscription during the alarm following Burgoyne's defeat at Saratoga, and the presentation of their colours in Liverpool in May of that year had been a splendid affair. The *Liverpool Advertiser* had reported their parade and the speech their commanding officer, Lieutenant-Colonel Crosbie, had made 'in very animated language' praising his men for the 'ZEAL and ALACRITY with which they had entered the Service' so enabling the regiment to recruit a strength of eleven hundred in four months. After saluting their new colours, 'the Blues' had 'fired three excellent vollies' and marched into the city, where the officers dined with gentlemen of the town at George's Coffee House, 'where an elegant entertainment was provided' and men were suitably 'regaled'.

While the rank and file had been recruited in and around Liverpool, the officers had been seconded from other regiments. Lieutenant Despard, formerly of the 36th, seemed particularly

[55]

promising to Colonel Crosbie, being appointed Quartermaster and given command of the light infantry company. This he led when, in June, the regiment, which, it was reported, was 'in great spirits and made a very martial appearance', marched down the road to Coventry and their way to camp in Essex. In February of the following year, the *Advertiser* printed a report from Portsmouth that 'The Liverpool Blues are here and in a few days will embark on board the transports for America.'

The regiment had first sailed to Philadelphia before continuing to Jamaica, where they arrived during the wet, sickly season of early summer. Within a month, the symptoms of malaria had appeared and they had already suffered their first losses when ordered to prepare for active service.

There were, in addition, locally raised troops commanded by both regular officers and those commissioned by the Governor. These included Dalrymple's Loyal Irish Corps, which had distinguished itself at Omoa, and was recruited from amongst the large numbers of Irishmen — mostly former indentured servants and sailors — who congregated at Kingston and reinforced from Ireland itself. Then there would be volunteers from the conscripted militia, who could be formed into companies, and other volunteers, attracted by the prospect of looting, who could be European, Negro, mulatto and Indian. Then these might be joined by 'freebooters' from privateers and numbers could be made up by offering prisoners of war their freedom in return for service on the expedition.

There could be a faint hope of reinforcement from North America. General Clinton in New York had been gratifyingly responsive during the invasion alarm of the summer and, in response to a call for help from Dalling, had actually despatched reinforcements, which had been recalled while still at sea when d'Estaing's destination was seen to be Georgia rather than Jamaica. So the Governor wrote to him again, pleading, 'If Your Excellency will send me only a single Regiment, I flatter myself I shall be able to cause such a diversion as will compel the Spaniards to turn their principal attention to their own defence.'

It was impossible to keep plans for the mounting of an expedition secret, particularly since Ross was busily assessing the necessary stores and shipping. Dalling himself was Commander-in-Chief of the land forces in Jamaica but all regular warships were under the command of Admiral Parker, who, when not in his flagship, lived ashore at Admiral's Pen and was available for meetings at Spanish Town.

When Parker was told the outline of the plan to attack Nicaragua as a first step in the conquest of Central America, he was aghast, but chose to put his objections in a tactful letter to Dalling. He pointed out that his squadron was already over-stretched. A convoy, about to sail for Europe, had been held back, because of the threat of interception, until a stronger escort could be assembled. Powerful French and Spanish squadrons were somewhere at sea and, on the Mosquito Shore there were no secure harbours to shelter the expedition's transports which could be harried by the six Spanish *guarda costa* brigs of sixteen guns that were known to be patrolling that coast. He agreed to provide naval escorts if asked by the Governor, but stressed, 'I have thought myself under the necessity of offering my sentiments on the intended Expedition, which, all circumstances considered, may be a detriment to this Island, and cannot, in my opinion, promise much to the adventurers; but in all these matters I shall willingly submit to your superior judgement and information.'

To this, Dalling replied icily, 'I cannot be so indeterminate and vague as to lay aside the Expedition, especially as an Invasion of this Island appears to me less likely than ever, and, in my opinion, employing a small force offensively will oblige our new Enemy, the Spaniard, to look at home and thereby eventually preserve us from attack.'

He then put forward an argument that he was hoping would avoid a confrontation with the Assembly over the despatch of regular troops. In Jamaica, they remained sickly; in Nicaragua, which, according to Lawrie, had a healthy climate, they would revive and so become fit for active service wherever they were needed. He wrote, 'The few Troops I am forwarding are only of the convalescent kind, the greater part of whom would probably die here, but, from the salubrity of the sea air, may recover and be useful there.

'Your idea as to weakening this island was also the idea of

[57]

some of the Assembly. . . . I trust you will give me credit for having very maturely considered this business; for, be assured, I would otherwise most cheerfully give up my opinion to yours.'

Having made his point, Parker determined to show himself more than willing to cooperate with the Governor, while leaving the Admiralty in no doubt of his disapproval of the adventure so that, whatever transpired, he could expect some of the credit but none of the blame. So, when Dalling asked him for a sloop to escort the troop transports to the Mosquito Shore, he responded by offering him a frigate and the one commanded by the Governor's young friend, Captain Nelson, at that.

'A sloop has been asked and I have given a frigate,' he wrote to Lord Sandwich, then went on to expound his fears. The expedition was being prepared without sufficient secrecy, he claimed, so that the enemy may well have had advance warning. In any case, such an operation would best be undertaken 'by the Indians, white inhabitants on the coast, freebooters, etc.' instead of regulars and volunteers. The force Dalling had in mind, he wrote, was 'six or seven hundred regulars and three or four hundred able volunteers, besides a number of seamen to be employed in the transports, small craft, etc.', which would be 'a great diminution of the strength of this island.' He concluded, 'My only reason for mentioning this affair is that your Lordship may know that I do not approve of sending so many people off this island till we are convinced of the disability of the enemy to attack it.'

Another reason for tension between Parker and Dalling was trouble over the distribution of the Omoa booty. The Navy followed its own regulations in the allocation of prize-money but this would have to be shared with the Army and a variety of volunteers and irregulars. All concerned were vigorously pressing their claims but there were neither laws nor customs to cover this contingency. The admiral wanted to ship all the plunder to England and the decisions to be taken there, but Dalling threatened him with legal action if he attempted to do so, maintaining that, as the King's representative, it was he who should be the final arbiter.

Major Dalrymple, the proposed field commander, was himself so embroiled in the division of the spoils that he might

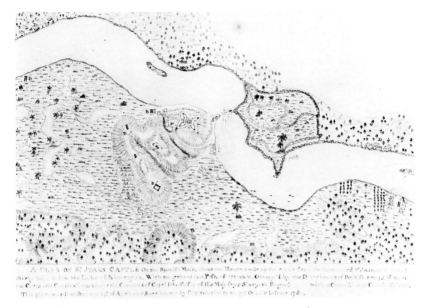

A PLAN OF St JUANS CASTLE On the Spanish Main, about one Hundred mile up the river from the mouth of St Juan, and about thirty miles below the Lake of Nicaragua, With the ground and Plan of attack & Occupied by the Detachment of British troops of war and the Corps and Complex siege under the Command of Capt John Polson of His Majesty's Sixty seth Regiment ... with a Council ... This place was Invested the 17 of April and Surrendered by Capitulation on the 1 of ... in front 178.

Plan of the San Juan castle said to have been drawn during the siege by
Captain Despard. The British batteries are on the hills to the immediate
south-west of the fortress.

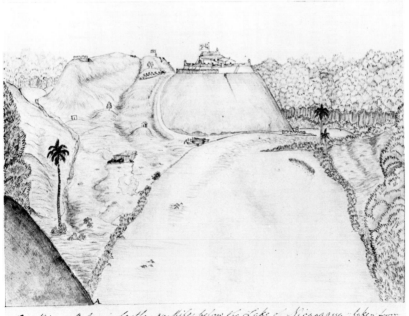

East View of St Juan's Castle, 30 Miles below the Lake of Nicaragua - taken from
the Spot of the Letter A, about 1400 Yards below the Castle —

The castle of San Juan as the approaching British would first have seen it
from the east. Believed to have been sketched by Captain Despard from a
point 1400 yards downstream of the fortress on the south bank.

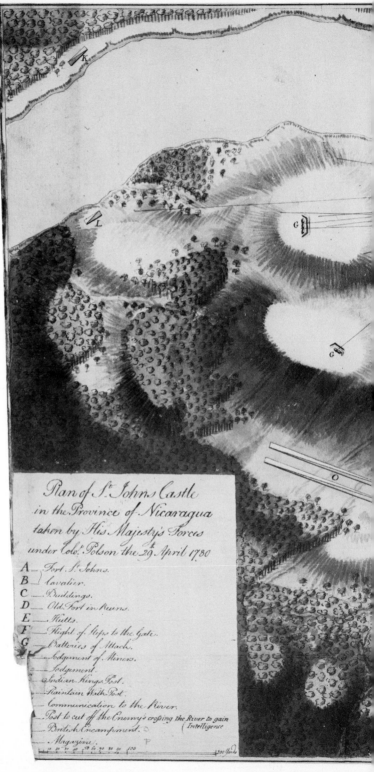

Plan of S.t John's Castle
in the Province of Nicaragua
taken by His Majesty's Forces
under Colo.l Polson the 29.th April 1780

A ── Fort S.t John's.
B ── Cavalier.
C ── Buildings.
D ── Old Fort in Ruins.
E ── Hutts.
F ── Flight of Steps to the Gate.
G ── Batteries of Attack.
── Lodgment of Miners.
── Lodgment.
── Indian Kings Post.
── Plaintain Walk Post.
── Communication to the River.
── Post to cut off the Enemy's crossing the River to gain
                                        (Intelligence
── British Encampment.
── Magazine.

Plan of the San Juan fortress showing the British emplacements
during the siege, drawn by an engineer officer and sent to Govern
Dalling with Colonel Polson's despatches.

Rapids *practicable for large Crafts*

Photographs of the San Juan castle taken in 1978.

top The author at the entrance to the castle.

below The castle seen from the river, upstream to the west, showing the village of El Castillo. The site of Nelson's battery is on the extreme right.

be required to return home for appearances in the law courts. He had been Dalling's first choice as being an officer equally at home in command of regulars or irregulars. His second choice would have to be an experienced regular officer — presumably from the Royal Americans — although this would inevitably draw attention to the loss of troops from the island's garrison and so intensify the criticism.

There were some fifteen hundred regular soldiers in Jamaica but a reinforcement of about three thousand was expected from England during the next three months. So if he launched his attack early in January, the spearhead only need be regulars — he had in mind about two hundred men — supported by double their number in volunteers and irregulars. In addition, Lawrie had promised to raise more than a thousand men on the Mosquito Shore. Most of these would be Indians to act as guides, boatmen and porters, rather than fight, because, as the Superintendent put it, 'when left to themselves they are not of a nature to occasion any great exertions on the part of the Spaniards.' But there would also be an independent company of one hundred and twenty British settlers, mulattoes, free Negroes, to whom could be added four hundred slaves. This force was short of suitable clothing and weapons (they preferred swan-shot to ball ammunition for their muskets), but, when suitably armed, Lawrie expected them to 'revive the ancient buccaneering spirit.'

Once this vanguard had ascended the San Juan river and captured the castle, there would surely be little opposition in the Assembly to the dispatch of reinforcements, which could include a stronger force of regulars. Not only would he be expected to exploit the victory, but the arrival of the reinforcements from home would be imminent, so allaying apprehensions.

For the command of the vanguard, Dalling now chose 'a Captain Polson of the 60th, a steady and good officer', who would be granted the temporary rank of lieutenant-colonel. His force was to be larger than originally planned, with about one hundred men of his own regiment and one hundred and forty of the 79th, under Captain Richard Bulkeley, a robust and enthusiastic officer, aged twenty-four, of Anglo-Irish stock, the son of the secretary to the colonial government of Nova Scotia.

According to an officer who visited them in their barracks they were 'a fine body of men, in good health and fit for the field.' This was embarrassing for Dalling who was assuring his critics that they were 'very sickly' and that sea air and exercise in the Nicaraguan countryside would restore them to health.

Indeed, the only sick men were about twenty-five of the hundred Loyal Irish, who were to sail with Polson, and even they were thought fit for garrison duties. The volunteers and irregulars, being mostly acclimatised to the tropics, were healthy, although often drunken when opportunity offered. These included some two hundred and forty men of Major James Macdonald's Royal Jamaica Volunteers, about two-thirds of them neutral seamen taken in prizes, and even prisoners of war released from Kingston gaol to enlist. More ruffianly was the Jamaica Legion, made up of unemployed sailors from privateers, loafers from Kingston waterfront, 'straggling sea-men' and other freebooters. Described by an inspecting officer as 'a riotous, troublesome set of people', they were said to muster about two hundred and fifty, but desertion, or just absence without leave, was so rife that their numbers fluctuated from one parade to the next.

In addition, there were the Royal Batteaux Corps of boatmen, said to number one hundred and twenty-five and be much like the Legion in character and reliability; and an unspecified number of volunteers in a Black Regiment, which had been raised despite the objections of planters fearing the consequences of arming any exclusively Negro force.

Dalling planned to send the Loyal Irish and about two hundred volunteers and irregulars with the first contingent, the remainder following with the second. So, together with Lawrie's force, the advance up the San Juan river would be made by about fifteen hundred men.

The commander of the naval escort and convoy was to be Captain Nelson. On sailing from Kingston early in January, he would be responsible for calling at the settlements on the Mosquito Shore to collect Lawrie's contingents, then conveying the whole force to San Juan del Norte — Greytown, or St. John's — where his frigate would cover the landing and remain as guardship until relieved.

Nelson was stimulated by the prospect and refused the offer from Parker of another, larger, ship. This was a Spanish storeship which he had taken in a brisk action off Omoa and brought into Port Royal. She was to be converted into a warship, as the *Hinchinbroke* had been, but would carry thirty-six guns. On Nelson's refusal, the admiral promised to give him the first true frigate that became available.

In January, he wrote to Locker, giving news of another £800 in prize money he expected from a ship taken on his last cruise, movements of ships of the squadron and their officers and that the pleasant little mess he had shared with Cornwallis was now to be broken up. Parker, he wrote, had 'appointed me to go with an Expedition which is now on foot against the city of Granada on the Lake of Nicaragua. How it will turn out, God knows. I do not expect to return before the beginning of June.'

But he was still troubled by the malaria that had recurred since his voyage to India. 'You must not be surprised to see me in England after this trip,' he continued. 'For if my health is not much better than it is at present, I shall certainly come home, as all the Doctors are against my staying so long in this country.'

One of these doctors was Benjamin Moseley, the Surgeon-General of the colony. Now aged thirty-seven, Dr. Moseley had studied medicine in London, Paris and Leyden before coming to Jamaica in 1768. He was another enthusiast, with a lively mind and wide-ranging interests that appealed to Nelson, and they became friends. Considered an authority on tropical diseases, he was also a practising surgeon, although many of his patients subsequently died of tetanus. His researches often strayed from the central disciplines of medicine, producing theories on the pathological effects of phases of the moon, studies of shark-bites and hydrophobia, superstition and black magic amongst slaves and the effects of coffee-drinking, which had led to the publication of his first book, *A Treatise Concerning the Properties and Effects of Coffee*, four years earlier.

His theories on treatment of tropical illnesses were sometimes controversial. He had little confidence of the use of quinine, made from powdered Peruvian cinchona bark, as a treatment for 'intermittent fever', or malaria, although he allowed its occasional use together with cinnamon, sweat-inducing diaphoretics and draughts of beer, finding that 'nothing was so grateful as London bottled porter.'

Dr. Moseley had been appointed chief medical officer to the expedition but decided to remain in Jamaica, his place being taken by a deputy, Dr. Thomas Dancer, an active man in his mid-twenties, whose interest in tropical botany was another reason for sending him into the Nicaraguan jungle. Dalling had stressed the importance of the expedition's medical services, but no abnormal problems were expected. Despite the Governor's public assurances that convalescents would be drafted from the two regular battalions, the contrary was the case. That any military expedition was likely to suffer from dysentery was taken for granted, but since the troops were to embark on a sea-voyage — a recognised means of restoring health in the tropics — and go ashore in what, according to Major Lawrie, was a dry, healthy and sparsely-populated country, they should avoid the malaria of swamps and the yellow fever and smallpox epidemics of towns.

The types and quantities of medical supplies were discussed by the two doctors with the Army surgeons at Castile and Up Park camps outside Kingston and the doctors of the naval hospital at Greenwich on Kingston Bay. They also met with Polson and with Hercules Ross, who was responsible for the ordering and shipping of all supplies and who was already facing severe problems.

Ross was working on the assumption that he would have to supply a force of between fifteen hundred and two thousand men for about six months. He had already bought all the salt beef and pork, flour and rum that was available in Kingston and there would not be enough. Polson had insisted that his men should have a daily ration of salt meat but had been told that this was impossible, since there was a shortage of Irish beef, and Jamaican beef could not be salted to keep for more than four days except in the cool of the mountains. So Ross suggested that the soldiers should eat the Jamaican beef on the voyage, fish and turtle meat on the coast of Nicaragua and save the salted Irish meat for the advance into the interior. He also advised the cutting of Jamaican beef into strips and drying it in the sun as a means of preservation.

An unexpected problem that beset him was that of prize money, hopes of which had induced many of the volunteers and irregulars to enlist. This was the Omoa troubles repeated because the Army and Navy held superior status to the rest — regular officers had been given automatic seniority to volunteer officers of their own rank — and there were demands that a scale of rewards be announced.

Those about to embark were, he reported to Dalling, 'greatly agitated in respect to the shares they were to be entitled.' He had tried to draw up a scheme for distribution but 'after much time and pain' had found himself 'unequal to the task.' He explained to the Governor, 'The mode prescribed for distribution to the Navy in eighth parts to the different classes of officers could not be followed with any certainty of distributive justice because the number of officers and men, and what proportion they bore to each other, could not be ascertained.' He had been 'confounded in such schemes by the medley of characters, which were likely to compose the Army on the Expedition: for instance, Officers by Sea and Land, Artificers, Gentlemen Volunteers, Indian Kings, Princes, Generals and Colonels of their class and colour. Every scheme he formed, he found subject to innumerable exceptions. It was a task beyond his abilities.'

Dalling did not reply to this letter and Ross noted, 'nothing was fixed or determined but left to future chance and events.'

Another problem was that the ships allocated as transports could not be got ready for sea, let alone sail, because Admiral Parker's press gangs, roaming the Kingston waterfront, had impressed so many of their seamen to man his warships. This was only overcome by Ross drafting the crews of 'his private vessels of war' — the privateers — to man the transports and store-ships.

Then there was a shortage of ammunition brought about by the late arrival of a convoy from England, and some of this was to be shipped in Nelson's convoy to the Mosquito Shore for Lawrie's irregulars. They had asked for cutlasses, as well as their swan-shot, together with canvas jackets, round hats, clasp-knives and iron cooking pots and the Superintendent-General had also asked for a variety of presents for the Indians.

Dalling had laid particular stress on the importance of good relations with the hundreds, if not thousands, of Indians whom he expected to be joining the expedition. In a note to Polson, he pointed out that 'the necessity of keeping such people in good humour is obvious. Inconsistencies, even absurdities, from them must not be combatted.' He also urged the colonel to 'avoid giving any distrust to the Indians by depriving them of their private plunder', thereby passing the problem that had been too much for Ross, to Polson.

The Agent-General had, however, been successful in providing the force with civilian artificers. Lieutenant Despard, who had been given the acting rank of captain, had proved himself as a resourceful military engineer, not only capable in building fortifications, but skilled as a draughtsman and something of a mathematician. He was to accompany Polson as his engineer officer, responsible for the siting and erection of batteries, camps and temporary barracks. He would be able to call on about twenty-five artificers, mostly British but with several Negroes and a couple of foreigners, whom Ross had recruited, amongst them.

These included five house carpenters, a bricklayer and two blacksmiths to work at the expedition's base on the Nicaraguan shore and about twenty shipwrights and boat-builders. Their task would be to realize Dalling's dream of launching a miniature fleet on Lake Nicaragua to command it and enable him to land troops wherever necessary on its shores. He explained to Germain, 'In order to be certain of securing command of the Lake, I have for some time given directions for building a vessel, which is to be sent down in pieces with ship-carpenters to put it together after getting it up the river St. John. The timbers for the above vessel have been all got ready.'

Others would be built at Greytown. In his original orders to the commander of the expedition, Dalling had said that, after landing at Greytown, ascending the river and capturing the castle of San Juan, the force was to continue up the river so that 'you will push for the fort at the entrance of the Lake and, after taking it, launch the vessels as speedily as possible so as to command it. Your next object, I should think, will be getting possession of the Town of Granada at the opposite end and, if possible, that of Leon.'

Dalling's knowledge of the lake was sketchy, being based on Lawrie's memorandum and the introduction to Jeffery's atlas. The latter had told him that the fort at San Carlos, commanding the northern end of the river, mounted twenty-five guns but was 'garrisoned mostly by criminals condemned to military service.' Similarly, there should be no serious opposition afloat since 'the seamen of the lake are the most awkward of any in all the Spanish settlements; the navigation of this little sea is of a tediousness as tiresome to the passengers as hurtful to the merchants.'

There were, he read, volcanoes around the shores of the lake and 'some of the islands in it are likewise burning mountains.' One of the islands was, apparently, cultivated and this, he suggested, could be occupied and used as a base from which the squadron could roam at will.

The flotilla was to be commanded by a volunteer officer, Captain Collins, and manned by sailors from the Jamaica Legion and soldiers. Nelson would have no part in this excitement, since his immediate task would end at the river mouth. This was hardly a role to satisfy his appetite for action as repeated delays in ·the sailing of the convoy seemed to confirm. Originally planned for the first week in January, the date for departure was finally postponed to the beginning of February.

Shortly before this, Nelson met Polson for the first time and the meeting was not auspicious. The colonel was a conventional soldier, trained to trust in the infallibility of superiors and tried tactics, and was probably irritated by Dalling's instructions on his relationship with the young officer he now met. The Governor had written, 'I need not point out to you, who have been so much used to service, the deference and respect due to the opinion of the naval power, which the Admiral may be pleased to send down with you.'

Then he had met Nelson, the twenty-one-year old post-captain. Later, Polson recalled, 'A light-haired boy came to me in a little frigate, of whom I at first made little account.'

The expedition was at last ready to sail. At Castile Fort and Up Park camp, the baggage had been loaded into waggons and hauled down to the Kingston jetties, where barrels of salt meat, boxes of biscuit, bags of flour and dried beans and kegs of rum were being loaded into the transports. Over at Port Royal, where powder and shot lay stacked at the gun-wharf, the *Hinchinbroke*, long ready for sea, was lying still amid the bustle, her ensign stirring in the warm wind.

When all was ready, and the Governor informed, Dalling was immersed in other problems. The trouble over the Omoa booty had worsened. The judge at the Court of Vice-Admiralty had failed to find a generally acceptable solution, and Admiral Parker had announced that he would indeed ship the captures to England, where higher authority would make a final decision. Dalling, furious at having his authority flouted in his own colony, in January ordered his Attorney-General, Thomas Harrison, to prosecute the Commander-in-Chief for interfering with Crown property. But Harrison was a particularly independent-minded member of the Assembly and, as as he was also Advocate-General, had doubts on the legality of the Governor's position. He therefore refused to prosecute until more evidence had been produced. Dalling summoned him to the King's House and, when persuasion failed, lost his temper and, shouting 'Drunkard! Liar! Impertinent!', had him hustled into the street.

Harrison thereupon resigned as Attorney-General. When tempers had cooled after a few days, a mutual friend nearly succeeded in restoring peace. He persuaded Dalling to reinstate Harrison if he would allow the quarrel to 'sink into oblivion', to which the latter agreed on condition that the Governor admitted that his accusations had been only 'words of anger.' At this, Dalling lost his temper again and dismissed Harrison as Advocate-General as well. In this, he had exceeded his authority, because this appointment was under the jurisdiction of the Admiralty and Sir Peter Parker would certainly bring the case to the attention of both Lord Sandwich and the Colonial Secretary.

So, while the Governor was preoccupied with political and

personal quarrelling, the formalities and ceremonial attending the departure of 'the Secret Expedition' devolved upon the recently-appointed Lieutenant-Governor, who had just arrived from London.

Like Dalling, Brigadier-General Archibald Campbell had served under Wolfe at Quebec, where he had been wounded in the fighting on the Heights of Abraham. But they had little else in common, for where the Governor was emotional, enthusiastic and quick to take offence, his deputy was cool-headed and shrewd. Now aged forty, he had had an active and distinguished career. He had been in Canada with the Fraser Highlanders throughout the Seven Years War, then, when that regiment had been disbanded, had gone to India with the 42nd Highlanders. Returning to Scotland in 1773, he was elected Member of Parliament for the Stirling burghs. A year later he returned to soldiering when the Fraser Highlanders were re-formed and he was given command of the 2nd Battalion, which was bound for North America.

Campbell's ship had arrived in Boston harbour just after the British had withdrawn and had been captured by the rebels, who had just entered the town. After months as a prisoner, the colonel had been exchanged for an American of equal standing, Colonel Ethan Allen, whose Green Mountain Boys had been at the capture of Fort Ticonderoga, but who had been taken prisoner in an attempt to take Montreal. On his release, Campbell had been promoted brigadier-general and given command of the expedition to Georgia, which seized Savannah. Returning home, he was received and congratulated by the King and, in 1779, married Amelia, daughter of the Scottish painter, Allan Ramsay. A man of strong character, with intelligent eyes, determined jaw and pursed mouth, he was a man of culture and political acumen as well as military flair; someone who could be considered as a stable successor to the temperatmental General Dalling.

So, at the beginning of February, 1780, Brigadier Campbell rode with his staff from Spanish Town to Kingston for one of his first public duties, the inspection of the volunteers and irregulars on the Grand Parade before embarkation and departure for the Mosquito Shore. As, resplendent in red coat, white breeches and tricorne hat, the Lieutenant-Governor rode out into the square, an extraordinary scene was presented, which he described in a letter to Dalling next day.

'Dalrymple's Legionary troops parading last evening in a ragged line, half-clothed and half-drunk, they seem to possess the true complexion of Buccaneers and it would be illiberal to suppose their principles were not in harmony with their faces,' he wrote. 'A hundred of them were only collected together and seemed so volatile and frolicksome, I thought it good policy to order 10 guineas for them to be drunk in grog on board their transports and embarked them with three cheers to the great satisfaction of the Town of Kingston.'

Once the expedition was on board the ships, Captain Nelson was ordered to sail with all dispatch. On the 3rd February, the *Hinchinbroke* cast off and made sail, gliding across the bay to round up her charges: one three-masted troop-transport, the *Penelope*, two brigs, three sloops and the tender *Royal George*.

Steering south-west, the convoy passed Portland Point and next morning the hills of Jamaica were out of sight. The talking was over and the action was about to begin and, as if in illustration of this, the Army officers, who were taking passage in the frigate, followed Nelson on to the quarterdeck to witness the flogging of a seaman and a marine, each of whom he had sentenced to a dozen lashes of the 'cat o' nine tails' for 'neglect of duty and insolence.'

Two days later, the officers were again mustered on deck by the captain. One of the soldiers embarked in the frigate, Sergeant Samuel Collingworth of the 79th, had been suffering from 'intermittent fever' since the regiment's first weeks in Jamaica. Although classed as 'convalescent', had been able to join the embarkation parade. But, below on the crowded gun-deck, he had been seized with the rigours and, according to Dr. Dancer, 'symptoms of immediate putrefaction' and quickly died. So, for the first time in the campaign which had now begun, officers and men stood bareheaded, while Nelson read the words of the burial service at sea, 'We therefore commit his body to the deep . . . and the life of the world to come, through our Lord Jesus Christ, who at His coming shall change our vile body that it may be like His glorious body. . . .'

More than two hundred young men, listening to his, words must have felt that this marked the end of their miseries. Around them blew the clean winds of the sea and ahead lay a promised land, healthful and fertile, where high adventure was certain and all things possible.

CHAPTER THREE

'Risques and Bugbears'

Although Nelson had had some experience of the Mosquito Shore, its few harbours were hedged about with shoals and sand-banks and not one member of the expedition had any knowledge of the San Juan river. Therefore pilots would be essential and these were known to be available at Providence Island, lying some hundred and fifty miles eastward of the mainland. So this was to be the first point of call for the convoy before it began collecting the armada of small craft that would carry many hundreds, if not thousands, of armed settlers and Indians to the scene of action.

The first week's passage from Jamaica had been uneventful. Nelson had devoted a day to gunnery and small arms practice and the soldiers were encouraged to exercise on deck – wrestling and skylarking with the sailors – for fear of the sicknesses that attacked those spending too much time in the damp and darkness below decks.

On the evening of 9th February, the *Hinchinbroke* anchored off Providence and, next morning, Captain Collins, who was to command the flotilla on the river and the lake, was sent ashore in search of a pilot. He returned with one Richard Hanna, who claimed to know the San Juan river well and heartened Polson by explaining that he could expect at least four feet of water in the main channel all the way up to the castle.

The need for pilots was demonstrated on leaving Providence, for, when the convoy sailed without Hanna and Collins, who were to follow in the *Royal George*, the *Penelope* ran aground on the La Maria reef and stuck fast. The ship's master fired several shots to attract attention to his plight but then panicked. Before Nelson arrived to take charge, he had all the ship's guns and those he was carrying for the expedition, except three, thrown over the side to lighten the ship.

When the *Hinchinbroke* reached her, Nelson ordered the shallow-draught schooners and sloops to run alongside and take off the troops. As this did not lighten the ship sufficiently, he ordered her stores and cargo of gunpowder to be unloaded into the smaller ships. When this had delayed the convoy for more than twenty-four hours, Polson began to worry. Dalling had stressed the importance of speed, writing in his orders, 'The more immediately you depart for the place of a general rendezvous the better, for the more feeble and less prepared you will find the enemy to be.' So, when it seemed that the *Penelope* might be stuck fast for days, he noted in his journal, 'Capt. Nelson and I agreed to send a sailing boat to Cape Graçias a Dios with letters directed to Major Lawrie . . . informing him of the situation we were in and desiring him to make every preparation possible for the intended Expedition that there might be no delay after our arrival at the Cape.'

For that was to be the first of the settlements where Lawrie's forces would be collected and it was only to be expected that, once the convoy was accompanied by a fleet of coastal craft, its progress might be slow. But when, on the morning of the 13th, the *Penelope* still lay aground, Nelson decided to sail the convoy in the hope that she could eventually follow. Shortly before noon, when the *Hinchinbroke* and her charges were less than ten miles to the north-west, her sails were seen to fill and, during the afternoon, she came up with them.

It was at Cape Graçias a Dios that Lawrie should have assembled his settlers, slaves and Indians from the largest settlements around Black River to the west. But when Nelson's telescope searched the bay where Wank's River ran into the sea, there was no sign of the expected flotillas. Hoping that these might have been moored out of sight in the river, Polson went ashore to be greeted by a Lieutenant Brown of the Royal Americans, who explained that neither Lawrie nor his forces had arrived. The letters Polson had sent to him from Providence had arrived the day before and Brown had just 'sent them off

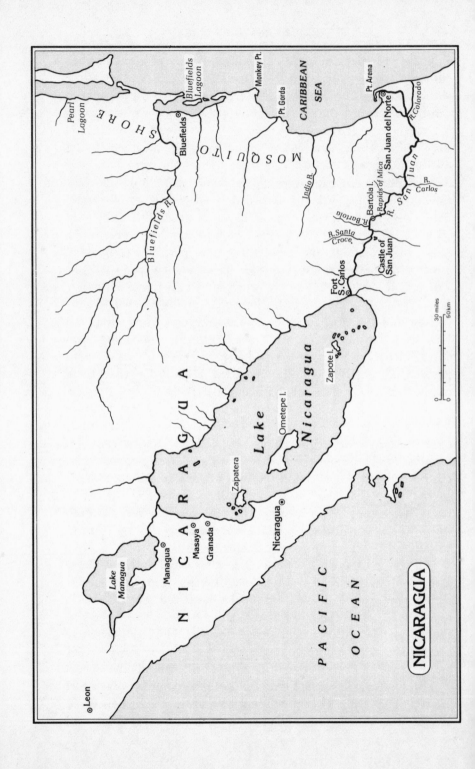

NICARAGUA

Express' to Black River, where the Superintendent-General was thought still to be.

Polson and Nelson were exasperated, particularly because the health of the troops was beginning to suffer from nearly two weeks' confinement to cramped and crowded ships in hot weather. Indeed, there had been a second death amongst them; a soldier, thought to be recovering from a bout of malaria but, as Dr. Dancer noted, 'being very weakly and not able to scuffle amongst the men on deck, remained constantly in his berth and, from lying always on the same side, got a mortification in the hip, which, notwithstanding the instant and free use of bark and wine, etc., soon carried him off.'

Despite this, the doctor's reputation stood high because he and an Army surgeon, Mr. Watson, had performed a remarkable and successful operation on board ship. During the salvage of the *Penelope*, one of the volunteers had fractured his skull in a fall. Operating 'under every possible circumstance of disadvantage', Dancer had extracted splintered bone and his patient seemed likely to recover.

So Colonel Polson agreed with his opinion that, as the convoy would probably have to await the arrival of Lawrie for a few days, it was essential to disembark the troops. It was decided that Wank's Savannah, the pasture that Lawrie had told Dalling could produce cattle worthy of Leadenhall Market, should make an ideal site for a camp and a party was at once sent ashore to survey it.

Although about a mile from the sea, Wank's Savannah at first seemed suitable enough; particularly so when Dr. Dancer announced that the fresh water there was strongly impregnated with iron salts which should be good for the soldiers 'by carrying off the bile and by a tonic power in bracing up the solids.' But he hoped their stay would not be prolonged because the site was sheltered from sea breezes by tall grass and dense mangroves and was so swampy that water lay only a foot or two beneath the surface, so as to 'generate an unwholesome air.' For every doctor, and, indeed, every soldier with experience of the tropics, knew that the cause of 'malignant fevers' was 'the poisonous effluvia, or miasmata, arising from the ground in all woody and marshy situations, particularly in warm seasons and in warm climates.'

There was another drawback but one that seemed no more than an irritation. This was the mosquito. In Jamaica, nights had been made restless enough by the whine and bite of mosquitoes, but Dr. Moseley himself warned that while they were 'a great vexation in all the islands, they are worse on the continent.' In Mexico they were thought to be able to kill men with their stinging and Indians were said to bury themselves to the neck in sand for protection at night. So Moseley advised those who could to wear 'loose linen buskins' to cover their legs and gauze curtains around their beds. Failing this, fire should be lit, as smoke kept the insects away.

But while mosquito-bites could cause 'an uncommon degree of itching', the Surgeon-General advised that they were only dangerous if scratched, when they might form 'painful acrid ulcers'. He recommended the use of oil, vinegar, lime-juice or camphorated spirits to relieve the itching but stressed that bites, 'though extremely disagreeable, will not long continue troublesome.'

Polson had more than mosquitoes to bother him. It had become increasingly apparent that not only had Lawrie failed to keep the rendezvous at the Cape, but that there was not a single British settler willing to join the expedition. Gradually it dawned on him that the arrival of regular troops on the Mosquito Shore, which was politically welcome to Lawrie, was not at all what the settlers wanted, as they feared that it would interfere with their busy and profitable smuggling trade with the Spaniards. Moreover, it also appeared that, in order to discourage the military, the settlers had been urging the Indians to avoid them because the true aim of the expedition was not the plundering of Spanish settlements but the rounding up of the Indians themselves to be shipped off to Jamaica and sold as slaves.

So, while awaiting the appearance of Lawrie from Black River, where it was hoped he had been more successful, Polson took matters into his own hands and wrote to the Mosquito chieftain known as 'the Duke of York', urging him to bring his fighting men to the Cape and to use his influence with the Mosquito 'King' and 'Admiral' to do likewise. But realising that it might be a fortnight before Lawrie could sail round from Black River, Polson decided to save time by ordering the assembling of the pre-fabricated flat-bottomed boat they had brought from Jamaica. Mr. Wright, the master carpenter, thought his men, helped by soldiers working as porters, could complete the work in ten days, so Polson ordered the frames to be landed and work to begin.

Next day, a violent storm – a north-westerly gale accompanied by rain – struck the camp, ripping open and blowing down many of the tents. While the colonel was assessing the damage, news reached him that Major Lawrie had at last arrived and would come to the camp from his house in the main settlement next morning. The Superintendent-General duly appeared to say that Polson's last letter had indeed reached him as he was preparing to leave for the Cape with about two hundred armed men. He had travelled as fast as possible but the gale had scattered his flotilla and he feared that some of the craft had been driven ashore.

The Mosquito Indians also began to arrive, responding to Polson's invitation as curiosity overcame their fears of enslavement. The King, attended by the 'Duke of York' appeared, followed by 'Admiral Dick Richards' and were presented with gifts that Polson had brought with him for this purpose. Soon afterwards, 'General Tempest', the most powerful Indian chief in the Black River district, arrived with news that four of their boats had been wrecked in the storm and some of their warriors lost. He agreed to help the British but his brother would command his contingent; he excused himself as being too old for war, and his son, as being his only child.

The surviving craft from Black River began to arrive, amongst them some bringing men of the 79th Regiment who had been there on detached service since the preceeding autumn under the command of Captain Samuel Dalrymple and Lieutenant Schomberg. Until their arrival, Dr. Dancer had been delighted by the health of the expedition, there being only thirty men in the field hospital. But the new arrivals he found 'in a most deplorable condition from old intermittents, dropsy and flux.'

On 28th February, Polson began re-embarking his troops

but, hampered by the lack of small boats, progress was slow and it was four days before they were all on board. He also loaded wooden gun-carriages and scaling-ladders, which had been brought from Jamaica in parts and assembled by the carpenters ashore. Finally, the prefabricated gunboat was pronounced seaworthy, although not complete, so was launched and named the *Lord Germain*. Nelson offered to take her in tow and she was got under the stern of the *Hinchinbroke* ready for departure.

About a dozen craft now having arrived from Black River, Polson decided to wait no longer and, on 7th March, after a delay of three weeks, 'the Fleet' sailed. The Indian and Black River craft were sent ahead to shelter off the small island of Water Key, while the main convoy sailed south down the coast to the next British settlement at Sandy Bay. It was a flat, featureless coastline, indented with estuaries and mangrove swamps and a challenge to Richard Hanna to demonstrate his skill as a pilot.

Lawrie had claimed that the Indians at Sandy Bay would have a war party ready to join the expedition but, when no native boats were seen, he was sent ashore to investigate. Meanwhile, the convoy, on Hanna's advice, anchored for the night off what he claimed to be Sandy Bay. But, next morning, it was discovered that they had passed their objective and neither Lawrie nor Indian allies were anywhere to be seen.

So they sailed on to another settlement named Tibuppy only to find, on sending a boat inshore, that it was a village called Ostara. An Indian guide eventually took them to the settlement and Polson sent a letter ashore to the senior settler, a Mr. Cairns, asking him to come on board the *Hinchinbroke* to report on the preparations for reinforcing the expedition that he and the local Indian chief had made. To this he received a short reply saying that, while he himself was quite ready to visit the ship, not one Indian would be available for the expedition unless the colonel himself came ashore to explain its purpose to the chief.

That evening, Polson and Nelson landed and, at a meeting in Cairns' house, assured the Indians that there was no threat to their liberty and that they could expect a share of future plunder. Unfortunately, all the remaining presents for the

Indians had gone into Sandy Bay with Lawrie, and there was still no news of him, so Polson felt obliged to remain ashore as a gesture of good faith, while sending a messenger to the Superintendent-General urging haste.

Three days later, Lawrie arrived and the presents were duly delivered. The Mosquito chief thereupon agreed to sail with the convoy next day but, in the morning, there was no sign of his boats because, he explained, provisions had to be collected before they could leave. The following day most of the Indian craft – except the chief's own and two others – were ready to leave and Nelson sailed, steering for the Pearl Key settlement on the mainland and hoping that the stragglers would follow.

The voyage took the convoy through coastal waters treacherous with shoals, so they were under way in daylight only and anchored for the night. The passage therefore lasted four days and was marred by two accidents. On leaving Tibuppy lagoon one of the carpenters was lost overboard. Then, on the third day, Hanna again demonstrated his inadequacy, when most of the ships ran on to a submerged reef, the *Hinchinbroke* tearing away part of her false keel and ripping off some of the copper sheathing from her bottom.

Lawrie had again been sent ahead to collect the Indians he had promised. The convoy anchored off the Pearl Key settlement on the 19th but there was no sign of Lawrie or his Indians. While Polson and Nelson impatiently awaited him, the latter was told by the masters of the transports that their fresh water supply was running dangerously low and that none could be found ashore. So, on the 21st, they sailed for Monkey Point on the mainland, where there was said to be water, leaving messages and sending instructions for Lawrie and other stragglers to join them there. One group of boats, commanded by Captain Campbell, was to call at Bluefields for any reinforcements that might be there.

Next day, the main force, having sailed past Bluefields, anchored off Monkey Point and the transports' boats were sent ashore only to find that there was no fresh water after all. Exasperated by the inefficiency of his pilot and the now apparent falsity of Lawrie's promises of massive support, both Polson and Nelson determined to press ahead with their own plans. Punta San Juan, the headland off the mouth of the San Juan river and the little port of Greytown, their final destination, was now only one day's sailing away.

Next morning they sailed southward again. The coast here was marked by a range of hills about four miles inland, rising above the trees to heights of five hundred feet and more, and by surf breaking on beaches of dark volcanic sand. Contrary winds forced them to anchor for the night about three miles out, so it was not until eleven o'clock on the morning of 24th March, forty-nine days after they had sailed from Kingston, that Nelson reached Greytown – or 'St. John's' – and the *Hinchinbroke* anchored in five fathoms at the harbour mouth.

Despard, as Chief Engineer, was immediately sent ashore to survey the beach where the landings would be made and choose a site for a shore battery. A wide sandy spit, nearly three miles in length, had formed across the bay, leaving an entrance about a mile wide and sheltering a large anchorage, which was mostly of less than five fathoms in depth. Where the San Juan river poured into the bay, staining the clear, peacock colours of the Caribbean with the muddy brown of its fresh water, low islands divided its flow into half-a-dozen channels. Of these, two debouched close to the mean little town itself, a collection of wooden huts thatched with palm leaves and standing on an isthmus that separated the sea from a shallow lagoon. The coast itself was low, its tall grass and scrub broken only by clumps of palms, bamboo and plantations of sugar cane.

While Despard was preparing his report, Nelson and Polson were worrying about their straggling convoy. Although the transports were all safely at anchor, the Indian craft had been caught at sea by the strong wind and some driven back to Monkey Point and Major Lawrie was thought to be trying to gather them together. Meanwhile, the troops, together with all their munitions and stores, had to put ashore and a camp and depot established.

Nelson's own orders from Admiral Parker were simply to escort the convoy and to remain at Greytown as guardship. So he had no part in the unloading of the transports, or the subsequent loading of the boats that were to make the advance up the river.

[78]

There was now a sense of urgency because the delays on the Mosquito Shore had lost a month of dry campaigning weather and the heavy rains of the wet season could be expected in six to eight weeks, by which time the expedition must have reached the healthy uplands of central Nicaragua. By now, Polson, exasperated by Lawrie's empty promises, was determined to begin the advance with what forces he had, leaving the Superintendent-General to follow with whatever stragglers he had been able to collect. He now found that, in addition to the force he had brought from Jamaica, the whole Mosquito Shore had furnished only twelve armed European settlers, sixty of their slaves and two hundred and twenty Mosquito Indians.

So, on the 26th, he ordered the Royal Americans and the Liverpool Blues to prepare for embarkation and departure next day, each man to carry five days' rations in his pack. The invasion flotilla that lay beached along the dark sand was a peculiar assembly. There were three large craft, the pre-fabricated *Lord Germain*, the tender *Royal George* and a Spanish vessel called the *Chichito*, together with a variety of Indian boats.

The largest of these was the panga — or bongo — the workhorse boat for trade and travel on the rivers and lakes of Nicaragua. Their hulls, usually about forty feet in length, were carved from a single cedar or mahogany trunk, and their sides built up and flared by stout planking, so giving them a beam of six to nine feet. They drew three to five feet of water and were pulled by sixteen to twenty-two oars and could carry about sixteen tons of cargo. Passengers were sheltered aft under a waggon-top canopy — the chopa — thatched and covered with hides.

In addition there were a variety of Indian boats, including the twenty-foot pitpan — or pipante — and the dory, the smallest of which could be stacked on the decks of the pangas. These, too, were dug-outs made from a single tree-trunk and with planking gunwales.

It was into such craft that Polson's volunteers and irregulars now began loading the military stores brought ashore from the transports. There were four-pounder cannon, with their wooden carriages, shot and powder; small arms and ammunition;

entrenching tools, tents and cooking pots; kegs of best salt beef and bags of dried peas, beans and biscuit; and, of course, Dr. Dancer's precious medical supplies.

Now that he was resolved to move without waiting for Lawrie, Polson was in a fever of impatience and, on the afternoon of the 27th, as soon as the boats were loaded, ordered the troops to embark for immediate departure.

So the soldiers clambered into the boats to sit, with their muskets upright between their knees, on or between the baggage and the guns. If they appeared somewhat overloaded, Polson could console himself that they should be travelling up a placid river with enough water beneath their keels. So, with much excitement, each craft, once loaded, was pushed off and rowed slowly out into the harbour and towards the mouth of the river.

It was now four o'clock and there would be only two hours before darkness would quickly fall. So Polson decided to beach his flotilla on one of the islands that separated the channels of the estuary and camp there, so as to be ready to enter the river at dawn next day.

To reach this island, the boats had to cross the brown water of the river, where it swirled and rippled into the bay, and they were unprepared for its strength. As they struck the current, boats swung violently and, as the soldiers struggled to steady themselves, cargoes shifted and some that were top-heavy, heeled and capsized. In a few moments, the triumphant departure of the expedition was a chaos of upturned boats, men struggling in the water and their baggage either sunk to the bottom, or floating out to sea.

One soldier of the Loyal Irish had been drowned but the rest were saved, the capsized boats taken in tow and the expedition returned to the beach it had left only an hour before.

It was now obvious to Polson that the boats, so easily over-turned, had been heavily over-loaded and that he dare not risk the ascent of the river until their cargoes and the number of passengers were reduced. He therefore resolved that the expedition should travel in two divisions. The first, commanded by himself, would consist of the experienced Royal Americans and just over half of the Liverpool Blues, together with some of

[80]

the Loyal Irish, volunteers and irregulars. Most of the Indians would accompany them as guides and scouts and to man the boats. So, when the first division had reached a suitable landing-place on the river, it would halt and establish a forward base, while the Indians would take the empty boats back down the river to collect the second division. This, commanded by Major James MacDonald of the Royal Jamaica Volunteers, would consist of the remainder of the 79th Regiment and the bulk of the volunteers and irregulars.

Polson wrote orders to be left for Lawrie, who had still failed to appear, ordering him to bring whatever force of Indians he had been able to recruit with him up the river as soon as he arrived at Greytown, but to leave enough guides for Major MacDonald's ascent.

Next morning, all was activity and zeal again as the cargoes were drastically reduced, several guns and much shot being left behind, together with much of the less-essential equipment, including the scaling ladders. As it was assumed they would be advancing into healthier country, most of the medical supplies were also left.

Nelson had been an appalled spectator of this confusion. Offically, it was no concern of his but it must have been clear to him that an expedition, which could not even begin its journey up an uncharted and virtually unknown river, could hardly be expected to reach its destination. He had come to like Polson – and the liking was, after the mistrustful start, mutual – but he seemed a commander without the imagination or initiative for such an enterprise. Among his officers, however, he recognised men after his own heart – Despard, the engineer, and his young brother, Thomas; Bulkeley of the 79th; Captain Harrison, who was considered an expert on Indian affairs; and Captain James Mounsey, the adjutant – and he longed to accompany them.

If the enterprise succeeded, the consequences would be almost beyond comprehension and would be matched by the glory. Were he, rather than a volunteer captain from Jamaica, to command the intended squadron on Lake Nicaragua, his name could become as famous as Wolfe's. He might even be known to history as the officer who severed North America from South America and made possible the conquest of New Spain.

[81]

Then there was the prize-money. General Dalling had been confident that, once the army could begin the ascent of the San Juan, there was little to halt their advance on the cities of Nicaragua and beyond. The booty would be enormous and Nelson could then, if he so wished, set up himself and his family as Norfolk landowners.

So it was that, on his own initiative and without authority from Admiral Parker, Nelson offered to accompany the expedition. Leaving the *Hinchinbroke* under the command of his first lieutenant, he would embark nearly fifty sailors and marines in the frigate's cutter and pinnace and put them and himself at Polson's disposal. The colonel, shaken by his first experience of amphibious operations, was effusive with gratitude and later wrote to Dalling, 'Captain Nelson . . . came up with thirty-four seamen, one sergeant and twelve marines; I want words to express the obligations I owe that gentleman.'

Now, with a naval officer to take charge of the travel by water, leaving the soldiers to concentrate upon matters they understood, new confidence urged forward the preparations. A final touch was given to morale when, on the morning of the 28th, just as Polson was about to give the order for the second departure, the sails of a sloop were sighted off the harbour mouth. She proved to be a despatch ship from Jamaica, carrying a letter for the colonel from Governor Dalling.

This was dated 17th March and began, 'From the time elapsed since your departure, I begin to be anxious for news from you.' Clearly, in the absence of news, the Governor's imagination had been stimulated to suppose that the expedition had already ascended the river, captured the castle of San Juan and entered the lake. But the importance of the letter to Polson was that it told him of powerful reinforcements soon to be on their way: 'I am now preparing a Corps of 300 Regulars and a number (I hope at least equal) of Volunteers . . . the whole will be ready to sail in about 3 weeks, or less, under the command of Lieut. Col. Kemble.' This was Lieutenant-Colonel Stephen Kemble, the commanding officer of the 1st Battalion of the Royal Americans, and a soldier of experience in the tropics.

Dalling continued, 'You will not therefore risque more than is necessary for the present, but, in case you should have fortified one of the little islands and are in possession of Granada, I would wish you to keep possession of the city, if without risque, and rather to instil into the inhabitants that no farther is meant. It will be proper to fortify passes and to collect horses for mounting a Corps I am raising here for Light Horse men . . . and as many cattle as possible in order to form a depot of Provisions in the first instance at or about the Fort of San Juan.'

Then, in his wildly optimistic assumptions, the Governor went on to apologise to Polson for the inevitable loss of supreme command, and his own future involvement in the great acts of war that he imagined to be unfolding. 'Colonel Kemble is sensible that he must be equally superseded in his turn,' he wrote, 'and should the King adopt the ideas I have had the honour to lay before him and still reinforce the troops on the Main, a superior officer must be sent to take command, likely it will be myself.

'I sincerely hope I may have given you time to gather the Laurels about Fort San Juan and the Lake. . . .'

These heady words had both an exciting and depressing effect upon the men in the boats off the mouth of the river. They were excited to know that they were the vanguard of a great conquering army: not just an expedition concocted by an enthusiastic colonial governor, but ordained across the Atlantic by the King of Great Britain himself. Yet they were depressed at the thought that what the Governor so blithely assumed to have been achieved with ease had not been begun. Before they had arrived off the mouth of the San Juan, the journey up the river had looked as if it would be a pleasant interlude before the campaign, but in their first brush with its waters, they had been flung into disarray.

For Dalling, the launching of the expedition had been both stimulant and palliative at a time of worry. As well as his feud with Harrison, and constant criticism and hostility from the Assembly, there was the abiding fear of a French, or Spanish fleet. Both, might re-appear in the Caribbean and the invasion of Jamaica might again threaten, while much of its garrison was away in Central America and before reinforcements arrived from home. This, indeed, was about to happen for, on 13th

February, the capable Comte de Guichen left Brest with sixteen sail of the line and steered for Martinique. Unaware of this, Rodney, who had just succeeded in relieving the besieged garrison of Gibraltar, sailed for the Caribbean with a smaller squadron a week later. Another confrontation at sea seemed inevitable and the numerical odds would be in favour of France and Spain.

The day after the expedition had sailed, the Governor had written to the Colonial Secretary to inform him, adding that he intended to reinforce it with a second contingent under Colonel Kemble. When the troop convoy arrived from England, he went on, it would be prudent to send them straight to Nicaragua because of the danger to their health in Jamaica from disease and rum. 'In short,' he wrote, 'comfortably hutted on the Main, warm clothing during the rainy season and good medicines bid fair to produce a more comfortable body for action.'

But he said nothing about his growing ambition to take command himself. The more he thought about this, the more attractive the idea became. He would assume supreme command in the field only if Polson and Kemble were successful in the opening stages of the campaign and final success seemed sure. He could then not only gratify his professional ambition but the consequent glory would wipe away memories of his political failures. Indeed, the conquest of Nicaragua, and the opening of direct communication with the Pacific coast of Central America, would be the moment to resign office and hand over to his Lieutenant-Governor, so returning home as a successful general instead of a failed colonial governor.

So, on the day he wrote to Polson, admitting this ambition, he wrote to Germain, 'Thank God, my health is in a tolerable state at present and were it not for the constant apprehension of that dreadful gout, I should yet think myself able to go thro' some service — but what a terrible disorder for a soldier!' Thus, he prepared Germain for what he hoped would be a later letter announcing that the gout was gone and that he, as Commander-in-Chief, had taken the field.

He also wrote to Admiral Parker stating baldly that the danger to Jamaica of invasion was now 'entirely removed' and, that he remained 'in hourly expectation of intelligence' from Polson. He forecast the opening of 'a free passage and intercourse to the South Sea' and the taking of Granada and Leon 'if not the whole Province of Guatemala itself.' Perhaps because he knew Parker to lack his own enthusiasms, he did not repeat the even more optimistic forecasts he had made in recent despatches to London, which included the conquest of Yucatan. He was careful neither to alarm nor alienate the admiral further, since he would shortly need his cooperation when the Colonial Office and the Admiralty responded to a suggestion he had made for a whole supporting squadron under a senior naval officer to be based on Greytown. Later, he might realise his dream of a two-ocean navy, and had already tried to excite Germain over this by writing that 'If we once fortify ourselves in Nicaragua, our ships in the South Sea may be very easily supplied with any kind of stores from the West Indies.'

But it was not only Dalling who had caught the fever of dramatic speculation. Even the shrewd General Campbell was infected. While awaiting news of Polson, he wrote to Germain, 'If the Administration mean to send a squadron of ships to the Pacific Ocean, the scene may open to a degree of importance to Britain beyond the power of human investigation; whilst Spain will feel its consequences terminal to her destruction.

'If the communication between the Harbour of St. John's and the Lake of Nicaragua can only be handsomely maintained, every intercourse with the Northern and Southern Continent may be effectively cut off and Forces thrown across to the South Seas in 30 days from Jamaica. Whether the object is therefore to attack the Northern or Southern settlements of South America, the rout of Nicaragua will effect it most completely.'

While such exhilarating theories were being bandied about in Spanish Town, the men who were expected to put them into practice were bracing themselves for a journey into the unknown. The two authorities, upon whom they relied for guidance on what to expect, had both failed them: Lawrie had not only failed to produce the promised men and boats but had not arrived himself for this critical day of departure; Hanna, the pilot, had, for all his boasts, proved unreliable. Even the Indians of Greytown seemed to have only sketchy knowledge of what awaited them up the river.

It had been said, on the one hand, that quite large vessels had ascended the river to the lake; on the other, that there were waterfalls along its course, or perhaps these were cataracts, as was noted on Jeffery's map. This seemed to show that the river was upwards of one hundred miles in length and was joined by tributaries but, although cross-hatching on the map indicated hills or mountains, there was no way of knowing whether it ran between swamps or cliffs, jungle or savannah. Somewhere more than thirty miles upstream was the castle of San Juan, which had to be taken, and there was also talk of outposts on islands downstream of it. Upstream, the river continued for an unknown distance until it reached the lake and the junction was commanded by the fort of San Carlos. The lake itself held fewer fears, because it would be deep, open water and, now that Captain Nelson and his confident sailors were with them, there was surely no need for apprehension.

Dr. Dancer, who was accompanying the first division of boats, was optimistic. The health of the troops remained better than might have been expected and they hoped to be far away from the unhealthy coastal marshes by the time the rains began and to have reached the bracing uplands around the lake. The most likely problem would be dysentery from drinking tainted water, but that was something to be expected by any force in the field. It was likely that they would come across biting insects and snakes, but the doctor remained sanguine and would probably have agreed with a contemporary, who wrote of such fears. 'The mosquitoes, sandflies and other insects, the poisonous reptiles and wild beasts, of which so much is said in England are . . . mere bugbears to frighten children.'

There was, however, one element of risk. Particular care had been taken by Dancer and Dr. Moseley, when the expedition was getting ready in Jamaica, that it should be well supplied not only with medicines and drugs but with rations suitable for the sick – such as vermicelli, sugar, sago, chocolate and oatmeal – and hospital bedding. But most of this had been left behind as being of less importance than ammunition.

On the morning of 28th March, Nelson tried to arrange his bizarre convoy into order for the start of the voyage. Indian canoes under the command of volunteer officers, and with pilots embarked, would go first to find the deepest channel and scout for possible enemy. Then would come his own cutter and pinnace, the boats carrying Polson, Despard, Dr. Dancer and the rest of the headquarters staff; next pangas and pitpans laden with troops, their rations and camp equipment; finally the heaviest craft, including the *Lord Germain* loaded with both stores and troops, the *Chichito*, carrying gunpowder; finally, the *Royal George*, laden with provisions and commanded by Captain Collins, who would bring up the rear.

When all the vessels were under way, their bows to the swirling brown stream, Nelson gave the order that was repeated by officers and coxswains and scores of oars and paddles plunged into the water. '*Hoo-pah! Hoo-pah!*' chanted the Indians in time with the stroke of paddles and oars. The long column of boats slowly moved westward into the river mouth, up the muddy channel between low banks thick with tall grass gently ruffling in the warm wind.

There were two principal mouths to the San Juan river; one narrow, one wide. The more southerly was nearly half a mile wide but so little water was flowing between its dried mud-banks, that its passage was impossible. The northerly channel was narrow — perhaps two hundred yards across — but there seemed enough water even for the biggest boats, so that was the channel chosen. Into this they headed, the energy of their enthusiasm moving them quickly upstream so that when the excitement of the start faded and the strokes of oars and paddles settled to a slower rhythm, they noticed that the banks seemed to have closed behind them, shutting off the reassuring view of sea and ships, and that they were embraced by surroundings both strange and remote.

There was no sign of human life or activity along the banks; no thatched huts, no cattle, not even a deserted fisherman's canoe on the shore. Perched on shoals, or old logs brought down by the current, cormorants spread their black wings to dry in the sun, watching the intruders with sharp, bright eyes but not frightened into flight by the splashing and the shouts. They, in turn, were ignored by the men in the boats, whose eyes were on the water, trying to judge its depth and where it

[87]

suddenly shelved.

The canoes leapt ahead but the bigger boats following would scrape their keels along the bottom and the heaviest craft astern would ground and swing broadside to the current, while their cursing crews thrust against the shoals with oars. The river was broken by sand-banks and low islands, thick with grass and scrub, its channels sometimes blocked with driftwood and flotsam, sometimes opening into a smoothly gliding reach where the oars could plunge deep. Where a backwater was bright with the blue of water hyacinth, the Indians would look instinctively for the swirl, or a glimpse, of the wet leathery back of a manatee 'sea cow', although there was no time to stop and spear them now.

Then there would be excited shouts passing from boat to boat as something was seen to move on a muddy shore and it would prove to be an alligator, or sometimes a crocodile. A traveller, who came up the river later, described how 'great numbers of large alligators were basking on the muddy banks, appearing at a distance like old decayed logs of wood or trunks of trees, but the noise of our boat ascending these rapid currents and the songs of our mariners invariably made these monsters take to the water.'

This was an excitement and for the young soldiers of the 79th, now safely seated in a boat with a musket between the knees and powder and shot in their pouches, would be something to boast about in the taverns of Liverpool. But excitement could quickly turn to fear when the boat jolted on to a shoal, began to swing with the current and the officer ordered everybody over the side to push her clear. This was when they would remember camp-fire stories by old hands in the tropics about crocodiles that could not only eat men but horses; giant leeches that sucked the blood and shoals of tiny fish that could strip a cow to its skeleton in a matter of minutes.

As the hours went by beneath a high tropic sun and the channels continued to wind and shelve, the boats grounded again and again, and their cursing crews and passengers scrambled over their sides to push. The canoes quickly floated free, the pangas were got off only after much labour but, one by one, the big craft at the rear stuck fast. By late afternoon, the convoy that had looked so orderly at the river mouth was straggling over many miles; the shallow-draught vanguard still darting ahead, the rear immobile. Nelson and Polson decided that it was time to stop and make an attempt to re-form.

Palms and flowering trees now grew along the banks, flocks of green parrots screamed and, where the water was smooth, turtles bobbed to the surface to thrust up a pointed head and cast a quizzical eye at the disturbance before disappearing with a splash. Polson waited until his boat came abreast of a gently shelving beach where palms and undergrowth were less thick and gave the order to halt and make camp. He estimated that they had covered six and a half miles on the first day.

Hot, tired and wet to the waist, the men of those boats that had managed to keep up, now struggled ashore and heaved the bows of their craft on to the sand. Fires were lit, some tents were pitched and Indians and sailors looked about for suitably-spaced trees from which hammocks could be slung. While the soldiers prepared to unpack, divide and cook their rations, the Indians settled down easily into making camp and preparing their food. They had brought with them strips of sun-dried 'jerk beef' to be cooked with plaintains and rice, *chanaca* cakes of unrefined sugar and *tiste*, a mixture of dried corn, cocoa and sugar to be mixed with water.

While the men in the stranded boats settled down amongst their cargoes as best they could, Nelson and Polson planned the next-day's operations, which would be devoted to lightening the over-loaded vessels and getting them up to their camp. At dawn, both of the *Hinchinbroke's* boats and several pitpans would be unloaded and sent downstream to collect most of the cargoes of the grounded vessels in the hope that these could then be got up to the beach by the camp.

The sun set at about six and darkness followed quickly. Immediately the hot air was whining with mosquitoes and the men huddled as close to the heat of the fires as possible in the hope that the smoke would protect them from the stinging bites. Then, as they tried to rest, the night came alive with noise: strange and alarming whoops and whistles, croaks and grunts, rustling and rattling, coughs and trills. The Liverpool Blues had never heard anything like it and had no means of

[89]

knowing what terrors could make such fearful sounds out beyond the wall of darkness. Bright eyes watched them: some proved to be fireflies, others might be the unblinking eyes of cayman alligators in the shallows; others, whatever they might be, watched from among the trees.

Lying wakeful in the heat, an officer who looked at his watch by the light of the fire could note that at about ten o'clock the torment of the mosquitoes began to ease. It became colder, and a mist arose from the river, but the wild night noises continued until, almost as if by agreement, they seemed to cease at midnight. Then the air became chill and dank and men who had sweated two hours earlier, now shivered. The first dim light came between five and six in the morning and men to whom exhaustion had brought sleep woke stiff in a heavy dew. A thick white mist lay over the river as they rose and tried to rekindle the fires, dry damp clothes and warm cramped limbs. Gradually the mist fell back and, by eight, the sun was burning in a bright and clear, blue sky.

By then, Nelson had led the relief flotilla downstream. He ordered the pitpans to stop and take aboard soldiers who had spent an uncomfortable night in the *Lord Germain*, while others embarked stores from other stranded craft and his own two boats loaded all the bags of gunpowder from the *Chichito*. Thus lightened, the big boats floated free and their crews began working them up the river, even now with the greatest difficulty. Meanwhile, Nelson returned with his cutter and pinnace to the camp, the laden pitpans following and sometimes running aground themselves.

Another night was spent at this first camp, some of the strange noises now being identified by the more experienced, for the benefit of the newcomers to the tropics, as being tree-frogs or insects; the terrifying shrieking whistle being only a whippoorwill calling to its mate, and the ominous roaring in the treetops from howler monkeys.

Along the banks, the palms had been giving way to tall jungle trees, their massive trunks rising straight for a hundred feet before throwing out great branches to form the canopy of the rain forest. One who followed them up the river described the trees standing 'like Gothic columns with evergreen arches, covering cool, dark vistas.'

At dawn on the third day, Polson decided to continue upstream, despite the fact that five or six of his craft carrying the extra loads quickly ran aground in the shallows and had to be left behind.

This was a difficult day for, while the lighter boats got several miles up the river, there were now two groups of stragglers to worry about. The big vessels had still been unable to get up to the camp, where the pitpans that had relieved them of some of their loads were now themselves stranded. So Polson, on Nelson's advice, again halted the expedition and sent back all the pitpans, canoes and dories to take yet more from the grounded craft, while his men unloaded twenty barrels of provisions and several gun-carriages and carts at the camp, where they could be left under a small guard until collected. The colonel also sent a canoe back to Greytown with a letter for Major MacDonald asking him to send up two empty boats for this purpose.

The next day, 1st April, was worse. The river was now walled by huge forest trees more than a hundred feet tall and shutting out any cooling breeze, while the sun beat on to shoals and sand-banks, throwing back reflected heat and dazzling glare. There seemed less water than ever and boats were constantly grounding, sometimes having to be unloaded and their cargoes heaved on to the bank while they were hauled into deeper water, then loaded again. There were islands as well and it was just below two of these that the river seemed to swing southward, becoming suddenly wide and deep. It was only after making easy progress up this reach for nearly three miles that it was realised that it was not just a meandering loop but another river into which they had blundered. It was, in fact, the Colorado river, which joined the San Juan about twenty miles from its mouth, but the men were so exhausted that Polson decided to camp there for the night before returning to their intended course in the morning. Now, any remaining faith in the pilots was lost, Nelson and Polson deciding to rely solely on Indian scouts accompanied by active young officers.

The shared hardship and successive problems had brought the officers closer together. Polson's initial doubts about Nelson

[91]

had long since disappeared and he had come to rely upon him to such an extent that later, when writing of his early reservations, he added that 'in two or three days he displayed himself and afterwards he directed all the operations.' Liking was mutual, but Nelson recognised that Polson, although an officer of the Royal Americans, who specialised in bush warfare, was now facing something far beyond his experience, or even his imagination.

Nelson's closest friend was Despard, whose enthusiasm was like his own and who was, above all, practical. It was he who advised the colonel on the choice of camp sites and it was he who often took a canoe ahead with the scouts to report on the state of the water. He was also busily engaged in surveying the river and evenings in camp would be spent drawing charts and writing reports that would, he hoped, one day find themselves on a polished mahogony table in the King's House at Spanish Town. He was also good company, debonair and stimulating, so that Nelson and he would eat together and shared a tent.

During these first days on the river, the rank and file of the expedition – the regulars, irregulars, volunteers, settlers and Indians – were too tired to want more than food and sleep and try to brush away the mosquitoes, when they stopped work for the night. But there were a few warning signs of discontent. It had been hoped to keep the regulars separate from the rest so as to avoid infection by their free and easy, and, when opportunity arose, debauched, ways. This proved impossible. Care had been advised in handling the Indians, but officers kept trying to make them conform to the disciplines of a military encampment and this they clearly resented. Yet, for all, there was still the prospect of plunder and glory – appealing to each man in accordance with his position – and this remained to bind them together.

Upstream of the junction with the Colorado, the banks were higher, the river deeper and the boats made good progress. Dancer, who later described the difficulties of the shoals when 'the men were frequently obliged to quit the boats and unite their most strenuous exertions in getting them along through a number of shallow channels, previously explored by Indians sent before for that purpose', was gratified by the sudden ease of deep water but worried that the men were suffering from heat exhaustion. 'Our men were much exposed to injury from the sun's rays beating violently upon them for seven or eight hours every day,' he noted, 'besides a still more intense heat reflected from the many naked shoals, covered with whitish sand, which rendered the air sometimes intolerable. This violent insolation during the day was followed by as dangerous an exposition to the heavy dews at night and it was surprising that the men continued so well, for as yet we had but few, and those trifling, complaints.'

For the next two days, they made up for lost time, covering, as Polson recorded, nine and a quarter miles on the first and ten and a quarter on the second. The river ran between what looked like solid walls of rain forest; gigantic trees trailing creepers and air plants, their sombre green lit by a spangle of orchids and the bright colours of parrots and kingfishers. To avoid the strongest current, the boats kept close to the shore so that sometimes, as that later navigator of the river wrote, 'vines loaded with gay and fragrant flowers trailed over the chopa . . . brilliantly-coloured birds sparkled in the cool, green coverts and, for the first time, we saw the ugly iguanas looking curiously down upon us from the projecting limbs of trees.'

The iguanas were among the strange creatures killed and skinned for the cooking pot by the Indians, and Nelson himself had an encounter with one that became the talk of the camp fires. After one particularly arduous day on the river, he was dozing in a hammock when an iguana slowly made its way from a tree to which it was hung, down the slinging ropes and across his face, waking him in alarm. He flung back his blanket to spring down, to see a large, poisonous snake coiled at his feet. At the time it was thought that the iguana was a 'monitory lizard' that was hunting the snake, whereas the reverse was more likely and the usually shy creature had forgotten its customary caution in flight.

A third day of easy going followed and they covered ten miles but now came the first suggestion of an enemy ahead. An Indian, who claimed to know the river, said that there was an old Spanish fort on an island some miles upstream, between two tributaries, one flowing north; the other, south. Nelson advised a cautious reconnaissance and a party of the most reliable Indians were sent forward in pitpans and dories accompanied by British officers. After they had set out, the main body camped for the night and next day covered another ten miles. On this passage they found their scouts awaiting them with the news that the fort had been sighted but was abandoned. As the boats drew level with the island, a small ruin could be seen already overwhelmed by the jungle.

A fourth successful day followed, Polson noting a passage of eleven and a half miles. Yet there was still no sign of human life, or an enemy. The river was becoming almost familiar: the white egrets and herons poised at the water's edge; the turtles basking on logs, or bobbing to the surface; monkeys swinging in the treetops. Often, huge tarpon leapt clear of the water, dropping back with a splash like falling shot.

There were other fish in the river. Some, like the tarpon, could be speared by the Indians in the shallows. Others were to be avoided at all costs. Among these, it was said, were sharks and sawfish making their way up from the sea to the great lake. But most dreadful were the shoals of *machaca* fish. When a fragment of food fell into the most placid deep water, it would suddenly boil with leaping gnashing fish. The Indians said that nobody should bathe in the river; a man swimming naked would invite castration.

So, much of the provisions having had to be left behind, the Indians supplemented the rations with fish as well as iguana, turtles, wild duck and large jungle rodents. At one camp, when rations had become short, Nelson was told that broth was being cooked; hungry, he approached the fire to find that stew-pot full of monkeys. So horrible did they look, he later said, that nothing could persuade him to eat.

The current was becoming stronger and then a new sound became apparent: the rushing of water over the rocks of rapids. This was the beginning of three sets of rapids where the river flowed through hills; those near the bank some two or three hundred feet high — although giant trees made them appear much more massive — but, to the north, sometimes rising to two thousand feet and more. This was by far the most formidable obstacle encountered so far and it seemed impossible that boats could pass it except in the rainy season when the river was high. While Nelson and Polson considered their position, the Indians, who had proved more reliable than the pilots, told them that about six miles upstream, beyond the rapids, there was a Spanish look-out post and that this was the first of the outer defences of the castle of San Juan, which lay farther still up the river.

At last, more than two months after the expedition had left Jamaica, action seemed imminent. In its planning and execution, Colonel Polson was resolved to rely upon the advice of his two most active young officers, Horatio Nelson and Edward Despard.

CHAPTER FOUR

Boarding the Enemy

On the morning of 1st April, 1780, Robert Hodgson, the deposed Superintendent-General of the Mosquito Shore walked through the streets of London to the seat of power in Whitehall with a deep sense of satisfaction. Since the demolition of the turreted Holbein arch and the widening of the street thirty years before, the place seemed to radiate an imperial confidence. The symbol of authority was no longer Inigo Jones's banqueting house, surviving from the old royal palace, but the new Admiralty, stern behind the Tuscan columns of Robert Adam's stone screen; the Army's headquarters elegantly housed in William Kent's Horse Guards buildings that opened on to the grand parade; and the opulence of St. James's Park.

The Colonial Office, whither he was bound, was a large, plain building in Downing Street. Certainly, for one whose life had been mostly spent among the jungles and rivers of Central America, it must have seemed the fount of all earthly patronage. Since he had been tricked out of his own position of power by James Lawrie, Hodgson had remained in England nursing his grievance and refusing – partly through pique but not without bitter satisfaction – an invitation to return to Jamaica to help with the early preparations for the expedition to Nicaragua.

Now, it seemed, he was about to receive his due as the originator – as he claimed – of the idea. He had been summoned, not by some unknown factotum of government but by the great Lord George Germain himself, to be entrusted with a mission of delicacy and significance.

Lord George was as imposing in presence as in stature, well armoured against the past scandal of his court-martial by the confidence arising from inherited wealth and aristocratic manner. His charm could be as inpsiring as his disdain could wither and, when he received Hodgson, his manners were at their most pleasant and easy. He was grateful to be able to entrust the secret despatches for the Governor of Jamaica to one so experienced and reliable and to know that his experience would then be available in the guidance of the great events that were now beginning to unfold on the Spanish Main.

Hodgson had finally agreed to join the convoy of troopships that had been preparing to sail for Jamaica with powerful reinforcements. These were to include four of the newly-raised infantry regiments – the 85th, 92nd, 93rd and 94th – under the command of Major-General George Garth. He had sent his luggage down to Plymouth in advance and was himself to follow that night with the dispatch-box in a fast chaise. The excitement of a secret mission was as stimulating as the confidence of the Colonial Secretary; Hodgson felt so flattered that he could not bring himself to be so presumptuous as to ask Lord George exactly what his official appointment would be when he reached his destination.

The audience over, Hodgson took to the road, reaching Plymouth in less than two days, and boarding General Garth's ship as the sailors were busy closing the gun-ports and stowing the last baggage in readiness for immediate departure. Exulting in the favour now shown to him and in the adventure now to begin, Hodgson 'set his mind at large from private cares', as he put it, 'and was ready for any exertion that might be required of him and, as he never doubted of fully repaying to his country any honour that might be done him, he chose to throw himself into the hands of Government with perfect confidence.'

It was therefore with heavy disappointment and sense of anti-climax that he heard, just as the ships' captains were about to give their orders to weigh anchor and make sail, that the wind had changed and was now so contrary and so strong that their departure must be indefinitely delayed.

Meanwhile, the first reinforcements had reached Jamaica with the arrival early in April of the 88th Regiment of Foot, commanded by Lieutenant-Colonel Sir Alexander Leith. Its appearance was timely because the Assembly and the Legislature, having heard no news of the expedition to Nicaragua and hearing that Governor Dalling was about to send most of the troops remaining in the island to join it, had become even more critical. Indeed, Dalling wrote that 'by the violence of their conduct I should have imagined them either to have been the Emissaries of an American Congress, or the Ambassadors of a discontented party at home, aided by the Spleen and Malgignancy of the late Attorney-General, (who has) endeavoured much to keep up the flame.'

His dismissal of Harrison had brought the anger of Whitehall — in the persons of the Colonial Secretary and the First Lord of the Admiralty — upon him and his response to such displeasure was, again, a mixture of self-abasement and self-justification. In a letter to Germain, he pleaded, 'I kiss the rod, not as a culprit, having intentionally taken a strong step, urged from vanity, self-conceit or the more ridiculous wish of empty popular applause, but for having been the means of trouble and uneasiness to your Lordship.'

But in his own colony, the Governor did not cringe and when he again drew criticism from Admiral Parker, his response was sharp. The Jamaica squadron was, as usual, under-manned and the Commander-in-Chief was having particular difficulty in finding either volunteers or men fit for impressment, because of the Governor's recruiting of seamen to man the boats that would accompany the reinforcements to the Spanish Main. So he wrote to Dalling, 'I cannot see the necessity of employing British seamen on the lakes and rivers in a country so baneful to European constitutions, when foreign seamen may be procured at Curaçoa and the neighbouring islands, who will answer the purpose better.'

He went on to complain that seamen from privateers and merchantmen had taken to roving the Kingston waterfront in armed groups to defend themselves against his press gangs and that they included deserters from his own ships. He therefore asked that regular troops be used 'to stop straggling seamen in all parts of the island and lodge them in the guard-house at Kingston, and, for their trouble, they shall receive twenty shillings Sterling for each straggling seamen and forty shillings Sterling for each deserter.'

The Governor's reply was brusque. The reinforcements – together with 'flat-bottomed boats, gun-boats and *batteaux* in frames' – were essential, he wrote, and 'should the climate, intended for the scene of operations, prove so baneful to the seamen as you imagine, we have only to lament the hardness of their fate; but British seamen, like British soldiers, will, I hope, ever be ready to pay the necessary obedience to the orders of their superior officers.'

He then, in turn, criticised Parker. He perfectly understood the need for recruiting seamen for His Majesty's ships but while the Kingston magistrates were quite ready to issue warrants for their impressment, 'they cannot, indeed, they say, they will not, encourage the mode of impressing lately adopted, so destructive of good order, so fraught with mischief and so repugnant to the spirit as well as the letter of a British Act of Parliament.'

Dalling was confident that there was no immediate threat of invasion to Jamaica, now that Rodney was back in the Caribbean, and, although he had so far failed to bring de Guichen to decisive action, held the initiative. So, together with Hercules Ross, he continued with his preparations for sending more troops to Nicaragua. Commanded by Lieutenant-Colonel Stephen Kemble of the Royal Americans, who would take over command from Polson, they would consist of two hundred and thirty-five regular soldiers – sixty-five of them from the 60th and most of the others from the Loyal Irish – and about two hundred and fifty volunteers and irregulars. The latter would include a second contingent of the Jamaica Legion, whom Brigadier Campbell found a 'riotous, troublesome set of people' (they included deserters from the Royal Navy, as well as privateersmen), under the command of Major William Dalrymple, whose dispute over the Omoa prize-money had now been settled. A somewhat similar collection of assorted seafarers had been brought together as the Royal Batteaux Corps, whose specific task would be to man boats on the river. While Governor Dalling publicly maintained that the regular reinforcement was largely made up of convalescents, they were nearly all reported as being 'a fine body of men, in good health and fit for the field.'

Although no word had been received from Polson, it was assumed that he had, at least, captured the castle of San Juan, and Kemble's orders from Dalling and Campbell were to exploit this success. On arrival at Greytown, he was first to fortify the port with a shore battery and stockade, then ascend the river to the castle and continue to the lake. There, he must occupy one of the most fertile of the islands 'possessing a safe, commodious harbour for your armed craft' and fortify it with redoubts. From this, he was told, 'your armed vessels must constantly be employed in sweeping the Lake of Nicaragua in every direction as well for the purpose of intelligence as for destroying any force the Enemy may attempt to show in opposition to you afloat.' From the island base an attack should be launched – if not already made – on Granada, then Leon, but, if opposition proved too strong, the western shore of the lake was to be occupied before advancing to the shores of the Pacific. Strategically, this would be more important than plundering towns and Campbell told Kemble to report urgently on the terrain between the lake and the coast – Was it healthy? How well supplied was it with wood and water? – and on anchorages in 'the Southern Ocean' suitable for warships.

Kemble was made aware of contingencies arising from a Spanish counter-attack, particularly an attempt to re-take Greytown, so cutting the expedition's communications. If that happened, Campbell wrote, 'you are not to think your situation desperate. The progress of the Enemy up the river may be disputed inch by inch . . . your forts and redoubts can be defended handsomely', and, finally, 'you can retreat to your island by means of the craft in your possession and maintain yourself there for a considerable length of time, dealing destruction to their army by fatigues and distress.'

But if retreat should become necessary this could be made across country and down another river that flowed into the sea at Bluefields. It was stressed, however, that the orders were flexible and that Kemble would be free to take the initiative in choosing other objectives as and when they appeared most promising. He was also urged to make the health of his men 'the chief object of your care.'

The expedition was due to sail in the second week of April but Parker had grudgingly allocated only the sixteen-gun brig *Victor* as escort and Ross had to commandeer armed storeships to accompany the convoy. The admiral was annoyed at having to keep a frigate immobile at Greytown as guardship, particularly because her captain was one of his best. He did not know that Nelson had gone up the river with Polson and determined to recall him to Port Royal at the earliest opportunity. This was because of the death in March of Captain Bonovier Glover, and the command of his ship, the forty-four gun frigate *Janus*, thereby falling vacant. She was to be Nelson's new command and Parker wrote to him accordingly, adding that his relief in the *Hinchinbroke* was to be Cuthbert Collingwood. So, on 10th April, Captain Collingwood sailed from Port Royal to take over an appointment from his friend for the fourth time.

Four days later, Colonel Kemble's convoy sailed from Kingston Bay and, within a week, the Assembly, aware that the Governor had again disregarded their wishes, passed a resolution that 'the Troops, or any of them now stationed here for our protection and defence, or any of the White Inhabitants or People of Colour be not sent off upon Foreign Expeditions.' But it was, of course, too late.

On 6th April, as General Garth's expeditionary force lay storm-bound at Plymouth and Colonel Kemble was reading his instructions for the advance across Nicaragua to the Pacific, Colonel Polson was giving his first orders for making contact with the enemy. His advance-guard, including his headquarters staff and Captain Nelson with his naval party, had made camp beside a small creek that flowed into the San Juan river just below the rapids. As he had been told that a Spanish outpost was likely to be sited on an island about six miles upstream, he decided that a patrol sent forward by water would lose all chance of surprise by struggling up the rapids. Therefore he decided to send them overland and, sure enough, an overgrown path through the forest beside the river – an old Spanish portage – was discovered.

The reconnaissance party was to consist of Captain Despard, Captain James Mounsey, the adjutant, accompanied by an officer and thirty men and the most reliable of the Indian guides. When they had disappeared amongst the tree-trunks of the rain forest, Polson settled down at the camp to await their report and hope that more of his straggling boats would appear. He waited that night and all the next day, until, after nightfall, a tired and jungle-stained messenger arrived from Despard. He reported that they had sighted the Spanish outpost on an island higher upstream than expected and round a bend of the river, so that it would be possible for the boats to attempt the ascent of the rapids without being seen. However Polson decided to march his men through 'these horrid woods', while the Indians tried to drag the boats up the rapids, which were estimated to be running at about seven knots. For most of the soldiers, this was their first experience of a jungle trail; the dangling creepers, the leeches and the ferocious thorns that ripped uniforms and skin; scratches often becoming inflamed and septic.

Farther along the trail, Polson and Nelson found Despard and Mounsey waiting for them. They had just returned from the river bank opposite the fortified island and the former made his report. The little island, he said, lay seventy to eighty yards from the north bank and he had seen three sentries, who appeared to be Spanish regular soldiers and much on the alert, on the horseshoe-shaped earthworks of a battery facing downstream. His Indians had bravely 'creep'd down to the river in the night to try if the river was fordable to the island but reported that at the very edge it took them up to their middle and therefore judg'd it impracticable to ford it.'

The best hope for a surprise attack, Despard suggested, was for 'light crafts to go up the river in the night and endeavour to pass the look-out by the south side of the river, that, in the morning, they should fall down to the upper end of the island and attack the post.' Meanwhile another party should open covering fire from the north bank.

Nelson agreed in principle but thought that a much stronger assault force should be sent upstream and volunteered to take them in his own two boats, pulled by his sailors. The colonel gratefully accepted his offer and gave him command of two officers and forty soldiers for the attack. Despard and

Mounsey volunteered to go with him.

The evening, the *Hinchinbroke*'s cutter and pinnace, packed with soldiers, and a flotilla of canoes manned by Indians, began the ascent of the rapids. It was far more difficult than expected and often every man was ordered over the sides of the two big boats to heave and drag them over shoals. In the darkness, some of the canoes went ahead and slipped past the island in the shadows of the far bank; before dawn, they were ready to sweep downstream to beach on the thickly wooded shore above the battery. Meanwhile Mounsey had taken his infantrymen up the northern bank to lie in hiding opposite the battery.

But, when the howler monkeys woke noisily in the tree-tops as the first dim light showed the outline of the forest on either shore and the wooded island in between, Nelson and Despard were still below the battery and one of the frigate's boats was firmly grounded on a shoal. But they still hoped that the Spaniards might be asleep and that they could pass the outpost undetected.

Together in the crowded boat, Nelson and Despard anxiously watched the silent island as the outline of its earthworks became increasingly distinct in the growing light. They were now in deeper water and the sailors were pulling their oars as softly as they could for every creak and splash seemed to proclaim their presence. This it had, for, just as they were coming within musket-shot of the island, there was a shouted challenge in Spanish. Nelson instantly ordered his men to pull furiously for the island, drew his sword and scrambled into the bows to be the first ashore. The sailors cheered as the boat swung out into the river and they heard the report of the first cannon-shot.

The Spaniards were ready for them and the water around the boat spouted with the fall of grape-shot and musket-balls. Sailors grasped their cutlasses and soldiers their muskets with bayonets fixed, as they swept into the enemy's gunsmoke. Two soldiers were hit, then the bows ran into the bank and Nelson and Despard leapt ashore with their men at their heels. The bank had seemed to be of firm, red mud but Nelson sank up to his knees into it and stood for a moment, a helpless target. But as he struggled to free himself, leaving both shoes in the mud

[103]

and scrambling up the bank on his bare feet, the enemy fire stopped. The sound of musket-fire was now coming from the opposite riverbank, where Mounsey's men had broken cover. As the cheering British bounded over the enemy's breastwork they found the battery abandoned.

Retreating through the woods, the Spaniards came under fire from Indian sharpshooters who had landed from the canoes farther upstream and, imagining themselves surrounded by a vastly surperior force, promptly surrendered. Nelson and Despard counted the cost of their success. One soldier had been slightly wounded in the hand and another had been shot in the abdomen; the ball had gone through his cartridge-box, spending its force, and his wound was not serious. For this small loss, they had taken fourteen prisoners and four swivel-guns mounted upon the fortification.

The island was named Bartola, they discovered, after a river of that name that flowed into the San Juan nearby, so the British decided to call it St. Bartholomew and, to Nelson, its capture and his part in it became a story that he loved to tell. In an autobiographical sketch that he wrote many years later for intending biographers, he told 'how I boarded, if I may be allowed the expression, an out-post of the enemy, situated on an island in the river.'

A boat was sent across to collect Mounsey and, after congratulations had been exchanged, Nelson heard that their first action had not been without its horrors. As Mounsey's Liverpool Blues had been trudging up the jungle trail to take up their positions on the river bank, one had screamed in agony. A snake, dangling from a branch above the track, had bitten him under the eye. 'He felt such intense pain,' noted Dr. Dancer, 'that he was unable to proceed; and when a messenger was sent to him a few hours afterwards, he was found dead, with all the symptoms of putrefaction; a yellowness and swelling all over his body; and the eye, near to which he was bitten, all dissolved.'

Later that day, Polson came ashore to congratulate Nelson, while his boat-crews and Indians tried to get their craft into the deeper water; one of them was stove in on a rock so that another had to be unloaded at the island and sent downstream in an attempt to salvage her cargo. Meanwhile, questioning of the prisoners had revealed that the castle of San Juan itself lay less than five miles upstream. Realising that their presence on the river might now be known there, Nelson urged the colonel to press ahead with urgency and he and Despard volunteered to make a reconnaissance. So, after dark, Polson sat in his tent by candlelight to write in his journal, 'This night, Mr. Despard, Chief Engineer, with Capt. Nelson of the *Hinchinbroke*, took one of the prisoners with them in a pitpan and went up the river very near the Fort. . . .'

On the morning of 10th April, as the rising sun burned the white mist off the river, Nelson and Despard watched from the wet leaves of the jungle the slow revelation of the place they had come so far to conquer. During the night they had paddled their boat between dark masses of towering trees and past islands thick with tall grass and palms, for more than three miles against swift currents to a bend in the river. There the prisoner had told them to wait in hiding until dawn. What they now saw upstream of them was a fine, straight reach of water and, at the head of it, less than a mile distant, a green, conical hill upon which stood a white fortress. From its keep flew the flag of Spain.

They could see the white water of rapids below the castle and countryside cleared of jungle for cultivation beyond. It was a striking view, as dramatic as theatrical scenery after so many miles of unbroken jungle. A later traveller, seeing it from this spot, described 'the fort-crowned hill and the little town clinging to its foot form the centre of the picture. The clear, sparkling, dancing rapids on one side contrast with the still, dark forest on the other, whilst the whole is relieved by the bright green, grassy hills in the background.'

From what Nelson could see, the habitations at the foot of the steep slopes of the hill were no more than wooden, thatched huts, which clustered most thickly just beyond the castle itself, where the river began to bend south and out of sight. There seemed to be a plantation of bananas, or cacao trees, below and downstream of the castle and, on both banks, ground appeared to have been cleared of all but a few giant palms, or old forest, trees for grazing cattle. Close behind the fort were a jumble of

[105]

little wooded hills and ridges and from these — if undefended —
it might be possible for guns to command it.

When Nelson and Despard returned to Bartola island with
their news, they were surprised to find that Major Lawrie,
whom they had not seen for nearly a month, had at last caught
up with them. He was telling Polson that Major MacDonald
was on his way up the river with the second division of troops;
he himself had left them at the point where the first division
had camped for their second night on the river, adding with
characteristic over-optimism, that they should therefore arrive
at Bartola in a couple of days.

Polson had decided to make the island the base for his final
advance on the castle and to leave a small garrison under
Lieutenant Colville of the 79th to guard it. He then sent a fast
canoe down-river with a letter for Major MacDonald, ordering
him to bring all his regular troops and a hundred of his best
volunteers up to the creek below the rapids. There they should
disembark and march along the portage to the point opposite
Bartola, where Colville would collect them with boats that
would be left for the purpose, and send them upstream after the
main force towards the castle.

Later that day, when enough boats had arrived from the
rapids, Polson embarked as many men as possible and set off
upstream. The river was now deep and about two hundred yards
wide, shut in by great trees standing at the water's edge and on
the little hills that rose from it, so appearing to be growing to
extraordinary heights. Sounds — the dipping of the oars and
paddles and the creaking of the rowlocks, even the splash of
leaping tarpon and the screech of parrots — seemed to be
muffled by the weight of the forest all about them.

After a passage of three miles, Despard told Polson that the
reach leading to the castle itself was beyond the next bend so
that, unless he planned a frontal assault from the boats, the
troops should be put ashore.

Since he and Despard had spied on the castle early that
morning, Nelson had become increasingly convinced that it
could and should be carried by storm without delay and had
explained this to Polson. But the colonel had seen too much of
the chaotic progress of his straggling fleet of boats up the river

Captain William Locker, Nelson's mentor, painted by
Gabriel Stuart at the time of their first meeting.

The portrait of Nelson begun by John Rigaud before his
departure for the Caribbean and completed on his return.
The castle of San Juan was then added to the background.

Captain Edward Despard at the time of the San Juan expedition.

COL DESPARD.

Colonel John Dalling, when Lieutenant-Governor of Jamaica, painted by the miniaturist John Smart.

Dr Benjamin Moseley, chief
medical officer to the San Juan
expedition, painted by John
Hoppner.

Lord George Germain, Secretary of
State for the Colonies, painted by
Thomas Gainsborough.

to dare risk his soldiers in an attack that could collapse into a ludicrous regatta of drifting or grounded boats in the unknown water below the castle and the rapids. So he determined to land his advance-guard, together with some artillery, on the south bank, just out of sight of the castle, and advance through the forest to cut its land communications. However difficult the terrain might prove to be, at least he and his men would have their feet on dry land and that was where they were trained to fight.

So the whole flotilla nosed into the bank and Polson ordered the Indians to clear the undergrowth from the shore so that unloading could begin. The guns — four four-pounder cannon — were hoisted ashore and artificers began assembling their carriages and making sledges so that they could be hauled overland. Meanwhile Polson ordered Captain Bulkeley of the 79th to take two subalterns and fifty men and advance through the jungle towards the fort, capturing and holding what commanding heights he could.

As the Indians hacked at the undergrowth with their machetes, the Liverpool Blues once again plunged into the damp, suffocating greenery. They struggled on until dusk, when Bulkeley ordered a halt to rest and light fires to dry clothes and in the hope of keeping away the swarming mosquitoes. With the memory of that ghastly death from snake-bite, every man's eyes were upon overhanging branches. But the next moment of sudden terror was something quite different.

Later, Bulkeley described to Dr. Moseley, 'A soldier having retired a little way from the rest, a tiger came behind him and struck him on the back with his paw and jumped on him. The man instantly started up, disentangled himself and ran to his companions, frightened almost to death, with the tiger after him. The man fell down and the tiger plunged headlong among the men, missed the one he was pursuing and caught another by the neck, tore his clothes and hurt his face; but, without doing further mischief, and from the noise and confusion of the whole party, he fled away.

'From these he ran to a party of Indians, who were accompanying them and were now resting at some little distance; but the Indians, seeing him approach, made a great howling, which is always their custom, and frightened the tiger away. He must have been much pressed with hunger, not being first attacked, to pursue a man where there were fires and a multitude of people.'

It was not, of course, a tiger but a jaguar – known on the Spanish Main as *tigre* – yet a lethal assailant nonetheless. Nor were snakes and wild animals the only terrors of the jungle. Usually there were Indians about to advise on which of the temptingly luscious wild fruit was safe to eat but when a fresh-water spring or stream was found and it appeared clean, the soldiers drank from it, hoping to avoid dysentery.

While ashore, Nelson and his men, thirsty in the heat of the day, came upon a clear jungle pool that did not appear stagnant and drank from it. Soon after, stomach pains, vomiting and diarrhoea began and Nelson feared that he, too, would now be brought down by attacks of 'the fluxes'. When the Indians were shown the pond they said that the water had been poisoned by local hunters with the manchineel apple which they used on the tips of their arrows. Indeed, so lethal are the secretions of this tree that even rainwater dripping from it can cause burns; or the poison may have come from another variety of poisonous tree, which the Indians used for fishing. A branch from it would be broken, splintered and twisted, then thrown into still water, where its sap would effect the nervous system of the fish, bringing them to the surface, unconscious but edible.

The effect of this upon Nelson was a violent form of dysentery. Yet the excitement at being so close to the first goal of the expedition was such that it could be borne with the other discomforts of the tropics.

Next morning, Polson, who had passed the night with the bulk of his force in camp at the landing-place, was told that the four little guns were now ready to be moved. Yet, at once, the difficulties became apparent. Not only was it far easier for foot-soldiers to push their way through heavy undergrowth than for guns to be hauled over roots, rocks and swampy earth, but most of the Indians needed for this labour, and for the hacking of a way through the matted leaves, stalks, trunks and creepers, had either gone ahead with Bulkeley, or taken their boats back to Bartola to collect more men and stores.

Eventually, enough Indians were collected and the hacking and hauling began. But, after two hours of exhausting labour, Polson realised that they had barely covered half a mile and saw that the terrain, which had become increasingly broken, was becoming a trackless jumble of steep little hills and gullies; the jungle, thick as ever. Short of ordering Despard to survey and plan a road, and then building it, the country was impassable for soldiers with baggage and artillery. So the colonel returned to the river-bank and, after consultation with Nelson, decided to re-embark and put his force ashore much nearer to the castle, even if this meant loss of surprise. So it was that, on the afternoon of 11th April, the boats of the expedition came in procession round the bend in the river and upon the striking view that Nelson and Despard had seen at dawn on the preceding day. In the hot sunshine, the castle gleamed white on its steep green hill. There was something sepulchral about it, for the tower of its keep, and the walls and bastions below it, sloped slightly inward to remind the more sophisticated, who had seen illustrations in recently-published travel books, of the gateway pylons of Egyptian temples, or the Mayan sacrificial pyramids of Mexico.

The boats, slowly appearing round the bend, oars working like the legs of water beetles, were watched with apprehension, but no longer with surprise from the battlements of that keep. The Governor, Don Juan d'Ayssa, had heard of the invaders' approach, and, perhaps, their gunfire at Bartola, two days before; then one of the island's garrison had escaped to give warning. He was as aware as any Spanish officer in Nicaragua of the French and Spanish declarations of war on Britain and the possible consequences, for he had just been entertaining distinguished guests – the President and Bishop of Guatemala, of which Nicaragua was a province – in whose honour he had had the stone walls of the castle freshly whitewashed.

His first act had been to write a report of the attack on his outpost and send it upstream after his departed guests by fast canoe, in which he also sent his wife to safety at Granada. He then ordered all the garrison within the castle walls and urgent preparations made to withstand a siege until help could reach them. Some of the cattle were herded into the fortress; the remainder, shot.

The castle stood upon the strongest natural defensive position on the hundred and eleven miles of the river, some thirty miles below the settlement of San Carlos at the junction with the lake. The steep-sided little hill rose about a hundred feet high at the crook of a bend above the fiercest rapids on the river. These ran, white and foaming, over rocks at about ten knots, leaving only a narrow navigable channel that could easily be commanded by guns, or even muskets, on either shore. The little hills that stood along the south bank of the river fell back a few hundred yards, except for one detached range, some hundred feet high, from which a ridge ran to the south and west of a castle and culminated in a slightly higher peak commanding the western approaches. Within a mile of this little hill, stretches of both shores were firm and fertile – as was the island of Juana about half a mile down-river – so providing secure farmland for crops and grazing cattle.

To prevent a repetition of buccaneer raids coming up the river to ravage the lake-side settlements, the fort had been built on its hill in the middle of the seventeenth century. After its vulnerability had been shown in another, almost successful, attack, it had been strengthened at the time of the Seven Years War – and named El Castillo de la Inmaculada Concepción.

The keep stood fifty feet, surrounded by oblong ramparts fourteen feet high and four feet thick and about two hundred and twenty-five feet long by one hundred and thirty-five feet broad and with triangular bastions mounting guns at each corner. The castle was armed at this time with twenty cannon, a dozen small swivel-guns that could be mounted on the walls and a brass mortar. Its garrison was about seventy-strong, including five officers and some sixty regular soldiers, seventeen of whom were gunners. Together with a few slaves, prisoners and the soldiers' families, the population of the castle and the thatched huts on the beach below, amounted to two hundred and twenty-one.

Strong as it looked – and was – the castle of San Juan had one weakness: there was no well within its walls. Because the river flowed fast and clean a hundred feet below and because more than a hundred inches of rain fell each year, it had been thought unnecessary. So, the garrison was at once put to work carrying kegs and skins of water from the river up the hill to the castle to replenish its cistern, which, at the end of the dry season, was far from full. Indeed, this was the first enemy activity reported by British scouts as they approached.

Captain Bulkeley's column had scrambled over the little lumpy hills and gullies that had thwarted Polson and through dense secondary jungle, where the great forest trees had been felled and thick vegetation sprung up in the unshaded sunlight. Then he had come to the edge of the jungle and could see across cleared ground to the castle, about half a mile distant. He had remained there and sent an Irish officer, Lieutenant James Fahy, of the Royal Americans, through the edge of the undergrowth to work his way round to the flank of the fortress, where it seemed to be dominated by the ridge and hills as high as that on which it stood.

After a few hours, Fahy reported back by messenger that there were indeed commanding heights to the south and south-west of the castle and that he could also see that 'the Garrison were very busy carrying in water.' Bulkeley and his men followed, but, when they reached Fahy, they could see that the Spaniards had occupied a small earthwork on the hill, which commanded the approach to the castle and the landing-place on the river bank to the west of it. He therefore sent a message to Polson, whom he assumed to be far back at the original landing-place, describing the position.

Polson, meanwhile, was busy putting his main force ashore some fourteen hundred yards from the castle, screened by a wooded headland and just beyond the range of its guns.

Despite the wear of more than a fortnight on the river, the soldiers were inspired by the sight of their objective; as Dr. Dancer put it, 'the animation excited by prospects of victory and success enabled our men to resist every impression from the fatigue and labour they underwent.' Even the Indians, who had had a surprising number of men sick with dysentery, became excited at the prospect of plunder.

But within the small circle of Polson's headquarters there

was disagreement. Nelson, supported by Despard, urged that the castle should at once be summoned to surrender and, if this was refused, should be taken by immediate assault. Polson thought otherwise: the enemy's strength was unknown and his own men were tired; moreover, neither had the scaling-ladders arrived, nor nearly enough cannon-shot to maintain a proper covering-fire. He decided that the commanding heights must be taken and batteries sited upon them; by the time that was done, the soldiers would be rested and the ammunition boats would have come up the river.

Nelson had no choice but to accept his orders and hope that his apprehensions would be proved unfounded. These were, in particular, that the rains might break before the castle fell and that the expedition, instead of breaking through to the lake and healthy highlands of central Nicaragua, would·be caught in the jungle. On their journey up the river, the lack of water in the channels had been the major obstacle, but at least the weather had been dry and health generally good. However, the dry season must be coming to an end and huge cumulus clouds had been gathering, gleaming white against the strong blue of the sky, on recent afternoons. There was no need to elaborate on what could happen to the health – let alone the comfort – of the expedition when those storm-clouds broke.

It had occasionally rained during the journey up the river. Instantly everybody would be soaked to the skin by the sudden downpour but the shower would pass and soon the jungle – and the men's clothes – would be steaming under the hot sun. Recently it had sometimes rained several times in a day as a foretaste of what could be expected when the 'periodical rains' set in.

Dr. Moseley, after hearing several first-hand accounts of such discomforts, wrote, 'The river has in its course many noisome marshes on its sides; and the trees are so thick as to intercept the rays of the sun: consequently the earth beneath their branches is covered with rotten leaves and putrid vegetables. Hence arise copious collections of foul vapours, which clog the atmosphere. These unite with large clouds and precipitate in rains: the rains are no sooner over than the sun breaks forth and shines with scorching heat. The surface of the ground in places not covered with trees is scarcely dry before the atmosphere is again loaded by another collection of clouds and exhalations and the sun is again concealed.'

Such forebodings were thrust aside in the mounting pace of activity. Polson at once set Captain Harrison and twenty-five of the Loyal Irish forward to reinforce Bulkeley, while he followed with the main force. This was now ashore and, as the advance-party's position at the edge of the jungle, five or six hundred yards from the castle, was near the river he decided to march along the bank, while the artillery and ammunition kept pace in the boats.

At four o'clock in the afternoon, Polson came up with Bulkeley and made camp on a small savannah by the river, shielded from observation and gunfire by a wooded spur. Just before nightfall, the colonel heard from Fahy's patrol that the enemy had abandoned the outpost and withdrawn to the castle. So he sent Lieutenant Leigh of the Liverpool Blues and thirty men to occupy it, while Harrison was ordered to take two subalterns and fifty of the Loyal Irish to work their way round the heights to the river bank upstream of the castle, so cutting its communications. This was achieved, but not before d'Ayssa had succeeded in sending another messenger up-river with the news of the impending siege and appealing for help.

Next morning, the artillery was brought up to the main position and, after dark that evening, dragged across the open ground east of the castle to the ridge commanding its approaches from the south. The slopes were steep, so Nelson and his sailors were called upon to hoist one of the four-pounders to the crest and, levelled the ground and threw up a breastwork for his battery of this one little gun. Meanwhile infantry reinforcements passed through his position to reinforce Leigh on the commanding hilltop.

Next day, 13th April, Polson wrote in his journal, 'At daylight, Captain Nelson opened his Battery of one Gun, which played with great success.' Encouraged, he had the other three guns dragged up the reverse slope and they were fired by the artillerymen, but 'to little effect,' doing no damage.

After this failure, the colonel ordered Nelson and Despard to take charge of the artillery. So, next day, a second gun was hauled up to Nelson's hilltop battery and two others were sited by Despard to the south of the castle. Nelson worked as his own gunlayer, aiming and firing several shot, all of which hit their target; one, to the cheers of his sailors, knocking down the flagstaff on the keep. Seeing what just a single well-directed gun could achieve, he decided to move one of his two on to the ridge between his own position and Despard's, so as to minimise the effect of counter-fire from the castle. Polson was delighted by Nelson's professionalism and noted, 'There was scarcely a gun fired but was pointed by him or Lieutenant Despard . . . who has exerted himself on every occasion.'

This achievement was all the more remarkable as Nelson was becoming increasingly weak from violent attacks of 'the fluxes'. Yet his expertise was in demand for only one more day, on which fire from the four guns severely damaged the parapets of both keep and ramparts, because ammunition ran out. Polson had been banking on the arrival of MacDonald's second division, which he knew to be bringing at least two hundred four-pounder shot. So he sent an 'express' dory down-river to meet the reinforcements and order the ammunition boats to be sent ahead with all possible speed. Indeed, such was his anxiety that, on the following day, he sent Captain Hallam of the Royal Americans down in another boat to stress the urgency.

The main camp with the stores depot and Dr. Dancer's hospital remained where the landing had been made on the small savannah beyond the headland. From there a trail led south-west through the trees and over the tops of the little hills before turning north and down to open ground, sheltered from the castle by the hills where the guns had been mounted. Here the main camp was established, tents were pitched – Nelson and Despard sharing one – and protocol observed as strictly as possible. It had not been possible to keep the regulars away from the raffish influence of the volunteers and irregulars, although the Indians were expected to camp some way apart but remain subject to military discipline.

Other than throwing up a breastwork nearer to the fort, from which more than forty men under Captain Harrison kept up harassing musket-fire – they over-optimistically claimed to have killed some Spaniards on the ramparts – there was little the British could do but await the arrival of the ammunition. The enemy, meanwhile, seemed to have plenty, keeping up a heavy fire from cannon and muskets. Although most of the besiegers were safely behind cover, a soldier of the Loyal Irish was dangerously wounded, and one of Nelson's sailors had a remarkable escape.

'A sailor of the *Hinchinbroke*,' recorded Dr. Dancer, 'being a little intoxicated, pursued down the hill, under the enemy's fire, a hog that he had endeavoured to kill. He received two or three shot; but one of them took a very extraordinary course, which I believe most people would think fatal.' He then described how a musket-ball had passed right through his lower belly, causing injuries beyond the doctor's surgical skill. So, giving the man up for lost, he simply gave him large amounts of wine and quinine, and, to his surprise, achieved a complete cure.

Unable to continue the bombardment, Polson consulted Despard about the possibility of mining: driving a horizontal shaft under the castle hill and exploding a heavy charge of gunpowder beneath the walls to make a breach. So, after dark on the evening of the 18th, three officers and fifty men began carrying picket-stakes and fascines – wattle fencing to shore up earthworks – and started to build a screen for the miners only forty yards from the castle wall. They did this under musket-fire, so close to the enemy that the Spaniards on the ramparts even threw stones at them.

At the same time, Polson stationed sharpshooters under cover between the castle and the river to stop the garrison refilling their water-casks at night. In this he succeeded, for that night a water-party with an armed escort did creep down the hill and a sharp skirmish drove them back empty-handed.

But there was still no news of the second division and the ammunition, despite a third 'express' that the colonel had sent down-river. Then at eleven o'clock on the night of the 20th news arrived that Captain Hallam had returned from his mission to Major MacDonald, bringing with him the cannon-balls and was now at the expedition's landing beach. Polson at once sent a working-party to help unload and, at one o'clock next morning, they returned with fifty-three four-pounder

balls. This, Polson was shocked to hear, was all that had
survived of two hundred shot that had been shipped from
Greytown. Some, he was told, had been lost in boats that had
capsized, or struck rocks and sunk, and some seemed to have
been aboard craft that had simply disappeared, probably by
following the wrong channel – as he had done up the Colorado
river – and becoming lost and stranded in deep jungle.

But Captain Hallam also brought the good news that, that
night, the bulk of the second division should have reached the
foot of the rapids and that their arrival would now be a matter
of days.

Yet this night was memorable for something far more
important to their prospects. All day, huge clouds had been
building up in towering thunderheads above the river and after
nightfall the rains broke in a terrifying apocalypse of thunder
and lightning.

There had been heavy showers before and they were
accustomed to being soaked through, but this was something
quite different. It was a solid, continuous downpour that beat
down tents and poured through canvas and thatching. Even
where there was a watertight roof, the drumming rain threw up
spray so that everything and everyone was quickly drenched.
When morning came, all was hidden by grey curtains of rain:
the far bank of the river was invisible and the castle itself only a
dim outline. Everywhere new streams and rivulets were running
down the gullies and into the camps.

'During the Periodical Rains, which begin about the middle
of April,' wrote Dr. Moseley after hearing Captain Bulkeley's
account of these miseries, 'the torrents of water that fall for
weeks together are prodigious, which gave the river a
tremendous aspect, and from their suddenness and impetuosity
cannot be imagined by an European to portend anything but a
deluge. This bursting of the waters above, and the raging of the
river below, with the blackness of the nights, accompanied with
horrible tempests of lightning and thunder, constitute a
magnificent scene of terror, unknown but in the tropic world.'

For Nelson himself the ordeal was made worse by an attack
of malaria. He had become accustomed to these 'intermittents'
but this time the bout was unusually violent. Indeed, as his

[116]

condition deteriorated, it seemed likely that the cold rigors and hot fevers, headaches and vomiting came from a new infection. This theory was supported by the number of men in the camp who were beginning to show symptoms of malaria for the first time. Many thought the infection to have come with the heavy rains but Nelson himself thought otherwise, noting that he and the others were falling sick between twenty and thirty days after arrival on the Spanish Main.

Despite the downpour, the besiegers worked hard. The first of the fifty-three cannon-balls were fired at the castle and knocked down a stone sentry-box on the south-west angle. Below, the miners struck hard rock, which meant that it would be long before they could hope to blow a breach in the walls above. Encouragement came late on the night of 21st April in the person of Major MacDonald, who arrived at Polson's tent with the news that some of his boats were already unloading and that the rest of those that had come up as far as the rapids should follow in the morning.

Next day, the last of the four-pounder shot was fired. but two carronades — short-barrelled guns, firing twelve-pounder shot, or grape-shot, at short range — had arrived with the second division. Nelson was too ill to oversee the fighting of these weapons, with which, as a naval officer, he was particularly familiar. So, when first fired, the shot fell short; then so much powder was used that it blew a gun off its mounting; when the castle was eventually hit, the balls seemed to have no power behind them. The shooting was even more erratic when nine-pounder shot was tried; the balls either falling short, or going over, although the same charge of powder and the same elevation was employed.

As MacDonald's boats arrived, Polson was appalled to find that they brought only enough rations for their own crews, so that his own men now had only enough food for three days. They were mostly on half-rations, but this could be extended to six and supplemented by fish, game and turtle-blood for the sick.

So he sent two volunteer officers down-river with as many light craft as could be manned to collect provisions from Greytown. He ordered another to be ready to follow with two big boats, which were due to arrive shortly and were manned by Negroes, because he had begun to distrust the Indians. Despite their early reluctance to join the expedition, those that had come up the river had proved their worth as scouts, boatmen and porters, but they had become increasingly moody and truculent. They clearly resented the British assumption that they should be subject to camp discipline and had to be urged on with promises of booty from the castle and the cities beyond. They also seemed less able to withstand the climate than the Negroes and men of mixed race, and had sickened as fast as any, dreading illness since it was their custom to abandon, rather than nurse, the incapacitated. Polson feared that if he sent them down-river without an armed escort, they would never return. The Negroes, however, had proved not only strong and healthy, but loyal.

MacDonald's division had all arrived in camp by the 23rd and seemed eager for action. Like Nelson, he saw the folly of a leisurely siege at this season and at once volunteered to lead his men in an assault on the castle. The colonel now agreed but, as no scaling ladders had arrived, ordered his carpenters to start making them.

Major MacDonald was proving a high-mettled man, both difficult and stimulating. When Polson decided that his Jamaica Volunteers should take over from regular troops in a forward position, and this involved MacDonald relieving a captain, he was furious, telling the colonel that he would be put in irons rather than accept a more junior officer's responsibility. Polson brusquely replied that he was surprised to hear that sort of complaint at such a time and, if he persisted in it, the adjutant would be ordered to put him under arrest. Then Polson saw a way of cooling his temper. Seeing Lawrie nearby, he called him over and asked MacDonald to repeat his objection. When he hesitated, the colonel himself explained it, making it sound petty in the telling. So, before Lawrie could comment, MacDonald interrupted and agreed to obey.

But he and his aggressive enthusiasm galvanised Polson into further action. As a start, he sent Captain Bertrand, a volunteer, across the river to snipe from the far bank at any Spanish water-carriers emerging from the castle. Then he began to plan for the next stage in the campaign and realised that he knew virtually nothing about the higher reaches of the river, and whether there were more rapids in its course. He did not even know how far upstream lay the lake. So he had two dories hauled out of the river below his camp and carried over the little hills south of the castle and put back into the river some way upstream. Lieutenant MacLean of the Jamaica Legion was then ordered to take twelve Indians and try to make his way to the lake, then return with his report as quickly as possible.

More empty boats were sent down-river for provisions and surprising news arrived that two of the heavy craft that had long been missing — one of them the *Royal George* — had been seen just below the rapids and a working-party was sent down to help them get up.

But still the castle loomed inviolate above them and there were reports that the Spaniards were still able to get water-carriers down to the river at night. Polson visited his forward posts, which had been positioned to prevent this, and reinforced them with a Sergeant Murray and twelve men of the Liverpool Blues. At eight o'clock next morning, Polson heard a sudden burst of musket-fire from the far side of the castle and, soon after, word arrived that Murray's post had been surprised, three of his men killed and the rest put to flight; moreover, the Spaniards were actually filling their water-skins from the river. The colonel at once ordered a counter-attack and the post was re-taken by the Loyal Irish under heavy fire. By the beach they found the three corpses, stripped of arms and equipment.

Polson now expected a sally from the castle and brought more infantry forward to meet it. At last the carronades proved their worth, lobbing hand-grenades over the enemy's ramparts to burst within. That night the riverside posts were reinforced and only just in time, for the Spaniards attempted a sally, which was stopped and driven back by the unexpectedly heavy fire. Yet the Spaniards were able to surprise the Loyal Irish guarding the miners and kill two of them.

On the 28th, events began to move fast. MacDonald reported his men ready for an assault and, on the strength of this and the repulse of the sally, Polson decided to summon the castle to surrender. His only officer able to speak Spanish,

Lieutenant Haldimand of the Royal Americans, being among the sick, he had the formal summons written in French and was having a white flag of truce made for Captain Mounsey, the adjutant, who was to deliver it, when a messenger arrived in the camp. He brought welcome news.

This was in letters from Colonel Kemble, sent from Greytown. He had arrived, he wrote, on the 20th, with five hundred troops to reinforce the expedition. But there was another letter, addressed to Captain Nelson. This was from Admiral Parker, informing him of his appointment to command the frigate *Janus*, in place of the late Captain Glover, and to hand over command of the *Hinchinbroke* to Captain Collingwood.

Nelson was now very sick indeed but had been unwilling to abandon his men, although his chances of survival in the continual damp – humid by day, chill at night – seemed increasingly slight. Yet these were orders and, particularly in coming from the Commander-in-Chief, were to be obeyed instantly. So Polson asked him to take with him his reply to Colonel Kemble and, while he wrote it, a boat was got ready. He made his farewells to the colonel, to Despard and his brother, Mounsey, Bulkeley and his own sailors and marines. Then he was helped into the boat and it was pushed out into the stream, where the swirling brown currents, swollen by the rain, caught it and carried it swiftly towards the sea.

Then exciting news reached Polson from his posts on the river upstream of the castle that Lieutenant MacLean had returned from his reconnaissance and that he had taken both prizes and prisoners. Sure enough, two large pangas lay off the bank, loaded with dried beef, bread, sugar, Indian corn and chocolate; under guard on the shore, were twenty-three dejected prisoners.

MacLean explained that he had made a quick and easy passage up-river in deep water and encountered no rapids. After about thirty miles, the river had widened and there, stretched before him, shone the great expanse of Lake Nicaragua. There he had sighted the two vessels at anchor, and, paddling silently towards them, had boarded and taken them without loss. Both had come from Granada with relief supplies for the castle and, more important still, were carrying despatches from Don Mathias Galvez, the President of Guatemala and Governor of Nicaragua, for Don Juan d'Ayssa.

But before Polson could read these despatches, he was interrupted by more dramatic news. Not only was the white flag of truce now ready and the formalities of a summons to surrender could begin, but the enemy, too, was ready to negotiate.

Just as the colonel was giving Mounsey his final instructions for the parley, they heard drums beating within the castle and a white flag was thrust from the battlements. Both sides were equally eager to arrange terms, it seemed, so the adjutant was sent forward up the grassy slope of the castle hill to the ramp and drawbridge at its gates, where he disappeared within. Soon he was back with a letter from the Governor requesting a cease-fire until eight o'clock the following morning so that terms for capitulation could be prepared.

Only now did Polson have time to have the captured despatches translated by the sick Haldimand. First, Galvez acknowledged the receipt of the two messages from d'Ayssa, reporting the British attack on Bartola and their arrival before the castle. Then he outlined his own plans. The militia of Nicaragua was being raised and he himself would lead it to the relief of the castle. First, the entrance to the lake would be fortified to prevent the British breaking into it from the river; then relief forces would move down-river and overland from the cattle-grazing centre of San Miguel, some forty miles distant by forest trail. Finally, Galvez told d'Ayssa that he was pressing forward with his plans for driving the British from the whole of the Mosquito Shore.

At seven o'clock on the morning of 29th April, as Polson was considering his response to the enemy's strategic plans, he was again interrupted by the drums of the castle. Again the adjutant was sent across and he returned to say that a Spanish officer wished to meet Polson and put their terms to him in person. Having expected Mounsey to bring written proposals that could be considered at leisure, the colonel became impatient and sent Despard over to the castle with instructions to question the officer, write down his proposals and return with them on his own. This Despard did, and when Polson had written his reply, took that back to the castle. When d'Ayssa read this, he sent his intermediary across to the British camp with Despard to ask the colonel for one concession: that, on surrendering, the Spanish officers should be released from captivity after six months, if they had not been exchanged for British prisoners before that time. To this, Polson replied that it was contrary to his instructions but that he would do his best to persuade the Governor of Jamaica to grant the request.

Polson then signed the instrument of surrender and, shortly after five o'clock in the afternoon, sent Despard back to the castle with a strong guard to take formal possession. Then, according to the terms of capitulation, d'Ayssa and his officers marched out at the head of some hundred and sixty men. When well away from the gates, they halted, grounded arms and marched back into the fortress that would now become their prison. The British busied themselves with the practicalities of taking over the fortress: Captain Hallam, of the Royal Americans, who was deputy quartermaster, was to take charge of documents and military stores; other officers were to report on the castle's artillery and the ammunition in its magazine.

The British now had two hundred and twenty-one more prisoners to add to those taken at Bartola and from the prizes. These included seven officers – among them, d'Ayssa, a chaplain and a surgeon – and about sixty regular soldiers. There were half a dozen slaves and about thirty women and children. The British loss in the siege – and in the skirmish at Bartola – amounted to nine killed and six wounded.

Yet the triumphant culmination of the daring and ambitious feat they had begun when they sailed from Port Royal nearly three months before now seemed hollow and abounding with horrors.

While they laboured up the river and lay in soaking tents behind their siege-works, it had always seemed that when the castle fell their troubles would be over. It would provide food and shelter and medicine for the sick. There would be prize-money, perhaps, for the British, and slaves for the Indians. Now, great was their disappointment.

'We hoped that our victory would furnish us, not only with

accommodation, but with many useful supplies, that might tend, in some degree, to stop our increasing sickness,' wrote Dr. Dancer. 'But, alas! the wretched state of the garrison, provided with nothing that could lend either them or us the least comfort; and the inconvenient structure of the place, which was worse than any prison and, as one would suppose, calculated only for the purpose of breeding infection, disappointed us in those flattering expectations.'

True, they had taken thirty cannon and a brass mortar but the castle, which was described as 'very dirty and stinking', had almost run out of provisions and, since the British had finally stopped water-carriers reaching the river, of water, since they had no effective means of collecting rainwater. Yet the lowering of the Spanish flag on the keep and the hoisting of the British was an impressive sight. It happened just as the head of the Spanish relief column of five hundred militia emerged from the forest on the far bank of the river. The effect was devastating and, as the British later discovered, 'when they saw the British colours, they fled with so much precipitation as to strew all the road with dead beasts and their burdens.'

Now, as Despard and MacDonald urged – and as Nelson would have agreed – was the time to follow up the victory with a swift advance up the river to the lake, before Galvez could bar the way. But, while the British flag hung limp in the drenching rain above the castle, Polson could only see ghastly predicaments. Dr. Dancer was reporting that the men were 'falling down in great numbers' from fever, as well as dysentery, and there were no medicines, let alone a hospital. The castle was too cramped, dark and dirty for habitation, so the sick, who had been brought up to it in the expectation of comforts within, had to be taken to the village below, which smelled as foul from the local industry of skinning cattle and drying hides.

'Our men . . . had no proper hospital,' wrote Dancer, 'the wretched houses or sheds, to which we were obliged to give that name, being from their situation, not only so nigh the river but under the castle hill and totally excluded from the sea-breezes; from the dirt and filth surrounding them, consisting chiefly of semi-putrid skins, yielding a most intolerable stench; from the insufficiency of the roofs, which . . . kept out very little rain, made them, I will not say merely an improper hospital, but a certain grave to almost all who entered them.'

The debilitation of the little army, was the first and most obvious handicap. The second was the shortage of boats for further advance, and the disaffection of the Indians. For, when the castle fell, the Mosquito headmen had gathered round to collect their slaves, only to be told that the garrison and their dependants were all prisoners of the British Crown, to which they had surrendered. Predictably, the Indians showed immediate anger at having been lured to join the expedition on false pretences, and the British officers could only wonder whether they would mutiny or desert.

However, Polson seated himself in the Govenor's room of the castle and addressed a letter to General Dalling, heading the paper, 'St. John's Fort, 30th April, 1780.' He began with pride, 'I have the honour to inform your Excellency that this Castle surrendered to his Majesty's arms yesterday at 5 o'clock p.m.'

It was his moment of glory.

CHAPTER FIVE

A Door Burst Open

On 1st May, Colonel Kemble and Captain Collingwood had been watching the mouth of the river for eleven days. Swollen by rain, it swirled from its mouths, clouded with mud and bringing down to the sea jungle flotsam but no news of Colonel Polson's expedition. On its banks, the black cormorants spread their wings to dry and the white herons stood elegantly poised, but there was no sign whatever of the hundreds of men who had disappeared into its unknown reaches.

The convoy carrying Colonel Kemble's reinforcement to the Spanish Main had arrived from Jamaica on 20th April. The troop transports had been escorted not only by the sloop *Victor* but, when Admiral Parker yielded to the Governor's pressure, by the small frigate *Resource*, commanded by Captain Patrick Fotheringham, and among the passengers had been Captain Cuthbert Collingwood, once again due to succeed Captain Nelson in a command.

Buoyed by expectations, their hopes had been high when Greytown had been sighted. But instead of a busy harbour with boats ferrying supplies from a depot to the expeditionary force, that they felt certain must by now be in command of Lake Nicaragua, the harbour seemed lifeless. The *Hinchinbroke* and the transports she had escorted lay at anchor 'too far up the harbour, by which means they were subject to the noisome smell of the lagoons.' Their crews seemed listless, the ships neglected and the frigate was leaking badly.

Worse, there was no news of the expedition. The officers of the *Hinchinbroke* reported that Major MacDonald and the second division had gone up on the river and nothing had been heard of them since.

The flotilla of river-craft that they had expected to find ready for their own ascent was nowhere to be seen and they learned that almost all of them had gone up with Polson and MacDonald. However, one that was ready was immediately manned and sent up-river with 'express letters' for Polson from Governor Dalling and one for Captain Nelson from Admiral Parker telling him of his new appointment.

However, Kemble did not worry unduly for there was much to be done. First, his troops and stores would have to be unloaded, a camp and depot established and then he was under orders to fortify the harbour. This seemed particularly urgent because, a fortnight before, an armed Spanish three-masted poleacre had appeared off the harbour mouth but had fled when two small craft manned by the *Hinchinbroke*'s sailors had given chase and opened fire.

On making their first landfall, they had seen the mountainous storm-clouds building up over the interior of Nicaragua and, the day after their arrival, the rains had broken. The downpour, which could blot out the view of one ship from another in the anchorage, made the provision of shelter the first priority and Captain Fotheringham put his sailors to work waxing sail-cloth for tents and for awnings to cover whatever boats might become available for the voyage up-river.

As the rains began, men in the ships that had been in the harbour for the past month began to die, the first being the first lieutenant of the *Hinchinbroke*. By the end of April, the frigate had seventy men sick with fever and the rest too sickly to pump out the water leaking through timbers eaten away by the teredo worm, which was particularly voracious in the warm waters of the harbour. Sometimes the rain eased and stopped, the ships steamed in the sun and, with the air washed clear and visibility sharp, eyes would strain towards the river mouth for any sign of those who had gone before. When day followed day without sign of craft emerging from the San Juan, Fotheringham offered Kemble all the boats of the warships in the anchorage and preparations began for sending more men in the wake of the expedition.

Then, on the morning of 1st May, shouts from one ship to another and along the shore, passed the news of a boat sighted, moving fast on the risen river towards the harbour. Telescopes were trained on her and they soon picked out the blue, white and gold of a naval uniform worn by her single passenger. As she entered the anchorage this was seen to be Captain Nelson.

Excitement was high. A post-captain of the Royal Navy was always an impressive figure but when such an officer arrived from the seat of war, he must be bearing news of the utmost importance. Had he come from the lake, or even from Granada itself? Perhaps he had actually set eyes upon the Pacific Ocean? Then, as the post-captain could be clearly seen, anticipation gave way to horror, for that brave uniform hung upon a near-skeleton of a man. Captain Nelson, haggard and almost drained of life, was clearly very ill indeed; by appearance, close to death.

However his mind was clear and at once he told Kemble, Collingwood and Fotheringham his news. Polson had not yet captured the castle, although, as he had left, a summons to surrender was about to be made. This he said was because an immediate assault, which he and Captain Despard had urged, had not been made, and siege operations had virtually petered out through lack of cannon-shot. It could only be hoped that the cutting-off of water supplies and the threat of the mine might induce capitulation. Meanwhile, the rains had broken and the besiegers were sickening with fever and the fluxes, of which he himself was a ghastly illustration.

His voyage down the San Juan had been swift, the full river sweeping the boat over the rapids and shoals, which had been the cause of so much labour and delay before the breaking of the rains. Indeed, the journey that had taken a fortnight in the ascent had been covered in only three days. But it was obvious that if the sick man was to have any chance of survival he must be got away from the lethal season in Nicaragua as quickly as possible. In any case, it was vital that his news of the expedition should be delivered to Govenor Dalling with the greatest urgency and Fotheringham ordered Captain Samuel Hood Walker, a nephew of Lord Hood, to prepare the *Victor* for sea.

Accordingly, Nelson was helped aboard the *Hinchinbroke* for the brief formalities of handing over command to Collingwood and signing her log-book. Then he embarked in the sloop, which sailed at once for Kingston Bay, the sick man being cared for by the purser, Tyson, who had served in the *Badger* under him. But, on arrival at Port Royal, he was so exhausted by dysentery, that he had to be taken ashore in his cot and there was no question of him being able to take the news of the victory to Spanish Town in person.

Luckily, his friend 'Billy Blue' Cornwallis, now commanding the third-rate *Lion*, was at Port Royal and urged that he should not be taken to hospital, which, because of its lack of hygiene, risk of cross-infection and air of doom, seemed little better than an ante-chamber to the cemetery. Instead, Cornwallis, an old West Indies hand, recommended the care of one of the black housekeepers, who had nursed many a sick naval officer back to health. Moreover, he insisted that Nelson be cared for by Cuba Cornwallis, who had taken his name after he had freed her from slavery and who was a friend and confidante to naval officers at the dockyard. Instead of conventional medicine and the debilitating bleeding of patients, Cuba used herbal remedies and such effective comforts as heating bricks to warm the feet during the chill shivering fits of malaria. But, above all, she was cheerful and confident. Being of African descent she was far less vulnerable to infection than a European and so did not treat fever as a sentence of death. Indeed, she infected her patients with her own optimism, giving them strength and the will to survive.

Three days after Nelson had left Greytown, another boat had appeared at the mouth of the river. This bore Lieutenant Thomas Mounsey of the Liverpool Blues carrying Colonel Polson's despatches reporting the surrender of the castle. But the news he could give Kemble and Collingwood was also ominous: the soldiers were increasingly sickly and the Indians discontented and deserting the expedition. He at once took passage for Jamaica, arriving at Port Royal and making the journey to Spanish Town, arriving to deliver the dispatches and present the captured Spanish colours to Governor Dalling on 2nd June.

Polson described the delays on the Mosquito Shore and the

absence of the Indians and the boats that Lawrie had promised; then, the laborious ascent of the river; finally the capture of the island outpost and the siege of the castle itself. Praise, he reserved for two young officers.

Of Nelson, he had written, 'He was first on every service, whether by day or by night; there was scarcely a gun fired but was pointed either by him or Lieutenant Despard, chief engineer, who has exerted himself on every occasion.'

'I am persuaded that if our shot had held out, we should have had the fort a week sooner. As Captain Nelson goes to Jamaica he can inform you of every delay and point of service as well as I can do, for he knows my very thoughts.'

Since Polson was well aware that Nelson would tell the Governor of his own rejected proposal to storm the castle – and the delay arising from that – these were remarkably generous words. He had, indeed, been well enough for several talks with Dalling and, on the day Mounsey's despatches came ashore at Port Royal, wrote to Polson to tell him so and that the Governor had 'expressed himself very much pleased with your conduct on every occasion.' But he had also left Dalling in no doubt as to a principal cause of the fatal delay so that the Governor would write in his report on the campaign that 'happy it would have been' if Polson had attempted an immediate assault.

But Nelson liked Polson and also spoke warmly of him to the Governor, who was now more than ever determined to take command of the army in Nicaragua as soon as the rein-forcements arrived from home. So, asking to be remembered to Despard, Bulkeley, Harrison and James Mounsey and hoping that the health of his friends would improve, he concluded his letter by assuring Polson that Dalling would be with him by the middle of July.

He also wrote a formal letter to Dalling and received the flattering reply, 'Thank you, my friend, for your kind congratulations. To you, without compliment, do I attribute, in a great measure, the cause.'

A week later, Admiral Parker invited him to continue his convalescence at his house, Admiral's Pen, in the foothills of the Blue Mountains behind Kingston. It was sumptuous in comparison with Cuba Cornwallis's lodgings but, as Lady Parker was away when he arrived, he was lonely and forlorn amongst the unaccustomed comforts, writing to Hercules Ross, 'Oh, Mr. Ross, what would I give to be at Port Royal. Lady P. not here, and the servants letting me lay as if a log, and take no notice.'

Even when the admiral and his wife returned to lavish care upon him, Nelson proved a difficult patient. At first he refused to take conventional medicines after Cuba's soothing remedies but Lady Parker, recognising his delight in small children, had them administered at his bedside by their youngest daughter and he proved willing enough, speaking of the children as his 'little nurse'.

Yet, despite occasional signs of improvement, his health continued to deteriorate and, while the dysentery eased, it was clear that he was suffering from multiple infections of a virulent strain of malaria and there was no question of taking up command of the *Janus*; indeed, Dr. Moseley had begun to doubt whether he would survive if he remained in the tropics.

Meanwhile, at the King's House all was euphoric. Dalling was now in no doubt that, despite the delays, disease and the disaffection of the Indians, the expedition could now sweep on to the lake and the healthy uplands, where health and morale would quickly recover. It would also be more than a victory that would soon be the talk not only of London but of Europe and America. It offered escape from his political embarrassments with honour; indeed, glory. Once the reinforcements had arrived from England, he would take command of a 'Northern Army' to advance across Nicaragua to the Southern Ocean. Having achieved this, he would hand over command to General Campbell and himself return to the acclaim of London, confident that petty squabbles with the Jamaican Assembly and Legislature would be forgotten amid the congratulations on his conquest of New Spain.

So, on the same day that he read Polson's despatches, he wrote his own formal announcement to Lord George Germain: 'I have the honour to congratulate your Lordship on the reduction of the important Fort and Post on the River St. John . . . And now, my Lord, the communicating door to the South

Sea having been burst open, what hinders his Majesty, should he so please, to carry the force of his Northern Army to the destruction of the Spanish Power, cooperating with a Southern Squadron. . . .?

'Everything I hold most dear is now at stake, I choose therefore to play the game as readily as possible myself,' and, making the assumption that Rodney had by now 'gained a decided victory' over the combined fleets of France and Spain, outlined the plans for 'the little army, which I shall have the honour to command.' He even went into details, telling the Colonial Secretary that Polson would be his quartermaster-general and asking for more prefabricated gunboats to be shipped from England.

His excitement was such that he could not stop writing excited letters to Germain and next day took his strategic plans a stage further. Once the Northern Army and the Navy's Southern Squadron had joined forces and severed New Spain, together they would be 'equal to the most serious attacks, from Chile to the Kingdom of Mexico.' He even suggested that while his own army advanced into Mexico from Nicaragua, another, composed of five thousand regulars and more volunteers, should be led by Campbell through Vera Cruz and both would march across the continent to Acapulco, which would have been seized by the Southern Squadron, this being 'abundantly sufficient to shake to the very centre the enormous, wide-extended and ill-constructed fabrick of Spanish dominion in America.

'At a further time, it may be found that Peru may become as easy a prey . . . whenever his Majesty's Ministers may please to try the experiment. In military affairs, it often happens that those things that seem of the greatest magnitude in point of difficulty are eventually attended with scarce any seeming hardship and fall with a facility that astonishes. The reduction of the New World will, I hope, effectually prove the truth of my observation.'

In another letter that month, Dalling included a fulsome tribute to Nelson and suggested him for the command of his proposed Southern Squadron in the Pacific. 'I have hitherto neglected a piece of justice to the service of Captain Nelson,' he wrote and described at length his services on the river and at the

[131]

siege. He then proposed, 'I most humbly entreat that his Majesty will be graciously pleased thro' your Lordship to manifest a satisfaction of his conduct, and, in case a cooperating squadron should have been determined for the Southern Ocean, that he may be employed on that service. As for the service under my direction on this Northern one, Captain Nelson's constitution is rather too delicate. But such minds, my Lord, are most devoutly to be wished for Government's sake.'

Campbell wrote a more realistic letter to Germain, regretting that the expedition had been 'so unfortunately ill-timed'; that it would not be possible to advance far until the rains had stopped; but that Polson's force would be reinforced so as to be ready for renewed operations in August. But even he had caught a little of the excitement, adding, 'I am only sorry it has not fallen to my lot to be fit to lead this Gallant Body against the Spaniards.'

Both men were enthusiastically preparing the next draft of reinforcements. Until Garth's troops arrived from England – they had, in fact, only just been able to leave Plymouth on 29th May – these would have to be volunteers. Lieutenant-Colonel Sir Alexander Leith, who commanded the newly-arrived 88th Regiment, would leave his regulars in Jamaica and take over more than a hundred boatmen. These were grandly called the Royal Batteaux Corps but, according to Robert Hodgson, who saw them later, were 'a worthless, nay helpless, set of people, the refuse of the other two bodies of volunteers.' Nelson had stressed the urgent need for more boats and boatmen to keep the expedition supplied and, as Dalling put it, they would 'save the soldiery from those fatigues which . . . have been the sole cause of their present sickness.'

The Governor also ordered Lieutenant-Colonel Richard Cribb, who commanded the Liverpool Blues, but who had been too ill to accompany them, to raise a regiment of Light Dragoons in the island, mostly from the mulatto population and with both European and coloured officers.

He was well aware that his grandiose plan of conquest would have the most profound effect upon events in North America, where the fortunes of war had just swung towards the British, with the surrender of Charleston in South Carolina to

General Clinton. Believing that the imminent annexation of New Spain would induce the American rebels to have second thoughts about the value of independence, he had already sent a Major Odell, of the Jamaican militia, to New York with a letter 'manifesting to the poor people of that continent . . . the great advantages that must result to them in settling the Province of Nicaragua, so well situated, of so excellent a soil and so good a climate.'

He now also saw North America as a source of manpower for his own armies and sent three other officers on a recruiting mission to Georgia with a letter of introduction to Sir James Wright, the Governor. 'I should be apt to imagine that among the many deserters from the Rebel Army, and even among the Rebel prisoners now in Carolina, many might be procured for the intended service,' he wrote. 'By thus removing such disaffected persons from your Government, two good effects must naturally result: viz, of lessening the Rebel Force on the continent; and of augmenting his Majesty's Army on the Spanish Main.' He also asked for weapons to be sent urgently, 'as I am informed that great quantities of spare arms are at New York and other places.'

Dalling knew what reinforcements were on their way from England and drew up an exact order of battle for his Northern Army, which he forwarded to Germain. It would consist of three thousand and fifty-three regulars, being the whole of the 60th, 79th, 85th, 88th and Loyal Irish regiments and companies from the newly-raised 92nd, 93rd and 94th, who would be formed into three brigades, two battalions of grenadiers and two battalions of light infantry. To these would be added four hundred and thirty-nine irregulars and whatever artillery and cavalry that could be found. Among the appointments, for which ambitious officers could compete, would be Adjutant-General, Captain of Guides, Physician-General, Surgeon-General and Captain of Spies, while Polson had already been appointed Quartermaster-General.

Campbell, who was in charge of this planning, estimated that this would leave nearly seventeen hundred regulars in Jamaica, which should be a garrison strong enough to satisfy the most demanding of the Governor's critics in the Assembly.

If the danger of invasion abated still further and Dalling's own army was seen to be victorious, this could form the nucleus of his own force for the attack on Mexico and it was for this army that the mission to Georgia had been empowered to offer a bounty of £5 to each American recruit.

But of immediate concern was the sailing of the third reinforcement to Nicaragua, under the command of Colonel Leith. A hundred and forty Batteaux men – racially mixed and including released prisoners of war – were embarked in the storeship *Hope*, together with several surgeons and artificers and a party of Negro slaves. Also loaded were camp equipment, boat awnings and warm clothing and provisions including sugar, vermicelli, coffee, wine and tobacco.

Once they had disembarked at Greytown, which, it was assumed, Kemble had already left, Leith would set up a main depot for the expedition. From there he would have supplies shipped up-river to form others at Bartola and at the castle itself. Sir Alexander had trained as a gunner, so was also to strengthen the defences of Greytown before joining Kemble and Polson and taking charge of their artillery.

Leith was also to do what he could to restore the loyalty of the Indians and the Governor had also decided that 'this is to be effected by plenty of presents' and, to this end, he was sending 'two Gentlemen of weight and influence amongst them.'

So, despite delays and setbacks, both Dalling and Campbell were confident in eventual success, the latter writing, 'I do not see how we can fail to bring about that grand object, a communication between sea and sea.' Since Rodney's return to the Caribbean, his recent relief of Gibraltar and its strategic implications had been the subject of much discussion at the King's House and the Governor found a parallel in that feat and his own. The castle of San Juan, he declared, 'may in some degree be looked upon as the inland Gibraltar of Spanish America, as it commands the only water pass between the Lake of Nicaragua and the Northern Ocean . . . by our possession of it, Spanish America is severed in two.'

It was this heroic mood that was shattered by the arrival of a letter from Colonel Kemble written on 19th May from 'the Gibraltar of Spanish America.'

Since the sight of the emaciated Nelson had shocked the soldiers at Greytown on the 1st of that month, their health and morale had steadily deteriorated. They began to go down with dysentery and the crews of the ships that had brought Polson's force began to die of malaria. In the *Hinchinbroke*, one or two men died each day and Captain Collingwood sent his fittest men ashore to pitch tents and build huts for a hospital. He was also having the frigate's lower deck washed with vinegar and kept fires burning in iron pots below in an attempt at fumigation and to keep away the mosquitoes that swarmed at dusk.

On the 5th, more boats had come down the San Juan carrying prisoners from the castle. These were, under the terms of capitulation, to be shipped to a Spanish port and Santiago de Cuba was chosen as the most convenient. Two transports, the *Monarch* and the *Venus*, prepared to embark them, while Captain Fotheringham, whose crew had not yet sickened, helped Collingwood to heel his ship in attempt to stop her leaks and make her ready for escort duty.

Little progress had been made in building a fort on the point because of heavy rain and the lassitude of the soldiers. Finally, Kemble, having sent an advance party up the river, decided that the time had come to go up himself with the main body, using both the warships' boats and those that had come down-river with the prisoners. Accordingly, on the 8th, he set out.

Polson's ascent of the San Juan had been fraught with difficulty and danger but Kemble's was far worse. With the river in flood, there were no rapids to overcome, but the water was swift and deep and, as the heavily-loaded pangas and pitpans were prone to capsize, accidents could, and did, lead to drownings. But natural hazards became disastrous when faced by drunken men. The morale of Kemble's men had been deteriorating since their arrival at Greytown and had sunk faster since the arrival of the sick Nelson. Now they were leaving the safety of a harbour, where delay seemed likely to mean death from disease, to struggle up an unknown river, raging with flood-water, to a castle and camp they knew to be already stricken with sickness. They were constantly rain-soaked by day, maddened by mosquitoes at nightfall and chilled throughout the night. Raw rum was plentiful and offered temporary escape; it also led to calamity.

Boats, manned and steered by drunken men, capsized, or were swamped and took the wrong channels, leading far into the jungle; men and cargoes were lost in deep water, or up a maze of tributaries. When accounts of this eventually reached Jamaica, Dalling wrote sharply to Kemble that 'much is said of the great irregularities and drunkenness of the Troops from the straggling manner in which they ascended the river, in consequence of which very many of them have been drowned.'

Some of the boats, manned by Europeans, took thirty days to make the journey to the castle, but Kemble himself managed it in a week, arriving on 15th May. He was appalled by what he saw, reporting to Dalling, 'I was greatly surprised to find the Troops under Colonel Polson's command, as well as those I had forwarded to him, in a most deplorable state, there not being a relief for the common camp duty and whole guards frequently forced to remain forty-eight hours; the reduction of them to almost nominal has not had effect, the sick increasing in proportion. As to officers, it is with difficulty that one subaltern can be found to mount the Castle Guard.

'From the foregoing reason, I found everything in the greatest confusion.'

The army that had been sent to conquer New Spain lay sick in its sodden, rotting tents, in the stinking huts that served as a hospital and in a few rooms of the dark and squalid little castle it had captured. Virtually no effort had been made to put the place into a state of defence against counter-attack, let alone begin the second stage of the advance to Lake Nicaragua.

Several officers were already dead; amongst them James Mounsey, the adjutant, who had been succeeded by Bulkeley. Almost everybody seemed to be sick in some degree with dysentery, or malaria, or both; among them, Lawrie and Despard.

There was an almost total lack of staple medicines for the treatment of the two principal illnesses: amongst them quinine bark, diaphoretic powders, purgatives such as ipecacuanha and opium; and in the widly exotic tangle of the jungle none of the familiar herbs from which healing draughts were brewed. Food thought suitable for invalids – like vermicelli, salt, sugar and chocolate – was lacking and much of the basic rations, particularly flour, had been ruined by rain.

Worst of all, no attempt was being made to man boats for the shipping of supplies from the depots down-river, for there were not enough men to provide crews. 'Soldiers would be a resource in other countries,' noted Kemble, 'but here they are incapable from indisposition even to help themselves.'

The over-worked Dr. Dancer was near despair, explaining to Kemble, as he later wrote, 'The question may be asked, "Why as there was no building fitted for the purposes of an hospital, was not one erected?" ' Polson had given orders for one to be built but 'sickness becoming so general . . . there was neither artificer to work, or soldier to assist him. Necessity then compelled us to make use of places that became a source of contagion and precipitated those who went into them out of the world.'

Asked about medicines, bedding and special rations for the sick, Dancer explained, 'We had them in abundant quantity, but not at our hospital where they were wanted: there being not a sufficient number of craft for transporting the ammunition and stores up the river, a certain quantity only of each could be put on board, which in many cases was not competent to the exigencies of the service.'

A principal cause of this was the defection of the Mosquito Indians. They had been even more sickly than the soldiery, several dying of dysentery during the siege, but they were also homesick and found military discipline irksome having, as Polson put it, 'the highest ideas of freedom.' They had remained with the expedition in the hope of the plunder and prisoners they had been promised, for one of their leaders, the 'Duke of York' swore that Governor Dalling had assured him that 'all Indians and Negroes are to be considered as slaves' and part of their reward. However, the colonel refused to hand over the non-European prisoners and Polson explained that the Governor had been referring only to slaves taken from the Spaniards. So the Indians, 'whose imaginations had been disastrously raised', as Dalling later put it, and who had been 'treated too much like soldiers and too little like savages', were not even given the half-dozen women and children of slaves, who had been taken, and were not allowed to strip and rob the prisoners, or even to enter the castle.

Thereupon 'the King, Duke, Admiral Richards and Colonel McFarlane', and the rest of the Indians, deserted in the night, taking their boats with them, only a few being stopped at gun-point. Their duties as boatmen were then taken over by Negroes from the Black River settlement. But they did not remain much longer themselves.

Soon after Kemble's arrival, Lawrie returned to the coast, whereupon almost all the Negroes, who had regarded themselves as under his personal command, also deserted in their boats.

The arrival of Kemble's troops should have provided some relief but their long delay 'amidst the pestilential vapours of the harbour . . . laid the seeds of a variety of diseases, which aggravated by the fatigues . . . in working the craft up the river, soon broke out in fluxes, dysenteries and other terrible disorders, which swept them off with such rapidity as to baffle all the skills and attention of the Medical Gentlemen.'

A month after his own arrival at Greytown, Kemble himself went down with a violent bout of malaria that, after six days, left him exhausted and delirious, unable to distinguish his own nightmares from the horrors around him.

The dead had been ferried across the river to the island of Juana for burial but when the few available boatmen were away trying to bring up supplies, the corpses were simply thrown into the water to be instantly torn to shreds by shoals of *machaca* fish, or laid out on the river bank where their bones were picked clean by carrion crows and turkey-buzzards and even eaten by jaguars. Black-winged birds of prey slowly circled above the Castillo de la Inmaculada Concepción.

Kemble had almost died and, as it was, the fever left him drained of energy and enthusiasm. But he was now in command and even sometimes known as 'the General', or 'the Commander-in-Chief', while Polson had become his Quartermaster-General, a task as desperate as that of the field commander. But on 6th June, the day he felt strong enough to get up and write another report to Dalling, he was urged towards activity by the arrival below the San Juan rapids of the *Lord Germain*, more than two months after she had left Greytown. Next day, Major Dalrymple and his contingent arrived at the castle.

He now had enough boats to attempt the further ascent of the river. If possible, the *Germain* would be warped up the rapids and, in the calm water above, be fitted out as a gunboat to lead a flotilla to the lake. Hauling tackle was rigged to great trees on the river bank and the healthiest of the new arrivals put to work, heaving the heavy vessel through the less turbulent water near the shore. By the 11th, she was past the rapids and, as the rains had somewhat abated, Kemble hoped to make her ready in a week. But she was in a poor state − much of her cordage lost or worn through on her long voyage up the river − and most of the carpenters needed to strengthen her hull for the mounting of guns were ill. 'If we employ two carpenters at a time, we are lucky,' noted Kemble.

He was in a dilemma. The orders from Dalling were clear: he was to continue up the river and establish a fortified post at the entrance to the lake; then he was to take and fortify the largest of the islands in it and, from there, launch his attack against Granada and its hinterland. By some accounts, this should be a simple operation. There were reported to be only about two hundred and fifty Spanish regular soldiers in the whole province and its vulnerability was suggested by Don Juan d'Ayssa having forwarding his wife's baggage to Granada, addressing it to 'the care of Colonel Polson.'

Yet, with only about seventy men unaffected by dysentery or malaria, the condition of his own force was so deplorable that he had, in a moment of despair, written to Dalling suggesting that he leave a garrison in the castle and withdraw not just to the coast but to the more healthful climate of Bluefields and nearby Corn Island. When he recovered his confidence, he wrote again, asking for all manner of supplies − 'tarpaulins, cordage, sail cloth, graplins, blocks, pitch, tar, oakum . . . plank and boards of all dimensions . . . a great number of house and ship carpenters, sawyers, smiths, masons, coopers and harness and collar makers for the artillery with abundance of tools for each and a quantity of nails and spikes of all sorts, also all sorts of entrenching tools. . . .'

There was a desperate need of clothing and boots, for the men still wore the tattered remnants of the uniforms torn on their journey up the river and through the jungle.

Although, in the middle of June, there was a slight easing of the rains, morale remained low. There was constant squabbling and drunkenness among the irregulars, and the volunteer officers were in continual rivalry over relative rank and whether any particular duty was beneath their dignity. Even the hard-worked Dr. Dancer broke out in a display of injured pride when a more senior doctor arrived from the coast and was only dissuaded from resigning by Kemble inventing the title of 'Physician to the Hospital' for him and promising that his pay would remain that of a Surgeon-General.

Discipline had almost ceased to exist in the Jamaica Legion and a soldier of the Loyal Irish was under arrest for planning to lead a mass-desertion. To tighten control of those fit for duty, Kemble formed them into two battalions: the Loyal Irish and the Jamaica Volunteers and Legion into one, commanded by Dalrymple; the Royal Americans and the Liverpool Blues into another under Polson.

There seemed some chance that this force might have the numbers and the energy to carry out the next phase of the campaign, when worrying news arrived from both down-river and up-river. From his convalescence on Corn Island, Major Lawrie had written on 9th June with the news that, in April, the Spaniards had attacked the Black River settlement and wanted urgent reinforcements for a counter-attack. He also said that the Mosquito Indians were 'much incensed' as result of what they considered their betrayal over the promise of slaves and plunder and that they might 'throw themselves into the arms of the Spaniards', and asked for one of the settlers with the expedition, Cairns, to be sent to pacify them.

Kemble complied with alacrity, ordering two officers and seventy men from among the healthiest invalids at Greytown to join Lawrie and sending Cairns down-river — 'tho' from character I doubt the efficacy of the emissary.'

The other news arrived with a returning reconnaissance

patrol led by Captain Despard, despite his fever, that had gone up-river at the beginning of June. Accompanied by a Captain Dawes, he had taken a canoe almost as far as the lake, then landed and continued on foot. On the return journey he suffered a relapse so that, on arrival at the castle, 'his indisposition rendered him unable to see, or make any remarks' so that Dawes had to deliver the report. This, Kemble sent to Dalling on 14th June, writing, 'Mr. Despard, the engineer, came yesterday from the head of the river, the north side of which he found occupied by the Spaniards, who possessed a breastwork . . . he was almost within arm's reach of a sentry, who gave the alarm, but he had the good fortune to retire without receiving any harm, tho' fired upon by one or two of the guard, who came to the sentry's relief. He is gone again this evening to endeavour to make such discoveries as will be of consequence.'

But instead of becoming infected by Despard's gallant enthusiasm, Kemble was depressed at the prospect of having to fight for entry to the lake and he wrote to Dalling, 'If we are able to carry 70 or 80 soldiers up the river — it will be as much as we shall — how inadequate to dislodge an enemy whose force we may reasonably suppose to be five times our number.'

This seemed like deliberate pessimism, because that was the number the *Germain* alone could carry and took no account of other boats that might follow, let alone any new reinforcement. This was now well on the way because, on the 19th, Leith and his Royal Batteaux men had arrived at Greytown. Like Kemble before him, he was appalled by what he found. The ships in the harbour seemed manned by dying sailors, the *Hinchinbroke* lying low in the water, and apparently slowly foundering. Since Collingwood had taken command, more than thirty of her men had died of 'fevers, fluxes and scorbutic ulcers' and about a hundred were desperately ill. Yet, in May, the ship had twice been able to put to sea, escorting the Spanish prisoners bound for Cuba, and once when she had to turn back as water in her bilges was rising fifteen inches an hour. Now her captain reported, 'The ship's company very ill and every day growing worse.'

The crew of the *Resource* were also sickening, as were those of the transports, of whom only about twenty men were fit for duty. Scores had been sent ashore. Although there had not been enough fit men to do more fortifying of the harbour than to mount three cannon on the point, Collingwood's foresight in building a hospital, before sickness had taken so calamitous a hold, had been prudent, although Leith found its stench, even at a distance, 'insupportable'. Of two hundred and forty soldiers ashore at Greytown, only ten were fit for duty.

Leith was able to collect ten boats, load them with seventy barrels of salt pork and flour, embark eighty men and send them up the river on the 25th. He himself accompanied a second division and took pains to ensure that the disaster of Kemble's ascent was not repeated by having two officers and a pilot in a light canoe constantly paddling up and down the column of boats to keep them on course. Even so, he reported, 'a boat containing thirteen barrels went up a wrong branch and was never heard of.'

It was worse than that. One account claims that not ten of their boats reached the castle. Knowing little of boatwork, they were unable to handle their craft and eventually gave up, exhausted and often stricken with dysentery, to drift with the current; several boats carrying only dead and dying men being swept back to Greytown. Of the boats that did arrive, most carried not food and clothing but ordnance stores, the gunpowder sometimes wet and useless. When seven craft appeared below the castle on 30th June, Kemble found that only forty of the gunpowder-filled shells they had brought were still serviceable.

On this dreadful journey, Leith himself went down with a first bout of malaria. When, on 4th July, after eight days on the river, he, too, arrived at the castle, he was as shocked as Kemble had been. As a professional gunner, he was particularly surprised to find that the principal prizes of the castle, the Spanish artillery, had not been touched, 'being in a very unserviceable state, every piece of ordnance being half full of water and the same charges of powder and ball as the Spaniards left in them at the conclusion of the siege.'

The smell was appalling. 'An intolerable stench from no sufficient regulation having taken place for keeping the castle clean,' he said, 'and the wrong situation for the necessary house, the stench of which was blown upon the castle by the breeze; the necessary house was extremely noisome from the number of fluxes that reigned at that period amongst the soldiery.'

Those soldiers still on their feet were emaciated and dirty. Their red and blue uniforms were stained and faded, usually lacking gaiters, stockings and shoes, so that their legs were bare below the knees, and they often wore rough sandals of cowhide. He was appalled to hear of the lack of medicines and any but basic rations, even then being at half the minimum level, and at once began sending his own boatmen out in search of fruit and plantains.

As the new second-in-command and commander of the artillery, Leith had naturally expected to be received with relief, if not warmth, by Kemble, whose letters had been stressing the need for his services. He was therefore surprised and hurt to find his commanding officer morose and in a strange mood that could only be explained by his recent delirium. He knew that the *Germain* had gone up-river on 15th June, two days after Despard had made his report, with seventy-two men embarked under the command of Major MacDonald, and that Colonel Kemble had been expected to leave the following day with the main force. But Kemble was still at the castle and there was no sign that he was preparing to leave. It was obviously essential for Leith to know what the plans might be, if only so as to be able to arrange for the necessary ammunition to be embarked.

When the commanding officer remained silent, he felt obliged to make enquiries, with a consequence he later described: 'The day after my arrival, I requested of him to inform me in what manner he intended attacking the Spanish post, hoping he would indulge me in giving an opinion on the subject. He evaded the question by rising from his seat and walking out. . . .'

Nor did Kemble ever confide his plans to his second-in-command but sent him signed orders for cartridges and gunpowder when embarkation was imminent. So Leith had to discover elsewhere that the *Germain* had been armed with two brass four-pounders, two twelve-pounder carronades and ten smaller guns, and that two four-inch howitzers were to be mounted in other craft.

The boats were available, but not the men. At the end of June not one officer of the 60th, or the 79th, had been fit for duty and the regulars from those regiments had had to be commanded by a lieutenant of the Jamaica Volunteers. Hopes of a reinforcement of healthy officers seemed dashed when Leith had arrived a sick man and Major Dalrymple went down with malaria. Then the rains eased, the sun shone and, during the first week of July, there was a slight improvement. Polson recovered from a bad bout of fever and it seemed that several other officers might be fit enough for the planned advance.

Although basic rations were not in dangerously short supply, none of the provisions needed for the sick — sugar, portable soup and coffee — or the urgently-needed medicines had come up the river. Five hundred pairs of shoes were known to be on board a transport at Greytown but, despite orders from Leith that they be sent up-river, there they remained. This, together with hopes of another reinforcement, provided Kemble with excuses enough for further delay.

Wistfully, Kemble wrote to Dalling, 'Could I have the pleasure of seeing your Excellency at the head of a good body of healthy troops coming up the river, I should be the happiest fellow on earth.' But he had no reason for such hopes beyond the knowledge that one day that year such an army might land on the Spanish Main. In his debilitated state, he had already decided that a successful debouching into the lake was almost certainly beyond his capability. His ragged and half-starved collection of soldiery — many of them drunken and undisciplined — could never become an offensive force fit to be commanded by a lieutenant-colonel accustomed to leading regular soldiers, even though he was a Royal American and so prided himself on his knowledge of unconventional warfare and bush-fighting.

He was now determined that the only course open to him was retreat to the coast and rest and recuperation for his men at Bluefields, Corn Island and other coastal settlements that were said to be healthier than Greytown. Then, when the rains had ceased at the end of the year and Governor Dalling had arrived with his army, another attempt could be made to invade Nicaragua. Yet this would be in direct contradiction to his orders and, in his weakened state, he lacked the resolution even for that.

Finally, Kemble decided upon a compromise. He would have to be seen to make an attempt to break into the lake but he would look for viable excuses for not doing so. Accordingly, on 7th July, he embarked with about a hundred and thirty men in a flotilla of pangas and pitpans and set off upstream. The water was higher, and the current stronger than ever but there were no islands or rocks in the river, which ran, two to three hundred yards wide, between low, thickly-wooded banks. But whereas the *Germain* had made the passage of about twenty miles, to within seven of the entrance to the lake, in nine days under sail, the journey took Kemble's boats twice as long.

Major MacDonald and Captain Despard had, meanwhile taken to canoes for another reconnaissance of the Spanish post. Landing at night on an island just below the lake, they had spent two days – 19th and 20th July – in watching the enemy at work on his defences. Four or five hundred men – including some Europeans, who were presumably regular soldiers – had almost completed a formidable fortification. It stood upon a ridge some sixty feet high and set back about a hundred and fifty yards from the northern bak of the river. It was an earthwork, braced with logs and protected by a stockade and abatis of sharp stakes. There were neither embrasures nor guns to be seen, although, as the trees had been felled to provide a clear field of fire to the river, these would presumably be mounted.

The two men also saw, riding at anchor, two Spanish ships – a brig and a sloop – but neither capable of defending herself against the guns of the *Germain*. While in hiding on the island, four hundred yards from the enemy, they were confident that they had not been seen but as Despard's canoe slid out from the cover of the heavy foliage along the shore, a Spanish patrol boat suddenly appeared and there was a sharp exchange of fire. Nobody was hit and the British boat escaped down-river; the Spaniard, upstream. Had Nelson been with Despard – as at Bartola island – they would have urged an immediate assault before the alerted garrison could make ready its defence and, on his return to the main force seven miles downstream, it is probable that Despard did suggest this to Kemble.

So when, on the evening of 24th July, Despard arrived with this news, it was, to Kemble, not a spur to action but a necessary excuse to retreat. His men were now in a worse state, some sixty of them ill. Most of the way up the river it had rained so heavily that it had been impossible to light fires when camping on the bank and fresh rations were so short that the best marksmen had been sent into the jungle to shoot monkeys. A boat bringing supplies up-river had met with 'some unaccountable accident *by the drunkenness of the hands* and had not been heard of.' When Polson, who had been fit enough to accompany Kemble, was sent back to the castle for food, he returned with some and the news that there was unlikely to be more because the troops at the castle had been without basic rations for two days.

Those of his men not sick were exhausted – the *Germain* had run aground on her way upstream and had only been saved by unloading all her guns and ammunition, floating her free, then loading again – and only twenty-four were considered fit for duty. Now, Kemble heard, he had also lost his advantage of surprise, which he thought essential to 'attempt boarding two armed vessels ready to receive you and to attack a post defended by three times your numbers and of difficult access.' All these factors combined, he said, in what 'I think to be a sufficient excuse for declining the attempt.' He did not even think it necessary to reconnoitre the enemy position himself.

Difficulties might arise with Leith, who had shown embarrassing enthusiasm for the enterprise before Kemble had sailed. He had since written to say that he was feeling so much healthier that he should be able to join the expedition up-river on about 25th July, when he hoped to be allowed to lead the attack on the enemy post. He would be bringing about forty of his strongest Batteaux men with him and, remembering details of Despard's first report on the fortifications, would have scaling-ladders made and also petard mines to sink any enemy ships that might be encountered. Kemble replied, making a pretence at gratitude, saying that he looked forward to having Leith with him yet urging him not to hurry because of the importance of a lengthy convalescence.

But Leith was even more optimistic than Kemble realised. The questioning of Spanish prisoners had convinced him that once the post on the lake — close to the settlement of San Carlos — was taken, it could be defended against any likely counter-attack as the enemy had little, if any, artillery in the province. The flotilla could then sail into the lake and take one of the islands as a base; he was told that one, within a few miles of San Carlos, was healthy and fertile, grazing ten thousand head of cattle. 'In my opinion,' he remarked later, 'there was no risque in advancing.'

So he was dismayed when, just as he was preparing to move up the river, Kemble's boats appeared above the rapids and it became clear that they had not even attempted to break into the lake. His commanding officer was now only too eager to converse with Leith, who later described how 'on his return to St. John's Castle, he introduced the conversation himself and informed me that the reason for his coming down the river was owing to Lieutenant Despard, who having been out on a reconnoitering party and met with a Spanish boat, whom he imprudently attacked . . . and as the enemy's boat returned up the river, General Kemble concluded that the Spanish officer must be acquainted with his intention to attack the post and therefore thought it expedient to return.'

Leith also noticed that the colonel had not given the shortage of supplies as a reason for his retreat; indeed he brought several unopened barrels of provisions back with him to the castle. But Major MacDonald told a different story: 'that sickness and want of provisions, together with the enemy's superiority in point of numbers, were the chief reasons assigned for not persisting in the attack.' He also said that the attempt was 'not weak in spirit, but in strength, for want of victuals.' Indeed, he suggested that some of the soldiers had actually died of starvation on the journey.

Leith was disgusted. Later, he brusquely answered the question, 'Was the force forwarded equal to the enterprise?' with, 'In every respect beyond it.' 'If equal, from what apparent cause, or causes, did it fail?' 'From the injudicious conduct of the commanding officers.'

But Kemble was now in full retreat. Without even knowing

whether there were any transports at Greytown to take his men to some healthier coast for recuperation, he set off down the river, leaving Leith in command at the castle with about a hundred and fifty men, a mixture of regiment and race, united only in having survived.

When news of the failure of the attack on the San Carlos post and the retreat to the sea reached him, Governor Dalling was furious, writing that 'the returning to the Fort without making the attempt, and then to the Harbour without even the hopes of getting away from thence, seems to be retiring from uncertain danger to certain destruction.' But Kemble had not acted wholly without authority. When Dalling had read his first pessimistic report he had, towards the end of June, sent him revised orders. These stressed that the eventual objectives remained but that if Spanish opposition on the river proved too strong, he could try to reach the lake another way. Indeed, some detailed instructions for the evacuation of the castle were included, involving the deception of the enemy – 'amusing them with false attacks' – while the garrison, guns and stores were quietly shipped downstream. The castle itself would then be blown up. The main force was then to be transferred to Bluefields and another attempt made by ascending the Bluefields river, then trying to drive a path through the jungle to the lake.

But when Kemble, accompanied by MacDonald and Dalrymple, arrived at Greytown on 9th August, the harbour was a scene of desolation. The flooding river swept them over the shoals of the estuary at eight knots to find that what had been the shallow harbour 'was now an ocean'. But it was empty of all but a few ships, listing, apparently derelict and manned by dying crews.

They discovered that some of Leith's reinforcement had never even tried to get up the river, lacking boatmen to man their craft, while a number of those who had and taken wrong channels had eventually returned 'worn out with fatigue and sickness.' One such party, which had mistakenly turned south into the Sarepiqui river had gone up it for twenty-six days during which, the young officer in command, almost incoherent with exhaustion, told Kemble that he had seen 'no traces of a human creature during the whole course of his wanderings.'

Dalrymple reached Jamaica first, having taken passage in the *Resource*, which was almost as sickly as the *Hinchinbroke*, having only seventy-five men on their feet. His reports were 'melancholy indeed', giving details of the 'uncommon mortality' among the troops in grim detail and maintaining that Colonel Kemble was 'determined to quit the country.'

Soon afterwards, Major MacDonald arrived and, while he confirmed Dalrymple's account of the failure to break into the lake and of the devastating epidemics, his emphasis was quite different; indeed, he was optimistic. Surprisingly, he reported that there were fifty or sixty boats on the river, capable of transporting five hundred men, with provisions for a month, and that, if these could be manned, such a force could reach the castle from Greytown in three weeks despite the strong current. He even suggested exact sites for four staging posts for another reinforcement on its way upstream.

Dalling seized on these high hopes. Now he would send more reinforcements; not only those few still available in Jamaica, but the thousands of fresh troops from England whose arrival was now imminent. The first to go would be the Light Dragoons – a mixture of Portuguese, Italians, Negroes and mulattoes and a few British. These had been raised by the ailing Major Cribb of the Liverpool Blues and, when he had died, their command had passed to his second-in-command, Major the Honourable William Lewis. About a hundred had been recruited, but when ordered to report for embarkation, only fifty-eight obeyed.

So impressed had Dalling been by Nelson's achievements that he appointed another naval officer to take command of the boats. This was Commander James Clarke, formerly first lieutenant of the frigate *Phoenix*, who had seen active service on the rivers of North America. Given the honorary rank of colonel, he was sent across to the San Juan with the initial task of assessing the chances of another attempt to break through to the lake.

All Governor Dalling's hopes now hinged on the safe arrival of General Garth and his army from England. It was not until 29th May that they had finally been able to sail from Plymouth and they had anchored briefly in Carlisle Bay, Barbados, on 10th July before moving on next day to St. Lucia. There, news awaited them from Jamaica that operations had begun ashore in Central America, described as 'beating up the Spanish Quarters'. But the soldiers were in no condition for any form of activity. Most of them had been on board their damp troopships for twenty-one weeks and many were rotten and debilitated with scurvy; one regiment was riddled with an epidemic of something akin to 'gaol fever'.

St. Lucia was particularly unhealthy at this season so the ships left quickly for Jamaica under the escort of Admiral Rodney's line of battle, since the enemy fleet was again thought to be hovering to strike. When a sloop was sent ahead to announce their arrival, Robert Hodgson sailed in her, reaching Kingston on 22nd July, twelve days before convoy at last anchored in the bay.

Hodgson considered himself the instigator of the campaign in Nicaragua and did not endear himself to Dalling by criticising the conduct of it. Indeed he was 'severely disappointed' by his reception at the King's House, where the Governor seemed to regard him as an interfering busybody with nothing to offer but hindsight and the news that he could not expect much help from General Garth. This proved all too true when the army began to disembark on 1st August. It was then discovered that of its two thousand, three hundred men, one hundred and eighty-six had died and seven hundred and eighty were sick.

To relieve the over-crowding on the troop-decks, the healthier men were put ashore. It was pouring with rain yet they had to sleep on the ground under canvas in such discomfort that they began to envy those who had remained on board. Fresh food and medical supplies were scarce; they had either been sent to Nicaragua, or the quartermasters were unwilling, or unable, to get them to the camp. So the soldiers continued to die.

This was the moment when even Governor Dalling lost heart. If his new army was withering away in Jamaica, how much more quickly would it wilt on the Mosquito Shore; the only hope for its recovery would have been a quick voyage to the healthy shores of Lake Nicaragua. The hospitals at Up Park and Castile Fort, outside Kingston, were, reported Dr. Moseley, 'small, boarded buildings . . . hot, crowded and unclean'. Into these were packed hundreds of men suffering from 'fluxes, bilious and remittent fevers'.

During the wet autumn months, a third of General Garth's army died in Jamaica. Of the seven and a half battalions that now made up the garrison of the island, eleven hundred died and fifteen hundred lay sick. Seeing his dreams of conquest collapse, Dalling remarked bitterly, 'Considered only as an article of commerce, these eleven hundred men have cost £22,000, a sum which, if laid out above ground, might have saved half their lives.'

Now, the only hope was that what remained of the expeditionary force on the Spanish Main might still be able to break through to the lake, either via the San Juan or Bluefields rivers. Yet, wherever they were, there was no escape from disease. Dr. Moseley, horrified first by reports from Greytown, then by the arrival of the first survivors, reported, 'Great as our inconveniences were in Jamaica, those who encountered the San Juan expedition suffered much more; and it was long doubtful whether those, who, after experiencing every hardship in life, were thrown into the river, or lay unburied on its banks, a prey to wild beasts in sight of their helpless companions, were not in a more enviable state than the survivors.

'Those who returned to Jamaica were harrassed with obstinate intermittents, or diarrhoeal, or dysenterical complaints; or with painful enlargements of the liver, or spleen. Their complexions were very yellow, and their bodies emaciated. Some, whom I attended after their return, that had been long ill on the Spanish Main, had their intellects impaired.'

Some were unable to shake off malarial delirium, which remained when attacks of fever had passed, and 'several men wandered about in a phrenzy and died raving mad.'

The sailors had suffered as much as the soldiers; particularly those aboard ships in the harbour at Greytown, where about a thousand died. Most of the Spanish prisoners from the castle – excepting the officers – were put aboard the transport *Hope* for passage to Cuba but, being turned back by bad weather, had to remain in that lethal anchorage, where they all died. Even Collingwood, who was aware of the latest methods of hygiene aboard ship, found himself commanding a dying crew.

Between 1st May, when he succeeded Nelson, to 5th August, when he sailed for Jamaica, ninety of his men died. In late May, they had been able to put to sea briefly to escort the Spanish prisoners on their way to Cuba, but the clean sea air had no remedial effect. On 18th July, Collingwood wrote in his log, 'The ship very leaky. The whole ships' company sick.' The frigate could only be worked with the help of drafts from the *Resource*, then, when her own crew became as sickly, from other ships.

When the *Hinchinbroke* was on passage to Port Royal, her captain was one of a handful of her original ship's company still on their feet. Twenty-one more men died on the twelve-day voyage and they continued to die in the hospitals ashore. When Collingwood gave up the command just before Christmas, a hundred and twenty-seven of his men had died. Later, he recorded that, of some two hundred men who had made up Nelson's original, healthy ship's company, only about ten survived.

Nelson himself had seemed to recover under the care of Cuba Cornwallis and Lady Parker, but suffered a relapse and Dr. Moseley feared for his life. There had been no question of his being able to take active command of his new frigate and, at the end of August, he had written to Admiral Parker, 'Having been in a very bad state of health for these several months past, so as to be unable to attend to my duty on board the *Janus* and the faculty having informed me that I cannot recover in this climate, I am therefore to request that you will be pleased to permit me to go to England for the re-establishment of my health.'

This was supported by a report of three naval surgeons, confirming that he was suffering from multiple infections of malaria together with 'Bilious Vomitings, Nervous Headaches, Visceral Obstructions and many other bodily Infirmities.' They declared their conviction that for him to remain in the tropics would 'be attended with fatal consequences' and recommended 'an immediate change of climate as the only chance he has for recovery.'

The Commander-in-Chief gave his permission to return to England that same day — adding his 'very sincere wishes for your speedy recovery' — but wrote despondently to the Admiralty, 'Captain Nelson is so emaciated and in so bad a state of health that I doubt whether he will live to get home. I wish much for his recovery. His abilities in his profession would be a loss to the Service.'

But he was now well enough to mount a horse and make a few parting calls and his spark of ambition had not been extinguished. So he wrote to Hercules Ross, 'I will ride over tomorrow and have a chat. Now assured I return to England, hope revives within me. I shall recover and my dream of glory be fulfilled. Nelson will yet be an admiral. It is the climate that has destroyed my health and crushed my spirit. Home and dear friends will restore me.'

Happily, the first suitable ship to leave for England was Captain Cornwallis's *Lion*, which was to escort an important convoy. On 3rd September, she embarked thirty invalids from the naval hospital, and Nelson himself was pulled across the harbour to her in the *Janus*'s longboat. Next day, she sailed for Portsmouth, a voyage which was to last nearly three months, during which the convoy was struck by an Atlantic storm so violent that the *Lion* was reported lost. After the ship finally dropped anchor at Spithead, he thanked Cornwallis for having cared for him with such attention, so, he believed, saving his life.

When he had left Port Royal seven months after leading the troopships towards the Spanish Main, the expedition that had then been so buoyant with optimism lay in total ruin and decomposition, most of its original members dead, or dying, racked with dysentery and malaria.

Yet Dalling refused to accept that his grand strategy had failed. He clung to Major MacDonald's false optimism and tried to give his opinions more weight by recommending him to the Colonial Secretary for promotion. Hodgson, on the other hand, he found increasingly irritating. Since his arrival, he had haunted the King's House, continually reminding all who would listen that the original concept of the expedition had been his and that, had his advice been followed, the present disasters would have been avoided.

The Governor now convinced himself that operations on the Spanish Main could be resumed when the rains ceased at the end of the year. A garrison would remain at the castle of San Juan and its communications with Greytown kept open but, meanwhile, a new attempt to reach the lake through Bluefields would be made. To this end, and to restore the British position along the Mosquito Shore northwards to Black River, a new military mission would be sent. This, Dalling decided, would be commanded by the tiresome, but unquestionably able, Robert Hodgson.

When the Governor's orders, together with the offer of a temporary colonelcy, reached Hodgson, he had mixed feelings. He was instructed to regain the confidence of the Mosquito Indians, for which purpose he would take with him presents, such as he himself had recommended, to the value of £3,000. He would recruit another Indian corps and also as many Negro slaves as possible, the best of them to be formed into a regiment of *chasseurs*. This having been done, he would urge the British settlers, who had fled on the Spanish attack in April, to return under his protection. While this was being done, a survey of the Bluefields river, and the terrain between its head and Lake Nicaragua, would be made, with a view to driving a military road between the two points when the rains ended.

It was a challenging proposal, but Hodgson did not want to face such a challenge so directly. One reason for this was his lack of confidence in those who would accompany him as temporary field officers. The two most senior of these, he noted, were 'a flighty Doctor of Physic', who was to be the colonel commanding the new corps of Indians, and the other, who was to be a major, 'a clergyman who . . . had been rung about with a bell for perjury.' So Hodgson prevaricated, writing long quibbling letters to the Governor, so that when his two curious brother-officers sailed for Bluefields on 6th September, he was still in Spanish Town making excuses for not accompanying them.

The outcome was as grotesque as might have been expected. On arrival at Bluefields, the doctor and the parson quarrelled and the latter was dismissed, while the former, taking an officer of the Royal Batteaux Corps with him as a surveyor, set off up the river. Later he claimed to have explored a hundred miles of its course and to have discovered not only that the building of a road through the jungle would be impossible but that it was swarming with Spanish troops and armed, hostile Indians.

The only claim, which was accurate, was on the prospects of road-building, but the doctor continued to report fantasies. He told Dalling that his mission to the Mosquito Indians had been successful and that he had recruited hundreds. In fact, he had not enrolled one, having encamped with the bundles of presents that had been intended for them on the far side of Bluefields lagoon from the garrison. He lived in a hut with 'a carpenter, who he called his secretary, tho' he could not write, and scarcely ever communicating with the military.'

Meanwhile, Captain Clarke, who had been promoted from commander to commodore and honorary colonel by Dalling, was conducting his survey of the San Juan river. Taking soundings and measuring the current with log and line, he found the river in ideal condition for sending another force up to the lake: nowhere was the channel less than five feet deep, nor the current running at more than four knots.

When Clarke returned to Jamaica at the beginning of November, crippled with dysentery and malaria, he was able to give the Governor a final, first-hand report on 'the shattered remains of his sickly army.' He had reached Greytown in the second week of September to find Kemble arrived there on his way to Bluefields with two hundred men, of whom only eighty were on their feet. The base depot itself had disintegrated, Colville, its commanding officer, was dead and he found 'the negligence of the officers and the drunkenness of the seamen remarkably shameful.'

Taking twenty-three of his own 'stout fellows' with him in a small flotilla of boats, the commodore set off up the river, seeing on its banks, as at the harbour, 'many traces of misconduct'. He described to Dalling 'barrels of beef lying in some places, flour in others, arms and camp equipage lay scattered on several parts of the banks from the river mouth to the castle. . . .'

[155]

Reaching it in less than a week, he found Despard in command, all but one of the other officers being sick. The garrison consisted of about a hundred dragoons of mixed race, including many of Spanish extraction, but only some twenty fit for duty. The castle itself was 'entirely dismantled' in readiness for the final evacuation in the *Lord Germain*, which lay 'in a very shattered condition' below of the rapids.

Despite this, Despard took Clarke on a three-day expedition up a tributary of the San Juan, the Rio Santa Cruz, that ran north-westward into the jungle towards the settlement of San Miguel on the lake. The commodore was convinced that the original strategy was sound and could succeed if the expedition could be assured of at least a hundred river-boats manned by a thousand Negroes. Failure had been caused by 'the troops delaying too long at the castle, which they might and ought to have stormed in the first instance, according to the plan proposed by Captain Nelson.' Disease had done the rest when 'the troops . . . about the twenty-third day after their arrival at the fort, all fell down sick.'

But there was no longer any army to launch another offensive. With remarkable optimism, Clarke again suggested the recruiting of Americans, saying, 'surely something might be done in America towards raising some troops for offensive operations on the Main, among the Continentals lately taken, most of whom are English, Irish and Scotch. Many might be found who, when withdrawn from the artful insinuations of a rebel Congress, might give fruits of loyalty and love to their country when transported to another region.'

When he returned to Greytown, the commodore found that Kemble had sailed, leaving 'nothing but some wrecked transports and perishing stores littering the country about.' He and his own 'stout fellows' had now been in Nicaragua for more than the fatal three weeks and they, too, began to sicken and die. Indeed, Clarke himself was the only one to survive.

Meanwhile, Kemble and the remanant of his force had sailed first to Corn Island, then to Bluefields, where they arrived on 8th October. He himself was worn out, cutting short the report to Dalling of his arrival with the words, 'Your Excellency will excuse me from further particulars as I am

[156]

obliged to lie down with the fever.' His command now consisted of four officers, thirty-four non-commissioned officers and men – mostly sick or lame – and about eighty Negroes.

The harbour beneath Bluefields Bluff looked almost as derelict as the Greytown anchorage; of the three small vessels lying there, only one could be manned for sea. Early in the month a catastrophic hurricane had struck Jamaica and caught many ships at sea; amongst them the *Hope*, in which the Spanish prisoners had died, while evacuating the artillery from Greytown, and the *Monarch*, with more prisoners embarked. Both were lost with all hands. But most disheartening of all was that Bluefields seemed as humid and unhealthy as Greytown had been and soon proved 'almost equally fatal to the soldiers.' Without ships, there was no escape.

Since February, between fifteen and eighteen hundred men and been sent to Nicaragua. Robert Hodgson, still in Spanish Town and privy to the returns and reports of the expedition, noted in November, 'There appears to remain of the Regular, Volunteers, Legion, Batteau Men, Horsemen and Workmen that were sent from Jamaica, about 70 Soldiers, and about 40 of the Horsemen, among which are many sick and dying, and also some few stores of small account may be saved out of the expensive profusion of them that was sent down to where but a few of them came into use.'

More than a thousand sailors had died in the ships and others had been lost at sea, and, of these, about four hundred had belonged to the Royal Navy. No warships had been lost but, the following year, the *Hinchinbroke*, worn out, foundered and sank.

Dr. Moseley estimated that there were not more than three hundred and eighty survivors of the San Juan expedition, including the crews of the warships. These he described as being 'in a miserable condition' and the soldiers, who were then sent to Bluefields, nearly all died. He recorded that sixty-nine officers died – six of them belong to the Royal Americans and ten to the Liverpool Blues – but this was an under-estimate since a number succumbed to fever and dysentery after their return to Jamaica, among them Sir Alexander Leith. Virtually all had been ill but most of the more senior officers survived.

[157]

Polson retired soon afterwards; Kemble rose to become a full colonel; Of Lawrie, Despard and Nelson more was soon to be heard.

Governor Dalling received a sombre reprimand from Lord George Germain, who wrote in December. 'I . . . lament exceedingly the dreadful havoc Death has made among the Troops . . . especially as from the entire failure of the Expedition no Public Benefit has been derived from the loss of so many brave men.' He said that he had realised that the enterprise would fail on hearing that the Indians had deserted and criticised Dalling for not making certain of their loyalties before the expedition embarked. Instead, he wrote, 'this undertaking was directed by desultory enterprises of Adventurers.'

But even Germain could not quite believe that so bold and promising a scheme had totally failed, particularly as it had held out hopes for relieving the mounting pressures of the American revolution. So, in this same letter, he urged a new attempt to be made through Bluefields, without realising that this was already known to be impracticable. Once Nicaragua, 'whose salubrity has been so much boasted of', had been conquered, he wrote, 'I have no doubt but numbers of Adventurers will flock into it from the Revolted Provinces in North America for the purpose of seating themselves there independent of the Spanish Government and, instead of Foes, become the Allies of Great Britain.'

But the final act of the tragedy had already been performed at the Castillo de la Inmaculada Concepción even before the rains had ceased. When Leith had followed Kemble down the river, he had left orders that, before the rearguard of Light Dragoons abandoned the fortress, it was to be destroyed. It was too massive a structure to be demolished by what gunpowder remained in the magazine, but charges were laid under the bastions and trains laid. Many of the dragoons died, others deserted, and there is no certain record of the fate of the few who remained, or whether they were able to blow up the bastions. Perhaps the charges were too weak, or too damp, to be effective, or perhaps they were surprised and captured by the Spaniards before they lit the trains. All that is known is that at the end of the year the royal standard of Spain was again flying over the Castle of St. John's.

In Jamaica, Governor Dalling was arraigned before a special Committee of Enquiry convened by the Council and Assembly to establish his degree of responsibility for the disaster and whether he had made any attempt to enrich himself from it. Among the witnesses who gave evidence were Polson, Bulkeley, Dalrymple, MacDonald, Collingwood and Hercules Ross and no serious degree of guilt could be established. The tantalising conclusion was that but for the initial delays on the Mosquito Shore and before the castle, the great endeavour might well have succeeded.

The blame for the former delays was put upon James Lawrie and, for the latter, upon John Polson. While nothing could have been done to rectify Lawrie's negligence in mobilising the Indians, Polson's decision to lay formal siege to the castle had been opposed on the day of their arrival before it by the two bold officers who had urged an immediate assault – Captain Nelson and Captain Despard. Had their advice been taken, it was said, the castle would have fallen, the lake reached and entered, and Granada and the rich and healthful uplands of Nicaragua taken before the onset of the rains.

The malaria, which was the prime destroyer of the expedition, was caused, all believed, by mysterious and lethal exhalations from swamps and rain-soaked jungle. Had the coast and the river been passed during the dry season, as had been planned, a strong and healthy expedition should have been able to conquer New Spain. Mosquitoes were, of course, regarded as an acceptable irritation; not as the bringers of fever.

This was the view of Dr. Benjamin Moseley, who became the recognised authority on the campaign, writing an account of it in his *Treatise on Tropical Diseases*. In his view Nelson himself had held the key to victory when 'his capacious mind gave, on this dangerous and dreadful service, an early specimen of those splendid elements, which have since decorated, with never-fading laurels, the English naval and military fame with deeds unparallelled in history with achievements beyond the hope of envy. . . .

'When they arrived at the castle – as prompt in thought as

bold in action – he advised the carrying of it instantly by assault. He knew the seasons were at hand and that there was no time to be lost. That his advice was not followed, this recital is a lamentable testimony.'

Soon, the expedition was relegated to the list of the tragic oddities of military history. As Dr. Moseley put it, the San Juan expedition had 'been buried, with many of its kindred, in the silent tomb of government.'

The few survivors were regarded as curiosities and not even Nelson could avoid a reflective shudder. He might boast to Hercules Ross that 'Dame Nature never failed me', but his darker thoughts turned to the naval cemetery at Green Bay near Port Royal just as they later turned to Westminster Abbey and St. Paul's Cathedral.

'Green Bay,' he told Ross, 'had very often its jaws open to receive me.'

CHAPTER SIX

'For Ever in Love'

On 22nd January, 1781 the *Bath Journal* published its weekly list of notables who had arrived in the city to enjoy its bountiful social life and healing waters. This list, headed by the Dowager Countess of Ilchester and Admiral Montagu, ran strictly according to protocol, keeping the new arrivals in their strata: royalty, aristrocracy, senior officers of the Navy and Army, clergy, gentry and trade. Gratifyingly high in the list was the name of Captain Nelson.

When the *Lion* had finally reached Portsmouth on 1st December, he had gone ashore, drained by illness and the exhaustion of a stormy passage and fit only for the relatively short journey to London. After a month's rest, staying first with Cornwallis and then with Captain Locker, who had lodgings at Gray's Inn, he felt able to join his father, who, as was now his custom, in Bath, avoiding the Norfolk winter. He had taken lodgings in the handsome terraced house of Mr. Spry, the apothecary, at 2 Pierrepont Street, which combined the convenience of proximity to the Pump Room, the medicinal baths and pleasant walks by the river, with economy, for the fashionable quarters of the city were now high on the slopes of Lansdown Hill, where the vast and elegant Assembly Rooms had recently been built. The circumstances of the Nelsons were modest indeed and his sister Susannah had been working as a shop assistant to a Bath milliner until given independence by a legacy from her uncle, Captain Suckling.

Horatio's weak and emaciated condition so shocked his father that an expensive physician, Dr. Woodward, was

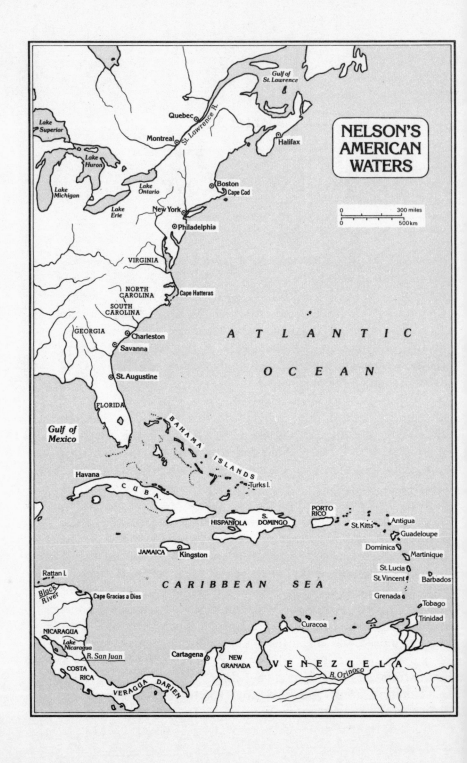

NELSON'S
AMERICAN
WATERS

0 ——— 300 miles
0 ——— 500 km

Lake Superior

Lake Huron

Lake Michigan

Lake Ontario

Lake Erie

Quebec

Montreal

St. Lawrence R.

Gulf of St. Lawrence

Halifax

Boston
Cape Cod

New York

Philadelphia

VIRGINIA

NORTH CAROLINA

SOUTH CAROLINA

Cape Hatteras

GEORGIA

Charleston

Savanna

St. Augustine

FLORIDA

Gulf of Mexico

ATLANTIC

OCEAN

BAHAMA ISLANDS

Havana

CUBA

Turks I.

HISPANIOLA

S. DOMINGO

PORTO RICO

St. Kitts

Antigua

Guadeloupe

Dominica

Martinique

St. Lucia

St. Vincent

Barbados

Grenada

Tobago

Trinidad

JAMAICA

Kingston

CARIBBEAN SEA

Curacoa

Rattan I.

Black River

Cape Gracias a Dios

NICARAGUA

Lake Nicaragua

R. San Juan

COSTA RICA

VERAGUA DARIEN

Cartagena

NEW GRANADA

VENEZUELA

R. Orinoco

summoned from his smart house in Gay Street up the hill to examine him. The doctor prescribed rest and then regular draughts of the unpalatable medicinal waters and frequent baths in the hot springs. When he was strong enough to make the short journey to the public baths, he avoided the fashionable morning, when the *bon ton* dressed in canvas bathing-clothes lowered themselves into the baths where, as had been said, 'is perform'd all the Wanton Dalliance imaginable; Celebrated Beauties, Panting Breasts and Curious Shapes almost expos'd to Public View; Languishing Eyes, Darting Glances, Tempting Amorous Postures, attended by soft Musick, enough to provoke a Vestal to forbidden Pleasures.' Instead, Captain Nelson bathed in the early evening when healthy and sociable visitors would be dining, at cards and on their way to the public balls.

He quickly showed some improvement and, a few days after his arrival,wrote to Locker, 'I have been so ill since I have been here that I was obliged to be carried to and from bed, with the most excruciating tortures, but, thank God, I am now upon the mending hand. I am physicked three times a day, drink the waters three times, and bathe every other night, besides not drinking wine, which I think the worst of all.'

Although of necessity a social recluse, Captain Nelson's arrival caused a stir in the city, where news of the expedition to Nicaragua had been reported in the two local newspapers and in those which arrived from London only twelve hours after publication. Indeed, the campaign had become a talking-point as result of contradictory reports published in the *Bath Chronicle* during November. One, from Port Royal, was 'melancholy indeed', giving details of 'an uncommon mortality, occasioned by the prodigious rains, . . . amongst the troops.' But, soon after, another announced that 'the rains have ceased, our troops are recovering fast and returning health has diffused fresh spirits through the army, which is now in airy and pleasant quarters.'

The newspaper had stated that the expedition should soon be on its way to Granada and Leon and when General Dalling arrived with the main force 'affairs will immediately assume a very different aspect and . . . besides gratifying the utmost wishes of the adventurers will be to Spain the most fatal blow she has suffered in this war.'

[163]

Subsequent reports, discussed in detail by senior officers on leave and veterans of the Seven Years War in the Pump Room, caused increasing concern and the final realisation that the enterprise had collapsed. No doubt attempting to analyse the degrees of blame that could fall to each of the senior officers involved, they could well have reached the conclusion that the two officers who survived the disaster with their reputations enhanced were Captain Nelson and Captain Despard.

At the beginning of January, the first eye-witness of these events became available for questioning with the arrival in Bath 'for benefit of his health' of Captain Harrison of the Loyal Irish and, a fortnight later, of Captain Nelson himself. His recovery was swift and, within a month, he was writing to Locker, 'My health, thank God, is very near perfectly restored; and I have the perfect use of all my limbs, except my left arm, which I can hardly tell what is the matter with it. From the shoulder to my fingers' ends are as if half dead; but the Surgeon and Doctors give me hopes it will all go off. I most sincerely wish to be employed and hope it will not be long . . . I must wish you good night and drink your health in a draught of my Physician's cordial. . . .'

He was now able to enjoy Bath. It was the busiest season for years, the weather so mild that he remarked that it was more like Jamaica than England. This may also have been an allusion to the company, for Bath was a favourite resort of rich West Indian planters on home leave and their ostentatious display of wealth was a popular subject for malicious gossip amongst sharp-eyed denizens of the Pump Room.

There were many social circles, separate or interlocking, who knew one another by sight or acquaintance at the round of public gatherings and entertainments. There were the rich residents and regular visitors, the landowning families and arbiters of fashion, officers recovering from active service, country parsons escaping rural winters, gamblers and courtesans, merchants and successful tradesmen improving their status, extravagant settlers home from the plantations, invalids and even intellectuals. Amongst the latter at this time was Fanny Burney, the diarist and author of the recently-published novel *Evelina*, who had been staying with Mr. and Mrs. Thrale, so that, as Nelson's father, a familiar figure in Bath, was both cultured and sociable, it is possible that the Nelsons were at least on nodding terms with the circle of Dr. Samuel Johnson.

He was an arresting figure: small and slight but his sallow, sunken face drawn into strong lines of experience and command around a wide mouth that may have already shown some promise of sensuality. In repose, his features were solemn, even forbidding, his manner grave; but, when his interest was aroused, the face would break into a charming smile, the eyes would light and his conversation could be alive with humour, opinion and unexpected knowledge. This, combined with the publicity accorded his exploits on the Spanish Main, gave him an heroic standing, particularly in contrast to the corpulent retired admirals and gouty captains on half-pay who had become stock figures in the caricaturists' view of Bath.

Consciousness of this prompted him to ask Locker if he would arrange for Mr. Rigaud, the painter, to complete his portrait, giving him the uniform of a post-captain and adding the castle of San Juan as his background. 'It will not be in the least like what I am now,' he wrote, 'but you may tell Mr. Rigaud to add beauty to it and it will be much mended.'

By March, he was so improved that he told Locker, 'I never was so well in health since you knew me, or that I can remember.' He was not particularly fond of dancing, or gambling, but the Orchard Street theatre, where Mrs. Sarah Siddons was playing in a popular repertory season, was a hundred yards from his door and evenings spent there may well have been the inspiration for his later encouragement of theatricals as recreation for young officers on long voyages.

He had struck up a friendship with his doctor although, as he said, 'I do not set under the hands of a Doctor very easy.' For his part, he boasted, Dr. Woodward had told him that 'he had never had a better patient.' So when Nelson called at the Gay Street consulting-rooms to pay for his treatment he was astonished by the modesty of the doctor's fee and queried it. 'Pray, Captain Nelson, allow me to follow that I consider to be my professional duty,' replied Dr. Woodward. 'Your illness, sir, has been brought on by serving your King and Country and, believe me, I love both too well to be able to receive any

[165]

more.' This was just the sort of spontaneous, generous gesture to inspire in Nelson the response of lifelong friendship.

Returning health, and the stimulus of reading reports on the war in the newspapers, induced restlessness. In March, the alternating good and bad news from America – and the reports of the trials and executions following the 'Gordon Riots' over religious reform in London of the previous summer – were interrupted by dispatches from Admiral Rodney. In January, as soon he had heard that Holland was at war with Britain, he had seized the Dutch island of St. Eustatius in the Caribbean and enormous booty. In Bath, church bells rang; on the lawn before the new Royal Crescent, the Inniskilling Regiment fired celebratory volleys; at night, the noble facades of golden Somerset stone were illuminated with oil lamps.

So, 'near perfectly restored' by mid-March, he decided to leave and accept an invitation to visit an old friend, a Captain Kingsmill, near Newbury in Berkshire, where Captain Locker was staying. He agreed to travel with another naval officer, Captain Kirke, who was returning to London with his invalid wife after the Bath physicians had pronounced her illness incurable. Because of her condition, the journey was delayed so that it was not until April that Nelson was able to begin his social calls; first on his naval friends and then on his uncle, William Suckling, in Kentish Town. Early in the month he heard that Admiral Parker had returned from Jamaica and, with hopes of the fruits of an expected recommendation for employment, sought an interview with the First Lord of the Admiralty. Lord Sandwich was not encouraging, offering no more than a promise of a future command. Nelson's disappointment was tempered by the knowledge that he was not yet fit for sea, since a relapse had partly paralysed his left arm and leg and he was under treatment by a fashionable London surgeon, Mr. Adair. So he had no choice but to resume his convalescence in the comfort of Kentish Town. There he met his favourite brother, Maurice, a clerk in the Admiralty, and together they planned a visit to their family home in Norfolk.

The weeks at Bath had been in sharp contrast to life in the Caribbean, but Norfolk was infinitely more so. Little seemed to have changed at Burnham Thorpe and the parson's other children were growing up into ordinary – sometimes dull – members of the rural middle class. Susannah, on her return from Bath, had married the previous year a merchant dealing in coal, corn and malt at the nearby seaport of Wells-next-the-Sea, Thomas Bolton. Anne, also freed from servitude behind a shop counter by their uncle's legacies, was living at home, as was Kate, who was aged only fourteen. Horatio still had social ambitions for his sisters, mentioning that, fond as of Susannah as he was, 'I should not like to see my little Kate fixed in Wells society.'

His two younger brothers had already fallen behind the family's standards: Edmund, as a clerk in his brother-in-law Bolton's branch office at Ostend; Suckling, apprenticed to a linen-draper at Beccles in Suffolk. But it was William, a year Horatio's senior, who was causing him concern, although he had succeeded in following so many of their forebears and relations in the clergy. William wanted his brother to take him to sea as a chaplain. In vain, Horatio stressed the poor pay, cramped quarters and miseries of being confined in them with a possibly disagreeable captain and officers. William's imagination had been fired – largely, perhaps, by his brother's stories of the tropics and his speculation over prize-money – so that, when news arrived that Captain Nelson was to command another frigate, he could only agree to take the restless curate with him if he could.

The new command was to be the *Albemarle*, which, like the *Hinchinbroke*, had been a prize converted into a frigate of twenty-eight guns. In August, Nelson travelled to Woolwich with Maurice to join her and at once fell in love with the ship, describing her build as 'clean' and 'bold', although he was soon to see her with a less ardent eye.

He considered his seamen 'as good a set of men as ever I saw' and his marines were 'likewise old standers' so that 'not a man or officer in her would I wish to change'. But there were not enough of them. The dockyard town was too wary for impressment raids on waterfront taverns so the only alternative would be to stop a homeward-bound merchantmen at sea and take off some of her crew. For this purpose there could be no better hunting-ground than the mouth of the Thames.

In mid-October, the *Albemarle* dropped down-river to the Nore, where Nelson received orders to take two other warships under his command and cross the North Sea to the Kattegat, where a large convoy was awaiting an escort. He was depressed by another relapse of his health, the foul winter weather and the bad news from America. 'I have been so ill as hardly to be kept out of bed,' he told Locker, and, referring to the news that Washington and de Grasse had trapped General Cornwallis in his coastal base at Yorktown, added, 'What sad news from America . . . I much fear for Lord Cornwallis: if something was not done immediately, America is quite lost.'

At the end of the month, he was joined by the *Argo* and the *Enterprise*, a fourth-rate and a frigate respectively, and found them to be seriously under-manned. So, on 28th October, when he heard that four big East India merchantmen were entering the estuary, bound for London docks, he did not hesitate to act. The four ships, well-armed and fully manned, were sailing in company for mutual protection not only against maurauding privateers from Dunkirk but from short-handed captains of the Royal Navy, such as the one they were about to encounter. In company and under full press of canvas, they could hope to ignore signals to stop and hand over prime seamen and do so with impunity.

The *Albemarle*'s press gang was mustered on deck as the frigate ran out into the channel towards the East Indiamen, who were bresting the current under full sail. Nelson picked the leading ship, the *Haswell*, and ordered a blank charge to be fired from one of his nine-pounders to attract her master's attention to the signal to stop, now flying from the frigate's halyards. But the merchantman swept on; her master had no intention of heaving-to and losing his best men; moreover, as could be seen from the frigate's deck, his crew were getting ready to defend themselves.

Probably the master of the *Haswell* expected his pursuer to fire a shot across his bows, which he could ignore as he and his three consorts surged up the river under more sail than a frigate could set. He may have been surprised to see the frigate's port-lids open and a row of black gun-muzzles run out. Certainly he was shocked when a broadside exploded along the frigate's side and the water around him spouted with falling shot. A second broadside followed and then a single heavy report from a bigger gun. The *Haswell* hove-to, as did the others, but Nelson, seeing that they still 'threatened resistance' showed that he, too, was ready for action, with gun-crews closed up and a boarding-party ready to jump. Then, he noted in his log, that having fired twenty-six nine-pounder and one eighteen-pounder shot at the *Haswell*, the East Indiamen 'finding the *Albemarle* yard-arm to yard-arm with them, they submitted.'

So, fully manned, the three warships, now under Nelson's command, headed across the stormy North Sea for the Baltic, arriving off Elsinore on 4th November. But their senior officer's belligerent mood had not moderated. The Danish admiral, conscious of his country's strained relationship with Britain, sent a mere midshipman to enquire the British ships' names and destination. Nelson received him personally and tartly answered his questions with, 'The *Albemarle* is one of His Britannic Majesty's ships; you are at liberty, sir, to count her guns as you go down the side; and you may assure the Danish admiral that, if necessary, they shall all be well served.' To stress his intended irony, he sent a message ashore after the midshipman had left, saying that his squadron would salute Kronenberg castle with nineteen of those guns provided the courtesy was reciprocated. It was.

After a month's wait, the whole convoy of two hundred and sixty sail had been collected and Nelson handed over command of the escort to a more senior captain of a third-rate. The convoy straggled across the North Sea without loss. Once, a notorious privateer, so unprincipled that he was regarded as a priate, got among the ships but was chased away by the *Albemarle*, which then escorted her charges safely into Yarmouth roads. Here the ship was visited by William Nelson, whose hopes of becoming a naval chaplain were strengthened by the display of maritime power. To his brother's relief, he was only able to reach the ship on one day as a rising sea made boatwork impossible and then the frigate was ordered south to the Downs roadstead off Deal. It was an open anchorage and, as gale followed gale, ships were dragging their anchors; the *Albemarle* was twice parted from hers and was in danger of being driven on to what her captain described as 'a coast full of wrecks.'

On 26th January, 1782, such a disaster seemed unavoidable. The East Indiaman *Brilliant*'s cable had parted in a violent squall and she drove down upon the *Albemarle*, snapping off her bowsprit and most of her foremast, breaking her yards, tearing away her standing rigging, and stoving-in much of her side. The wind was so violent, and her remaining masts so unstable through loss of rigging that she was in danger of capsizing and carpenters stood by to hack away the remaining stays and shrouds to let the mainmast fall rather than turn the ship over. Nelson, it is said, was ashore at the time and had to bribe a Deal boatman with fifteen guineas before he would take him out to his ship.

The crippled frigate was ordered to Portsmouth for repairs once her damaged side had been plugged and temporary jury masts, yards and bowsprit rigged. There, she was fitted with shorter masts which so reduced her capabilities under sail that she only handled well when running before the wind, prompting her captain to joke that the French, her original owners, had only taught her to run away.

While in the dockyard, he heard with apprehension that his brother William's prospects ashore remained modest and wrote, in an effort to improve them, asking him to tell his only possible patron, Lord Walpole, that he would send him 'some of the best wines' when he called at one of the wine-producing countries. He also joked about ecclesiastical vacancies arising through deaths, adding, 'I got my rank by a shot killing a Post-Captain and I most sincerely hope I shall, when I go, go out of the world the same way: then we go all in the line of our Profession — a Parson praying, a Captain fighting.'

He was still there on 9th March, when the *Ranger*, an armed merchantman which had survived an attack on her convoy from Jamaica by Spanish squadron, entered the harbour and one of her passengers proved to be General Dalling. His news was uniformly bad, the most recent being that Hercules Ross had been in another ship of the convoy and was thought to have been captured and taken into Havana. Since the collapse of the expedition to Nicaragua, the Governor had been fighting for

Nelson's frigate, the *Boreas*, cruising off Nevis. Painted by
Nicholas Pocock who, as a ship's captain, had known these
waters well.

overleaf: The map in Jeffery's *West Indies Atlas* with which
Governor Dalling planned the expedition to Nicaragua. (For
convenience, the two pages have been aligned but, in the atlas,
they were printed back to back.)

Rio de Nueva Segovia

N I C A R A G U A

el Realejo

Volcan de

Los Ancoradero
Puerto de Cardon
P. del Carbon

Laguna de Leon or
Lake Lindiri

LEON

Plain of Leon

Volcan de Leon

P. de los Descolados

Volcan de Momotombo

Granada

Laguna de Nicaragua

Volcan de Granada

las Islas

la Trinidada

Chomal Tenamit

Puerto de S.ͭ Juan

S.ͭ Bernardo

Volcan de Mombacho

Mangua

Chomal Tenamit y P. del Zapatero

GOLFO DEL PAPIGAYO

Villas Nicaragua

Omotepe

L A G U N A D E N I C A R A G U A

S.ͭ Sebastian

Volcan de Papagayo

Rio Zapote

P.ͭ de Cruz

Boca del
Rio Juan

Rio de Nicoa

P.ͭ de S.ͭ Catherina

Entrer de la Caldera

Rio de Nicoa

C O S

C H O M E S

Sierra de Esperanza

Nicoya

Mirualla

Ensenada

Deseado

Rio de Canta

Puerto de Vdas

R. de Barranca

R. de Guanabacal

Rio de Mandagua

Barranca

Puerto

T A

Mero Hermoso

P.ͭ de Cuiema

Ensenada
de
Nicoya
or
GOLFO DE LAS SALINAS

S. Domingo

Ganabacal

Barba

Rio de Cartago

los Buxos

Puerto de la Herradura

Cabo Blanco

Punta de la Herradura

Rio la

S O U T H   S E A

Ballencia de Quepo

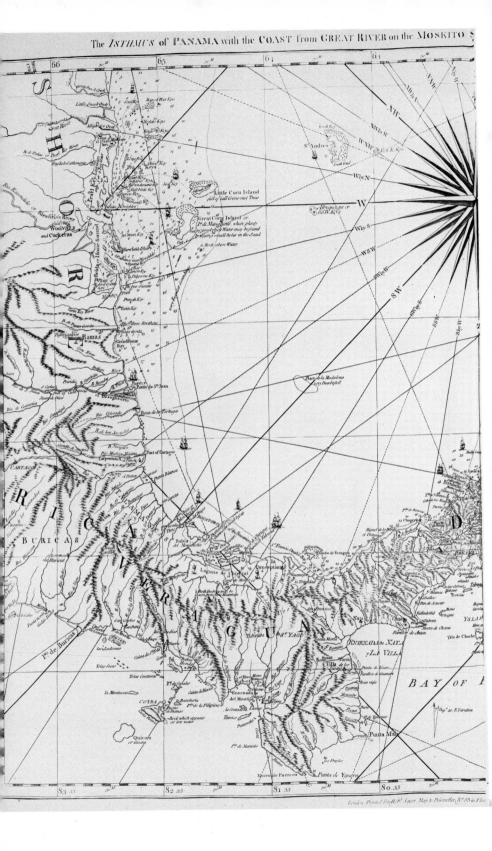

The ISTHMUS of PANAMA with the COAST from GREAT RIVER on the MOSKITO S

Fanny Nelson painted in the early years of her
marriage by Daniel Orme.

political survival and had finally lost.

At the end of 1780, the Jamaican Assembly had convened the Committee of Enquiry to examine the causes of failure and had interviewed the surviving senior officers. Finally it had been agreed that disaster had been brought about by delays and, for these, blame could only be attached to Major Lawrie and Colonels Polson and Kemble.

But his dispute with the judiciary continued. Protests and counter-protests over this to the Colonial Secretary, and the First Lord of the Admiralty, combined with the failure of the expedition and the Governor's quarrels with the Commander-in-Chief, only served to irritate ministers at a time when their attention was concentrated upon the war in North America. Moreover, they had heard that, on Holland's entry in the war, he was planning another expedition — this time to the Dutch island of Curaçoa — against the advice of both General Campbell and Admiral Parker. So, as Dalling had previously applied for home leave, this was now granted. But, fearful of what his political enemies might achieve in his absence, he changed his mind and remained in Spanish Town. In June, 1781, Germain sent him a letter of recall, which he ignored until the end of the year, when, as the Colonial Secretary was writing to dismiss him with the formality of an Order in Council, he prorogued · the Assembly and, on 24th November, boarded the *Ranger*, bound for England.

Although, he did not, of course, know it, the day before he sailed, Cornwallis had surrendered Yorktown, so starting the process of bringing down the British Government and, with it, Lord George Germain.

Nelson, of course, heard all this from Dalling's point of view but, as he liked the man, he was inclined to accept it and, in any case, was glad to hear news of old friends, among them Edward Despard. When he had returned to Jamaica at the end of 1780 he had found his regiment virtually destroyed and, despite drafts of soldiers from the 93rd Regiment, no longer a fighting formation. The Governor had, however, remembered his skill as a military engineer and, doubtless, Nelson's commendation of his initiative, so he promoted him to the provincial rank of lieutenant-colonel and appointed him com-

[171]

mandant of Rattan island and its dependencies.

More news of old friends might soon be forthcoming because now Nelson heard that he was to return to the Americas. In March, he received orders to escort a convoy to the St. Lawrence and then prepare himself for a Canadian winter. Cornwallis had surrendered Yorktown and both Charleston and Savannah had had to be evacuated; therefore land operations were almost halted, but there was plenty of action at sea from the Arctic ice to the Caribbean. Indeed, on 12th April, less than a week before he sailed from Portsmouth, Rodney had fought the long-awaited battle at sea and swung the fortunes of war in favour of the British.

At last, he had brought Vice-Admiral the Comte de Grasse to action, with thirty-six British sail of the line against thirty French, escorting a convoy of troopships destined for the invasion of Jamaica. The French were intercepted off The Saints islets near Guadeloupe and, in a day-long action, defeated; their flagship being among the five ships of the line captured and de Grasse himself a prisoner. What particularly fascinated Nelson, when detailed reports eventually reached him, was that Rodney had ignored the rules of the Navy's *Fighting Instructions*, which insisted on the use of the line of battle as the essential tactical formation. He had sent his ships bursting through the enemy line, so bringing about a confused close action in which superior British gunnery was decisive. Rodney had not only saved Jamaica and the West Indies, but had begun a new evaluation of established tactics by the more thoughtful naval officers; amongst them, Nelson.

But while prospects of action and prize-money improved, an abiding worry remained. For just as Dr. Moseley had warned that further service in the Caribbean would prove fatal to his health, now his London doctor, Adair, was uttering similar warnings about the North Atlantic. 'I want much to get off this d--- voyage,' he wrote to Locker, for the doctor had told him 'that if I was sent to a cold, damp climate, it would make me worse than ever.' However, he argued, he could hardly ask for another appointment since his present orders came directly from the First Lord of the Admiralty.

So Nelson sailed for Cork from whence he was to cross the

Atlantic with nearly forty sail and, after a stormy voyage of three weeks, anchored off St. John's, Newfoundland, which he found a 'disagreeable place'. Finally, at the beginning of July, he delivered his merchant ships safely into the mouth of the St. Lawrence river and was himself ordered to cruise off Boston and Cape Cod in search of American and French shipping.

Despite the apprehensions, his health was improving and he had written to Locker, 'I know your goodness will say, "I wonder how Nelson does?" I say, I am quite well, better than for a long time past.' It was stimulating to be cruising again, chasing strange sails, sighted on the horizon, in the knowledge that they might equally well belong to a rich prize, or a fierce frigate. These waters were also a challenge to his seamanship because he did not know them, they were perilous with shoals and sandbanks and the charts were unreliable.

Experience on the Norfolk coast, in the Thames estuary and even on the San Juan, had made him familiar with difficult inshore waters, but these present hazards were in the open sea.

The *Albemarle* had become so clumsy a frigate that her captain was determined to take an enemy ship which he could use to chase and board others. On 13th July he sighted such a vessel — a fishing schooner — and next day had her in tow. When the prisoners were questioned he found that she was the *Harmony*, from Plymouth, Massachusetts, famous for having been the final landing-place of the Pilgrim Fathers. Her master proved to be one Nathaniel Carver, who quickly revealed himself to be a skilled pilot, for both ships lay dangerously close to shoals and, in the interests of captor and captured alike, he guided them out into 'blue water'.

Nelson liked Carver and was impressed with the stoicism with which he received the orders to remain on board the frigate as her pilot, despite his despondency at having lost his ship while homeward bound and his worries over his large family ashore. Moreover, his sympathies were clearly loyalist. During the next few days he again proved his worth through a succession of violent gales, squalls and thunderstorms and Nelson was relieved at no longer having to rely on soundings taken with lead and line. Meanwhile, British sailors had manned the *Harmony*; carpenters and gunners had converted her

[173]

into a fast gunboat, and she was becoming invaluable as a scout, chasing and identifying strange and elusive sails.

Another fishing schooner was taken and a third chased but run ashore by her crew before she could be boarded. On 14th July, in Boston Bay, when the morning fog cleared, Nelson and Carver sighted sails that could never be confused with those of merchantmen: they were those of four ships of the line and, as they drew nearer from the direction of Boston, their colours could be seen to be those of France. With her stunted masts, there seemed no way that the *Albemarle* could escape these avengers with their towering tiers of taut canvas. To stand and fight the frigate that accompanied them would have been an equal match, but there would be no chance against ships, each of which could fire a broadside three times the weight of the British.

But Nelson had his American pilot on board and it was, presumably, at his suggestion that the bold gamble was taken to run the frigate towards the dangerous waters about St. George's Bank in the hope of finding refuge amongst the shoals, where ships of the line would not dare to follow. Even so, the chase was long and, as Nelson put it, the French 'gave me a pretty dance for between nine or ten hours.' Then the *Albemarle* was amongst the choppy, breaking water above the shoals, and her pursuers sheered away in alarm, all except the frigate, the *Iris*, whose captain steered resolutely in her wake.

Nelson needed no further advice from a pilot, for there was only one thing to do and that was to give battle. So, at sunset, when the *Iris* was almost within gunshot, he ordered his ship's main-topsail to be backed and, as she lost way, put her helm over to present his broadside to the enemy. The French captain was startled; the ships of the line he was accompanying were out of sight, while he was threatened with what could become a night action amongst unfamiliar shoals, which could result in his ship being crippled, then wrecked. There would be no glory in that, so, without firing a shot, he tacked and headed back to the safety of deep water.

Three days later, when there was no further sign of the French squadron, Nelson sent for Carver to express his formal thanks. 'You have rendered us, sir, a very essential service and

[174]

it is not the custom of English seamen to be ungrateful,' he said. 'In the name, therefore, and with the approbation of the officers of this ship, I return your schooner and with it this certificate of your good conduct. Farewell, and may God bless you!'

He thereupon handed Carver a note to be produced in the event of his again being captured by a British warship. It read, 'These are to certify that I took the schooner *Harmony*, Nathaniel Carver, Master, belonging to Plymouth; but, on account of his good services, have given him up his vessel again. Dated on board His Majesty's ship *Albemarle*, 17th August, 1782. Horatio Nelson. Boston Bay.'

Watched by his captors, who had thus deprived themselves of prize-money, Carver and his crew boarded their little ship and set sail for Cape Cod. But this was not the end of the friendship between the English captain and the American fishermen. The frigate had been at sea almost continuously since April and, because she was cruising off the enemy's coast, had been unable to take on fresh meat and vegetables. So most of her crew, including Nelson, were suffering from the debilitating early symptoms of scurvy, which was almost inevitable after more than six weeks on salt provisions and without fruit or vegetables.

Then, the day after the schooner had been released and while the *Albemarle* was cruising five miles off Plymouth, the *Harmony* was sighted coming out of the anchorage. Running alongside the frigate, Nathaniel Carver shouted from his deck for permission to return on board. Nelson greeted him and was presented with four sheep, poultry and sacks of vegetables with the compliments of Carver and his ship's owner, Thomas Davis. Refusing any payment, Carver accepted the captain's invitation to dine before returning to harbour; his reward, the good conduct certificate that should allow him — and often him alone — to fish the St. George's Bank with impunity during the British blockade.

Despite the fresh provisions, most of which were reserved for the most ill, the ship's company was now so sickly that Nelson determined to lose no time in following his orders to make for Quebec. There was now no sign of the French squadron, which proved to have been one that had escaped destruction at the Battle of the Saints, and been chased into Boston by Admiral Hood. Even so, it proved a difficult passage, lasting a month because of contrary winds, and, once in the St. Lawrence, calms when the frigate almost drifted with the current on to shoals. A river pilot urged Nelson to wait for favourable winds but he refused, saying, 'I have a great number of men sick on board. I am bound for Quebec, and there I will go.'

Slowly they glided up the great river between bluffs upon which the forests of maple, spruce and birch were beginning to change from the green of summer to the reds, browns and gold

[176]

of autumn. The water was deep and cold, the air crisp and clear; indeed, no scene could have been more in striking contrast to memories of the San Juan. Ahead lay the city of Quebec, captured by Wolfe twenty-three years before, standing on its headland above the wide and noble river that led to the heartland of America. Fortified with walls, batteries and citadel, it stood like a stronger, grander, northern counterpart of the little Castillo de la Inmaculada Concepción at the far extremity of the theatre of war.

Finally, the *Albemarle* passed the Ile d'Orleans and entered the great basin below the city. On 17th September, she anchored off Quebec and, next day, twenty-two of her men were sent ashore to hospital, while her captain, himself 'knocked up with the scurvy', supervised the loading of fresh beef, bread and beer. Quickly, good food, rest and the bracing air took effect so that, only a month later, Nelson was confiding in a letter to his father, 'Health, that greatest of blessings, is what I never truly enjoyed till I saw Fair Canada. The change it has wrought, I am convinced, is truly wonderful.'

Another change had become apparent five days after his arrival. It was the twenty-second anniversary of the coronation of King George III and the occasion was marked by celebrations at Quebec. The *Albemarle* fired a salute of seventeen guns and the day's events would have included a military parade and a ball. It was in all probability at the latter that Horatio Nelson fell in love for the first time.

The social life of Quebec was mid-way between the prim yet *louche* formalities of Bath and the hectic routs of Spanish Town. As in the former, there was ordered hierarchy, strict protocol and a sense of Georgian discipline. As in the latter, there was a *frisson* of warlike immediacy, for the American rebels and their French and Indian allies were only just out of striking-distance beyond the great forests. But, whereas Bath was claustrophobic in its deep valley and with its air of self-indulgent convalescence, and Spanish Town was heavy with the foreboding of sudden, mysterious and fatal epidemics, the open prospects and brisk air of Quebec sharpened the senses and lifted the heart.

Society was as lively as it was mixed. Since Wolfe had taken it from Montcalm, English-speaking settlers – including many

American loyalists fleeing from New England – had arrived and had begun to impose their customs just as they were adding handsome white door-cases to the fronts of the grey stone houses of French provincial design. To these were added enterprising British merchants and the military garrison and it was to one of these Army families that Mary Simpson belonged.

Aged sixteen and the daughter of Colonel Saunders Simpson, the Provost-Marshal of the Garrison, she was one of the belles of Quebec. 'Sandy' Simpson, who had fought with Wolfe at Louisbourg and Quebec and had served at Montreal, was also the cousin of the city's overseer of works, and so was well placed in its society, his handsome house near the St. Louis Gate a centre of fashionable activity.

His daughter was something of a beauty, descriptions of her suggesting a handsome and healthy girl, rather than pert and pretty in the manner of some of her French rivals. Certainly she was aware of her charms, if only because she had been one of the few girls identified in a hymn of praise published in the poetry columns of the *Quebec Gazette*:

> *Sure you will listen to my call,*
> *Since beauty and Quebec's fair nymphs I sing.*
> *Henceforth Diana is Miss S--ps-n see,*
> *As noble and majestic is her air. . . .*

Young Captain Nelson, now a week short of his twenty-fourth birthday, attracted her. He was later remembered in the city as 'erect and stern of aspect', but there was something curiously old-fashioned about him and he still wore his hair in a queue, or pigtail, although this was no longer the fashion amongst naval officers. Yet he could be amusing in conversation and this, combined with his air of command and the aura of one who had survived extraordinary adventures, made him far more desirable company than the stiff young officers of the garrison, whose talk tended towards social gossip and horses.

Quebec was a beautiful and fascinating city in which to be in love. The leaves of the surrounding woods turned more flamboyant in flaming colour with each day and the great sheet of river below the city reflected the clear blue of the sky. Here, too, General Dalling's stories of Wolfe, the scaling of the

Heights of Abraham and the battle that won Canada for King George could not only be remembered but discussed with Mary's father, who had also been there. Indeed, the battlefield itself was only a few minutes' walk from the Simpsons' house and upon it, in the shelter of slightly rising ground, still lay a rock that British soldiers had rolled there to mark the place where Wolfe had died.

While his thoughts were centred upon Mary, Nelson also met many 'Quebecers of note', amongst them Alexander Davison, to whose company he was drawn for much the same reason as to that of Hercules Ross. Aged thirty-two and also a bachelor, Davison was a prosperous merchant, shipowner and government contractor, as Ross had been. Also a Scot by ancestry, he was a man of culture and struck up an immediate friendship with Nelson, who spent much time in his comfortable house, in the lower town near the waterfront, to escape from his own cramped quarters and, no doubt, to confide in him and seek his advice in the unaccustomed arts of courtship.

It was as well that he did become so reliant upon Davison's advice, for he was beginning to convince himself that his future could hold nothing more important than Mary Simpson. His thoughts were less with the frigate anchored in the river and more up among the steep, narrow streets, where she lived. A certain coolness on her part only served to stoke his infatuation; for she was very young and in no mood to exchange the reign of the belle for the uncertainties of a life of housekeeping and bearing children for a naval officer of no fortune. It was far too soon to be forced into such a decision.

Winter gripped the St. Lawrence early, perhaps giving Nelson a sudden hope that his ship might be locked into Quebec by ice for the winter. But, before he had been there a month, a sloop arrived with orders for him to leave: transports were to be fitted as troopships and he was to escort them to New York. Dreams of a cosy winter at the Simpsons' fireside ended and he complained, 'a very *pretty* job at this late season of the year, for our sails are at this moment frozen to the yards.' So Nelson made his sad farewells, returned aboard his ship and took her down-river to the anchorage where shipping awaited a fair wind to carry it through the narrows and out into the Gulf

[179]

of the St. Lawrence.

On 14th October, the day after his departure, Alexander
Davison, walking by the waterfront, was startled to see Nelson
walking towards him from one of the *Albemarle*'s boats. When
asked the reason for his unexpected return, Nelson was said to
have replied, 'Walk up to your house and you shall be
acquainted with the cause.' He then explained, 'I find it utterly
impossible to leave this place without waiting on her whose
society has so much added to its charms and laying myself and
my fortunes at her feet.'

Davison tried to disuade him, supposedly saying, 'Your
utter ruin, situated as you are at present, must inevitably
follow.' 'Then let it follow,' replied Nelson, 'for I am resolved
to do it.' 'And I also,' said his friend, 'positively declare that
you shall not.'

Words such as these certainly were exchanged and the
argument continued until Davison and reason prevailed and a
forlorn but resigned Nelson returned to his boat and his ship.
Happily, there was news to occupy his thoughts, for sailing
orders had now arrived and he wrote to his father, 'I think it
very likely we shall go to the *grand theatre* of Actions, the West
Indies.' A few days later, his ship and another frigate were
shepherding twenty-three transports towards the open sea and,
after an uneventful passage, were, on 12th November, beating
up to New York.

Unrequited love could now be sublimated in the familiar
yet ever-changing excitement of commanding a ship and joining
a fleet. For when the *Albemarle* anchored off Staten Island next
day, she was surrounded by the noble shapes of twelve sail of
the line. This was Lord Hood's squadron of Rodney's fleet,
which had fought in the victory at The Saints, then chased the
division of French ships that had escaped to Boston. Subsequently it had come close to capturing the *Albemarle*.

Nelson's first official call was upon Rear-Admiral the
Honourable Robert Digby, the Commander-in-Chief of the
North American Station, who was also at New York. 'You are
come on a fine station for making prize-money,' was the
admiral's hearty greeting, to which the young captain somewhat
priggishly replied, 'Yes, sir, but the West Indies is the station

for honour.' This remark was pointed, for Lord Hood was present and it was thought that his squadron would be sailing for Jamaica within a week, and that would be the place to forget an unhappy love affair.

Rear-Admiral Lord Hood was now meeting his old friend Captain Suckling's nephew for the first time and, liking what he saw, invited him aboard his flagship, the *Barfleur*. Soon afterwards, when his barge was pulled alongside the great ship, a seventeen-year-old midshipman on deck–duty watched the visitor come over the side and exchange salutes with the officer of the watch and he remembered vividly what he saw and the man he then met.

'Captain Nelson . . . appeared to be the merest boy of a captain I ever beheld,' he recalled, 'And his dress was worthy of attention. He had on a full-laced uniform: his lank, unpow-dered hair was tied in a stiff Hessian tail of an extraordinary length; the old-fashioned flaps on his waistcoat added to the general appearance of quaintness of his figure and produced an appearance which particularly attracted my notice; for I had never seen anything like it before, nor could imagine who he was, nor what he came about. My doubts were, however, removed when Lord Hood introduced me to him. There was something irresistibly pleasing in his address and conversation; and an enthusiasm when speaking on professional subjects that showed he was no common being.'

The admiral had introduced them because the midshipman was an heir to the throne: Prince William Henry, the third son of King George, who had enthusiastically embarked upon a naval career as training for future royal duties. He and Nelson liked one another on meeting. The prince was intrigued by this strange yet stimulating young officer, whose mind was as lively as his appearance was archaic. The captain was pleased to find a prince so full of professional enthusiasm and glad to be able to focus his ardent loyalty to the monarchy on a person rather than an idea.

Nelson's ambition was, firstly, to accompany Hood to the West Indies and, secondly, to command a ship of the line and it seemed that the one was likely to follow the other if he could persuade Admiral Digby to let him go. While awaiting

[181]

permission, there was much to do in preparing the ship for another long spell at sea. Instead of lying alongside, the *Albemarle* moved up the East River and anchored half a mile from what her captain called 'York Town' largely because of the risk of her men deserting to join the American insurgents. Even so, two of them managed to desert from boats sent ashore for provisions and water; one of them a corporal of marines, whose duty was to prevent desertion.

There was an uneasy atmosphere at New York for it was clear that the rebels were about to achieve all that they had hoped. The Royal Navy – challenged by the French on virtually equal terms in European waters, the Atlantic, the Caribbean and even the Indian Ocean – had not been able to maintain unquestioned command of the sea. When it had put armies ashore in America, they had floundered across a seemingly boundless battlefield, exhausting themselves without being able to inflict a sharp and decisive defeat in the manner for which they had been trained. Although Spain, having conquered Florida, was anxious for peace, and France was threatened by political upheaval, it looked as though the British Government might at last be willing to grant the colonies their independence. So naval officers in New York were thinking of prize-money rather than glory and Nelson noted with distaste, 'Money is the great object here, nothing else is attended to.' He was delighted therefore to obey signals made by Hood's flagship on 21st November and next day drop down the East River and sail in the wake of the fleet, steering south.

In the event, the cruise to Jamaica was a disappointment. The French squadron from Boston, also bound for the Caribbean, eluded Hood, prompting Nelson's weary comment, 'Where they are, God knows. We are all in the dark in this part of the world, whether it is Peace or War.' When the fleet finally anchored off Port Royal, they found the new Governor, General Campbell, who had been Dalling's deputy, equally in the dark.

The next three months were a mixture of frustration and satisfaction. While cruising with Hood, towards the end of February, the *Albemarle* chased and captured a French supply ship, belonging to the fleet they were hunting, with a cargo of more than a hundred top-masts for big ships. It so happened that the British fleet was in urgent need of sixteen topmasts, and had not been able to find one at Port Royal, so not only did this capture delight the admiral but was assessed as being worth £20,000. But as she had been taken within sight of the fleet, the prize-money would have to be shared amongst all, the major portion going to the admiral. 'They do not deserve to share for her,' complained Nelson. 'She had passed every ship in the fleet without being noticed.'

Soon after he suffered an actual reverse, if not a defeat. Hearing that the French had landed a detachment of troops on Turk's Island at the south-eastern extremity of the Bahamas, he took another frigate and two smaller ships under his command and attempted a landing. On 7th March, he sent an officer ashore under flag of truce to summon the garrison to surrender. This was contemptuously refused so, after a night spent shooting at whatever lights were shown on the island, landing parties were embarked in the ships' boats and pulled ashore.

But this time the boldness, which might have accomplished so much in Nicaragua, was simply rash for it was not supported by any thorough assessment of the enemy's strength. This proved to be far greater than expected, with a hundred and fifty French regular troops behind well-sited, and sometimes concealed, guns, and earthworks. When the assaulting British received their first volleys of accurate fire, they stopped for further orders and Nelson realised that such a petty prize was not worth heavy casualties when a peace treaty might already have been signed in Europe. So, next morning, after a face-saving bombardment of the defences, he ordered his men to re-embark.

On the other hand, Nelson was delighted by the attention of Lord Hood, which, he told Locker, 'must be in the highest degree flattering to any young man. He treats me as if I was his son and will, I am convinced, give me anything I can ask of him: nor is my situation with Prince William less flattering.'

This brought out a certain courtliness in him, which he displayed when, while cruising off Curaçoa at the end of March, he took a small Spanish vessel carrying a French scientific expedition. The most distinguished of his prisoners called

NELSON IN THE AMERICAS

himself the Marquis de Deux Ponts and he went out of the way
to show him every courtesy, entertaining the party to the best
dinner the frigate could provide before allowing them to
proceed.

The next display of such manners was in peacetime. News
reached the Caribbean that the preliminaries of a peace treaty
between Britain, France and Spain had been signed at Versailles
on 20th January so that hostilities should cease pending a final
agreement. A courtesy visit to Havana by Prince William
Henry was therefore in order and the *Albemarle* was chosen as his
temporary royal yacht, while the main fleet hovered tactfully in
the background.

It was a simple matter of entering the great harbour on 9th
May and leaving two days later, of firing salutes and providing
smart boats' crews. But it served to cement the friendship and
mutual respect between the prince and the captain. It was also a
pleasant ending to years of arduous sea-keeping in wartime. For
now the ship was only sent with Lord Hood's dispatches for the
garrison of St. Augustine in Florida before she sailed for
England on the 25th of the month.

'After all my tossing about in various climates, here at last
am I arrived, safe and sound,' he wrote to Locker when his ship
finally anchored at Spithead on 25th June. A few days later he
had paid off the *Albemarle* without regret, although touched
when the entire crew offered to follow him to another ship. But
he was in no mood for further seafaring. He had been lucky to
survive the war – albeit without a fortune in prize-money – and
was now ready to enjoy the pleasures of peace and resume old
friendships at leisure.

On arrival in London, he was commanded to accompany
Lord Hood to a levee at St. James's Palace, where he was
presented to the King, who was pleased to speak kindly to a
friend of his son's. Then he was summoned to Windsor by
Prince William himself, who was about to leave on an educative
tour on the Continent and probably advised Nelson to do the
same.

There was news of other old friends. Admiral and Lady
Parker were in Essex, building a new house with their West
Indian prize-money; Hercules Ross had survived the attack on

the Jamaica convoy and was staying in Scotland; Alexander Davison was in London. This latter friendship, Nelson was particularly delighted to renew for the two had reached an unusual degree of mutual confidence in Quebec, and they met again when he called on his way back from the palace to his Salisbury Street lodgings at Davison's rooms in Lincoln's Inn. There was much news to exchange – Nelson's royal friendship and Davison's political aspirations – and Nelson gratefully threw off his best 'iron-bound' uniform coat to put on one of his host's dressing-gowns and they talked for hours.

Nelson was content. 'I have closed the war without a fortune,' he wrote to Ross. 'But, I trust . . . that there is not a speck in my character. True honour I hope predominates in my mind far above riches.' One professional shortcoming, of which he was much aware, was his inability to speak French and he determined to emulate Prince William in visiting the Continent for this purpose. He was granted six months' leave, found an agreeable travelling companion in Captain James Macnamara, with whom he had been shipmates in Parker's flagship, and in mid-October they set out.

It was a delightful tour. On the road to Dover, they dined with Locker at West Malling in Kent, then boarded the Calais packet and crossed the Channel in three and a half hours. They had no definite plan, so they took the stage-coach to Marquise, then Boulogne and Montreuil. It was an adventure to be exploring what had so recently been enemy country, and they noted its pecularities with perceptive and amused eyes, comparing it all unfavourably with England. In several long and entertaining letters, Nelson described the beauty of the countryside and the abundance of game but also the squalor and the social inequalities. 'We stopped at an inn – a clean pig-sty is far preferable,' he told his brother William. 'However, after a good laugh, we went to bed and slept very soundly.'

After stopping at Abbeville they chose to stay at St. Omer, a handsome town where they took lodgings with a French family, whose two pretty daughters kept them company. 'I exert myself, you will suppose, in the French language,' said Nelson, 'that I may have the pleasure of talking to them.' There were other English visitors in St. Omer, among them two other captains of the Royal Navy and a clergyman, a Mr. Andrews, 'who has two very beautiful young ladies, daughters.'

Soon after his arrival, he was shocked to hear of his sister Anne's sudden death at Bath, after a short illness brought on by walking in chill night air immediately after dancing in a heated ballroom. The Andrews family was a great comfort, the daughters playing the piano and singing to the two young officers, who became daily visitors. 'My heart is quite secured against the French beauties,' Nelson could write, 'I almost wish I could say as much for an English young lady . . . She has such accomplishments, that, had I a million of money, I am sure I should at this moment make her an offer of them: my income is at present far too small to think of marriage and she has no fortune.'

But this obstacle did not deter for long – particularly after a happy Christmas in the Andrews' company – and on 14th January, 1784, he wrote bluntly to his well-to-do uncle William Suckling in Kentish Town. He asked for money, explaining, 'The whole of my income does not exceed £130 per annum. Now I must come to the point: – will you, if I should marry, allow me yearly £100 until my income is increased to that sum?' He made it difficult for his uncle to refuse, pleading, 'The critical moment of my life is now arrived, that either I am to be happy or miserable: – it depends solely on you.'

Mr. Suckling was ready to help but other factors intervened. Miss Andrews does not seem to have refused him finally, or unkindly – for he remained friendly with her family – but he returned to England soon after because of 'some little matters in my Accounts', possibly connected with his uncle's response. This also led him to refuse a surprising invitation to visit Paris from the 'Marquis de Deux Ponts', whom he had captured and released off Curaçoa, and who now turned out to be the future King Maximilian of Bavaria and a French general, who had been second-in-command at the fall of Yorktown. He was anxious to repay hospitality and, hearing that he was in France, asked him to stay. Perhaps misinterpreting Nelson's kindliness to his youngest officers, he added, 'You shall see here very pretty little midshipmans which I dare say will teach you French with a method which will please you.'

There was another reason for his sudden return to London. Weariness with the sea had combined with an interest in politics and, with a general election imminent, he was hoping to be adopted as a Parliamentary candidate. For a few weeks he dreamt of a London life as a Member of Parliament, with a beautiful, accomplished wife and friends at Court. It was not the dedicated naval officer, who wrote to his brother, 'My time has been so much taken up by running at the ring of pleasure, that I have almost neglected all my friends — for London has so many charms that a man's time is wholly taken up.'

He was soon disappointed, both in his political aspirations and in his hopes of marriage. He thought of returning to the Continent for the summer, adding sadly, 'I return to many charming women, *but no charming woman* will return with me.' But, once again, the Admiralty settled his future for him and on 18th March he was told that he had been appointed to command another frigate of twenty-eight guns, the *Boreas*, which was lying at Woolwich ready for sea.

The ship was well-manned but, when she sailed for the West Indies on 12th April, the start of the commission was not auspicious. It was not only Nelson's anger that the pilot should immediately run her aground so firmly that it was possible to walk round her at low tide, but that this was done before such an audience, for the frigate was packed with passengers. Foremost amongst these was Lady Hughes, the wife of Rear-Admiral Sir Richard Hughes, the Commander-in-Chief of the Leeward Islands Station, whither the ship was bound, and her husband-hunting daughter Rosy. Then there was his brother William who had finally succeeded in getting aboard as a naval chaplain and was far from stimulating company. And there were thirty midshipman — including a young brother of the lovely Miss Andrews — destined for ships in the Caribbean. The captain remarked that the frigate was 'pretty well filled with lumber' and must have been relieved when a hard gale and snow-storm off the Thames Estuary put a stop to Lady Hughes's 'infernal clack.'

During the long voyage to Madeira, then Barbados, Nelson's temper moderated with the weather and he devoted much time to the welfare of his midshipmen. 'The timid he never rebuked but always wished to show them,' noted Lady Hughes. 'I have known him say, "Well, sir, I am going a race to the mast-head and beg I may meet you there." No denial could be given to such a request, and the poor little fellow instantly began to climb the shrouds. Captain Nelson never took the least notice in what manner it was done, but, when they met in the top, spoke in the most cheerful terms to the midshipman and observed how much any person was to be pitied who could fancy there was any danger, or even anything disagreeable, in the attempt.'

On 14th June, they crossed the Equator and, when the ship's company were skylarking as Neptune and his court in the 'Crossing the Line' horseplay, their captain lectured them on the importance of hygiene and suitable diet in the tropics. Twelve days later, they arrived off Barbados and anchored in Carlisle Bay.

'The Grand Theatre of Actions' was now lacking all the excitements of wartime, whether glory or prize-money, and Admiral Hughes appeared a suitable commander for so dreary a prospect. 'The Admiral and all about him are great ninnies,' wrote Nelson to Locker. However, he was to be his second-in-command and therefore responsible for the northern islands of the chain, basing himself on Antigua, while Hughes remained at Barbados to the south. Yet even this independence would offer little freedom for several months, as his first task on arrival would be to lay his ship up in harbour for the three or four months of the hurricane season.

Professional, and, perhaps, sexual, frustration shortened Nelson's temper again and any sign of inefficiency, presumption or lack of courtesy in others brought sharp reaction. In Carlisle Bay, he gave the garrison a prompt lesson in etiquette; noting in his log, 'Sailed the French Schooner of War. Fired two 9-pounders at the Fort for not hoisting her Colours to the French King's vessel going out.' Stopping at Martinique on his way to Antigua, he gave the French a brusque, but only verbal, rebuke for neglecting a similar courtesy to himself.

On arrival at English Harbour, he saw that the Commissioner of the Dockyard, Captain John Moutray, who had long retired from active duty, had presumed to hoist a commodore's pendant, so implying that he was the senior naval officer. Nelson immediately ordered the pendant to be struck and returned to store in the dockyard, leaving no doubt that he himself was in full operational command.

English Harbour – a series of almost landlocked basins among high, scrub-covered hills on the south coast of Antigua – had been a British naval base for forty years. A small dockyard had been established for the re-fitting and replenishment of warships and a resident community of officials and artisans had grown up. However, it lay twelve miles from St. John's, the capital, and its social life, so that, particularly during the hurricane months, it became lonely and claustrophobic. Nelson's first impressions were, however, softened on meeting the Commissioner's attractive young wife at their residence, 'Windsor', on a hill behind the dockyard. 'Were it not for Mrs. Moutray, who is *very, very* good to me, I should almost hang myself in this infernal hole,' he wrote to Locker.

This flirtatious friendship helped while away the dreary hurricane months but the hot wind, the mosquitoes and the boredom were too much for William Nelson, who now decided that his true vocation was in a Norfolk parsonage and gratefully sailed for England at the end of September. But when the gales abated and the *Boreas*, freshly painted and ready for sea, sailed on her first cruise, her captain's mood was as touchy as ever.

Off the island of Nevis he sighted a French frigate that was clearly engaged in espionage; or at least making a survey of the coast for intelligence purposes. With elaborate courtesy, Nelson told her captain that his ship would accompany them so 'that attention may be paid to the officers of His Most Christian Majesty, which he was sure every Englishman in the Islands would be proud of the opportunity of doing.' So, 'determined not to be outdone in *civility*', he escorted the angry and embarrassed Frenchmen back to Martinique.

On another occasion, he refused an invitation to visit the President of St. Kitts, who was flying an Irish flag on St Patrick's Day, 'only to show the principle to these *vagabonds*.'

Such behaviour could entertain, or irritate, those in a position to influence the course of a career but, in themselves, would not make, or break, an officer's reputation. Yet such

[189]

dangers now lay ahead, like sharp coral reefs in these placid seas, and, in taking the stand he did, Nelson showed faith in his idea of patriotic duty rather than awareness of political realities. It was to do with the enforcement of the Navigation Act which now insisted that American merchants trade with British colonies as foreigners rather than as favoured compatriots. 'The station opened a new scene to the officers of the British Navy,' said Nelson. 'The Americans, when colonists, possessed almost all the trade from America to our West Indian islands; and on the return of peace, they forgot. . . . they became foreigners and, of course, had no right to trade in the British Colonies. Our Governors and Custom-house officers pretended that by the Navigation Act they had a right to trade, and all the West Indians wished what was so much for their interest.'

In the Leeward Islands, as in Jamaica, he found that 'the residents of these islands are Americans by connexion and by interest and are inimical to Great Britain. They are as great rebels as ever were in America, had they the power to show it.' Certainly their mercantile contacts with North America were intimate: American ships brought down flour, timber, whale-oil, tar and tobacco and returned with sugar, rum and coffee. Since it was in the interests of both that this should continue as before, there was understandable anger in the islands when zealous — or, as they saw it, officious — naval officers tried to enforce an unrealistic law dictated by politicians in London.

The first of these officers to attract wide attention was Cuthbert Collingwood, now a frigate captain in these waters, who, at the end of 1784, stopped an American sloop from entering St. John's harbour at Antigua. The American master claimed that he must go in for essential repairs to his mast, to which Collingwood replied that this could be attended to by his carpenter and ordered the ship under his guns. As result, the Governor of the island, General Shirley, complained of high-handed action by the Navy and was supported by Admiral Hughes, who ordered his captains to refer all such cases to the Governor, or President, of the island concerned.

Nelson and Collingwood refused to comply, the former writing to Shirley on 29th January, 1785, 'Captains of Men of

War receive orders and make reports to none but the Admiralty, Admirals or Senior Officers in their own Service. Therefore it is totally out of my power to send any reports to Mr. Presidents . . . . ' The Governor complained that he was 'hurt and insulted' by this letter, which he forwarded to Hughes for 'proper redress for such indignant behaviour.' Nelson replied in his earlier uncompromising manner and Shirley protested that 'old and respectable officers of high rank. . . . are very jealous of being dictated to in their duty by very young gentlemen.' To this, Nelson is said to have replied that he had the honour of being as old as the Prime Minister and thought himself as capable of commanding one of His Majesty's ships as was Mr. Pitt in governing Great Britain.

'I, for one, am determined not to suffer the Yankees to come where my ship is,' Nelson told Locker, 'For I am sure that once the Americans are admitted to any kind of intercourse with these islands, the views of the Loyalists are entirely done away.' So, together with Collingwood and his younger brother Wilfred Collingwood, who was commanding a smaller ship, the letter of the restrictive law was enforced in the teeth of opposition from almost all the authorities and interests in the British islands.

Nelson's attitude was only hardened by hostility. As he explained to a friend, 'I did my duty. No mean consideration of gain actuated my conduct. I wish most sincerely they may always be able to say the same of all officers put into office in the Islands. My conduct arose from an Honest Principle and the same principle shall actuate me when I may be sent at a future date to defend them.'

The most serious single incident took place off the small island of Nevis. After seizing four American merchantmen off Charlestown, the capital, he was surprised to find himself the object of litigation, when their masters, with the support of the island's merchants sued him for assault and imprisonment, claiming damages of £40,000. To have gone ashore without an armed escort of marines would have invited arrest, so, for eight weeks, he remained on board his ship and the risk remained for three months. Then a letter from the Admiralty informed him that his defence costs would be paid by the Treasury and, with unconscious irony, congratulated Admiral Hughes on his zeal in protecting British trade.

A strange and gratifying aspect of these wranglings was that the President of Nevis, John Herbert, who stood to lose by the hampering of American trade, supported Nelson and even offered to stand bail for him should he be arrested. Moreover, he invited him up to his estate, Montpelier, three miles out of Charlestown and seven hundred feet up a green hillside, where trees, soft winds and a house provided with louvre-boarded balconies, offered cool shade and relaxation after the hot and worrying weeks on board ship.

Nevis was an idyllic island, rising in a great volcanic cone to more than three thousand feet above the sea, its well-watered slopes studded with white plantation houses, and fields of sugar-cane rippling in the sea-wind. Although covering only thirty-two square miles, it was one of the richest islands in the Caribbean, its British planters considering themselves a social elite.

Charlestown, with its trim, stone houses along the waterfront between the flanking forts, was pleasant enough for ships' companies allowed ashore. For the sailors, there were grog-shops, flirting with Negro slave-girls, and the cool of the coconut groves around the fresh-water spring, where watering-parties landed to fill the casks. For the officers, there was the newly-opened, three-storey Bath Hotel above the thermal springs that were said to heal manchineel poisoning such as Nelson had suffered in Nicaragua. Most delectable of all were the plantation houses and their gardens of flowering shrubs, alive with humming-birds, the beauty of which could bemuse and enchant a visitor from the sea.

On his early visits to Montpelier, Nelson was impressed by the cool elegance of its life: the shine of silver and polished mahogany in shaded rooms, and the blazing colours of its flower-gardens against the bright blues and greens of sea, sky and mountain. He was also delighted by a little boy of five, Josiah Nisbet, the son, he was told, of the young widow of a doctor and a niece of Mr. Herbert, who had acted as housekeeper for the President since the death of his wife.

When Horatio Nelson and Frances Nisbet finally met in March, each was already aware of the other. She had had a letter from a friend on neighbouring St. Kitts telling her, 'We have at last seen the Captain of the *Boreas*, of whom so much has been said. He came up, just before dinner, much heated, and was very silent; yet seemed, according to the old adage, to think the more . . . . It was impossible, during this visit, for any of us to make out his real character; there was such a reserve and sternness in his behaviour, with occasional sallies, though very transient, of a superior mind. Being placed by him, I endeavoured to arouse his attention by showing him all the civilities in my power; but I drew out little more than "Yes" or "No". If you, Fanny, had been there, we think you would have made something of him; for you have been in the habit of attending to these odd sort of people.'

Fanny Nisbet, the daughter of a judge, William Wool-ward, was a little older than Nelson and had so pleasant a way with her that he was at once reminded of Mrs. Moutray, whose manners had taken him back to Bath and, perhaps, even to dim memories of his mother. She was charming — gentle grey eyes set off by dark curls and a clear complexion, sheltered from the burning West Indian sun — but, met in the voluptuous groves of Montpelier, she must have seemed a goddess. It was not, therefore, surprising that Mr. William Suckling of Kentish Town should receive another letter from his nephew asking for money, with the excuse, 'you will smile . . . . and say, "This Horatio is for ever in love." '

His courtship was conducted in the quiet house to the soft coo of mountain doves and rustle of its sheltering trees; at dinner-parties in candle-lit dining-rooms; at matins among the elaborately-carved armorial monuments in St. John's parish church. His absences at sea only served to heighten the passion, protestation of esteem quickly warming to love. With the seemly formalities out of the way, he was able to write, 'As you begin to know something about sailors, have you not often heard that salt water and absence always wash away love? Now I am such a heretic as not to believe that faith: for, behold, every morning . . . . I have had six pails of water at day-light poured upon my head and . . . . perceive the contrary effect.'

Unhappily, he still had to spend the hurricane months at English Harbour. But the *Boreas* was a healthy ship for he kept his men busy working her at sea and exercising tactics when in company. When possible, 'she was always on the wing' and four days was usually the longest she lay at any port except Charlestown and English Harbour. When laid up in the latter, her captain 'encouraged music, dancing and cudgeling, etc., and the Officers and Young Gentlemen acted plays, which kept up their spirits . . . . which is of the utmost utility in preserving health in these climes.'

While the *Boreas* was occupied by shipwrights and carpenters, he lived alone in the senior officer's house, plagued by 'woefully pinching' mosquitoes, which bit him through his clothes and penetrated his mosquito-net at night. Mindful of his coming union, he assured Fanny that 'a pint of goat's milk every morning and Beef Tea will make me what I wish to be for your sake.' But he revelled in small domestic missions, such as trying to buy a pet parrot for Montpelier and having a piano tuned and shipped to Nevis: 'All the news I shall tell you is that a man is cracking my head with tuning your pianoforte. However, be assured there is nothing in this world I would not bear to please my dearest Fanny.'

For her part, Fanny fussed about her fiancé's almost universal unpopularity for his persistence in chasing, turning away or arresting American ships. She was well aware that, but for his friendship with her uncle, he would be ostracised, even on Nevis. But when she pleaded with him to follow his admiral's advice, he was adamant, writing from sea, 'Had I taken your advice and not seized any Americans I should now have been with you, but I should have neglected my duty, which I think your regard for me is too great for you to have wish'd me to do.'

But rescue from fears of social rejection came when, in November, 1786, Prince William Henry suddenly arrived in the frigate *Pegasus*, which he was commanding, from Nova Scotia. He was about to begin a seven-week tour of the Leeward Islands and was insistent that he should be attended throughout by his senior officer and friend, Captain Nelson. At once, those who had abused him now sought his company for, through him, royal favours could be sought.

The two enjoyed each other's company: the prince teasing

the captain about his coming marriage and insisting that he be best man; the captain admiring the prince for his seamanlike qualities and as a disciplinarian. He also found him a considerable ladies' man – 'a gallant man . . . . volatile but with great good nature' – and quite ready to cut short a drearily formal occasion at the sight of a pretty face. Everywhere they were entertained to a round of receptions, dinner-parties and balls, broken only by the short voyage to the next island. From English Harbour, Nelson wrote to Fanny, 'We returned last night from St. John's and I fancy many people were as happy to see His Royal Highness quit as they were to see him enter St. John's. For another day of this racquet would have knocked some of the fair sex up. These nights' dancing was too much and never broke up 'till near day . . . . I have not more than twice or thrice been in bed 'till morning.'

His own bachelor days were almost at an end and, on 11th March, 1787, the couple married at Montpelier. As the guests chattered happily in the shade of the spreading silk cotton tree in the garden, all his hopes seemed to have been realised. A charming and ladylike wife; a seven-year-old stepson, whom he adored; a royal best man, whose friendship would continue to bestow reflected glory; these combined with eight of his own twenty-eight years spent as a post-captain could only mean future success.

Yet, only the next day, one of his brother-captains was beginning to say to others, 'The Navy, sir, yesterday lost one of its greatest ornaments by Nelson's marriage. It is a national loss that such an officer should marry; had it not been for that circumstance, I foresaw Nelson would become the greatest man in the Service.'

Soon after, bride and groom left for England; the former by merchant ship, the latter in his frigate. The *Boreas* reached Portsmouth on 4th July and was finally paid off at the end of November. But there was no new command ready for her captain; indeed, the Admiralty seemed only interested in sending him nagging letters about complaints from the West Indies over his enforcement of the Navigation Act; and there seemed a surprising reluctance in Whitehall to confirm the temporary appointments he had made in the ships under his command. A West Indian writ even followed him to Norfolk, when he and Fanny eventually settled at Burnham Thorpe to live frugally on his half-pay of eight shillings a day and an annual allowance of £100, which both he and Fanny received from their uncles.

Year followed year and his letters requesting employment were ignored or brought no result, until he began to talk of becoming a naval mercenary in the service of the Tsar of Russia. Revolution broke out in France and the Admiralty began to bring ships out of reserve and recall officers for active service, yet no letter of appointment came to him. 'My not being appointed to a ship is so very mortifying that I cannot find words to express what I feel,' he wrote to Prince William Henry, who was now the Duke of Clarence.

Even such an appeal could not help, for talk of Nelson's high-handed officiousness in the West Indies had earned him the reputation of a trouble-maker, and word of this had reached King George. This was confirmed by Lord Hood, now a member of the Board of Admiralty, so that he admitted, 'The King is impressed with an unfavourable opinion of me' and that this was because of 'a prejudice at the Admiralty . . . . against me, which I can neither guess at, nor in the least account for'.

Five years after he had stepped ashore from the *Boreas*, Nelson was still unemployed. The King of France was about to stand trial for his life, war seemed imminent and the newspapers were reporting the mobilisation of the Royal Navy. But still he was not recalled to duty.

It then seemed that the years of effort and endeavour, daring and danger, the risk of life and reputation – the high stakes he had hoped would win so much – had been in vain.

CHAPTER SEVEN

Hero and Traitor

When Colonel Edward Despard crossed the Atlantic — bound for England — at the end of May, 1790, he had more than a month at sea in which to muse upon past triumphs, present frustrations and future uncertainties. To him, as to many forceful officers, seasoned in war, peace had brought seemingly trivial but deeply unsettling problems of politics and commerce, whether on a private or public level. He must have known that, three years before, the most professionally promising of his friends, Captain Nelson, had, while doing his duty, been hounded by writs around the Leeward Islands and finally back to England, where he was said to have retired on half-pay.

But Colonel Despard did not seem likely to risk so humiliating a fate. His responsibilities had been far more important than those of a frigate captain and squadron-commander, for he had been equivalent to a commander-in-chief although, as everyone destined for high office knew, the privileges of power were always accompanied by problems.

In assessing his present difficulty, and ways to settle it to his advantage on arrival in London, Despard was able to look back on the decade since he had fought beside Nelson in Nicaragua with reasons for satisfaction. The first of these was that he had survived. On his return to Jamaica at the end of 1780, he had been something of a celebrity, having been one of only four British officers to reach Lake Nicaragua and one of the last to leave the castle of San Juan when all hope of success was finally lost. He had been praised publicly by Colonel Polson in the *London Gazette*, and, amidst all the recriminations, the only two officers who appeared not only to be blameless, but to have enhanced reputations, were Nelson and himself.

After a short convalescence, he was confirmed in his rank of captain and returned to work on the island's defences. His reward came a few months later, in 1781, when Governor Dalling chose him for an appointment that could lead to the very highest; even, eventually, to the governorship of a colony. With the local rank of lieutenant-colonel and field-engineer, he was to take command – as 'Commandant and Commander-in-Chief' – of the island of Rattan, (or Ruatan) in the Bay of Honduras.

His stay on the island was short. It was a primitive place and had become the refuge for British timber-traders and logwood-cutters, driven from the mainland coast of Honduras by the Spaniards. They were unruly, living much as the Indians, and Despard realised that, without some military force and administration, it would be impossible to control them, let alone to defend the island against Spanish attack. So he decided to appeal to the Governor of Jamaica and, although it was late summer and the hurricane season had begun, he took passage for Kingston.

On arrival at Spanish Town, he was congratulated by General Campbell, who had just replaced Governor Dalling, for taking his responsibilities so seriously but told that there were now other plans for him. The threat of invasion had, after lurking so long, finally taken a tangible and terrifying shape. A massive French and Spanish fleet, under the Comte de Grasse, was reported to be escorting an armada of troop-transports with an invasion force embarked and their destination was Jamaica. So he ordered Despard to return to the planning and building of defences throughout the island and particularly in defence of Kingston. As reports of the enemy became more precise, the prospects seemed worse.

Then, on 12th April, 1782, the danger was removed. Admiral Rodney had intercepted de Grasse at The Saints and destroyed his fleet; on that day, Jamaica became as secure as it had been since the American rebellion had begun. But, a month before, the Spaniards, taking advantage of the British preoccupation, had launched their own offensive against the Jamaican dependencies. A small invasion fleet had taken Rattan, then continued to the Mosquito Shore, where it joined with a strong force of Spanish militia from the hinterland, and attacked the Black River settlement.

Major Lawrie, who was still the Superintendent of the Mosquito Shore, realising that his own twenty-one regular soldiers, and the armed settlers, slaves and Indians, were heavily outnumbered, spiked the guns of the little fort and set sail for safety at Cape Graçias a Dios. There he remained until, after Rodney's victory, Governor Campbell ordered a counteroffensive on the Spanish Main and sent a hundred and thirty Loyal Americans to join some eight hundred armed men Lawrie had assembled at the Cape. But the Governor, remembering Lawrie's part in the failure of the expedition to Nicaragua, decided not to trust him again and ordered his old enemy, Robert Hodgson, to take command.

But, as was his wont, Hodgson found reasons to prevaricate and delay, so that the Loyal Americans sailed and arrived at the Cape before him. Lawrie was aghast to hear that he was to be superseded by his predecessor, whom he had ousted with such guile, but could hardly disobey the Governor's instructions.

However, at this moment, Colonel Despard, who had been on unspecified 'private affairs' on the Mosquito Shore, arrived at the Cape and a means of forestalling Hodgson came to mind. Lawrie and his cronies had no difficulty in convincing Despard that Hodgson, because of his 'pride, caprice and misconduct', was so obnoxious to the inhabitants that they positively refused to serve under him.' So, when Hodsgon finally arrived, he found that Despard had been offered and had accepted the command. In vain did he protest, and present his commission from the Governor of Jamaica; the Mosquito Shore had always been a law unto itself. So, in August, one of Lawrie's henchmen could report gleefully that the expedition was about to sail for Black River under Colonel Despard's command 'in spite of Colonel Hodgson's arts, who had thrown every possible impediment in their way that a Jesuitical head of a malignant heart could suggest. Thus did Mr. Hodgson – long distinguished as the Evil Genius of the Shore – well nigh overset the union, order and strength of the present Expedition.'

The attack on Black River was as dashing as anything that Despard had planned with Nelson. The Spaniards were taken by surprise as he, at the head of his little army of regulars and irregulars, took the village by assault and surrounded the fort. On 31st August, the Spanish commander surrendered and the British found themselves with no less than seven hundred prisoners and no further opposition along the whole of the Mosquito Shore. Hundreds of imprisoned or fugitive settlers were able to return home. It had been a remarkable little victory.

The irregularities in Despard's assumption of command were forgotten in a flurry of congratulations. The Assembly of Jamaica passed a resolution praising him for his 'gallant and judicious conduct' when in command of his 'undisciplined and inferior force'. When the news reached London, the King himself was pleased to offer his congratulations through his new Colonial Secretary, Thomas Townshend – later Lord Sydney – who wrote that 'His Majesty has received the highest satisfaction . . . at the success of his arms on the Mosquito Shore under the conduct of Lieutenant-Colonel Despard, by the total defeat of the enemy', going on to convey 'his royal approbation of the judicious and gallant services of Lieutenant-Colonel Despard.'

There was particular satisfaction that the colonel was establishing such friendly relations with the bizarre court of another King George, the Mosquito Indian ruler at Black River. Despard's secretary and friend, James Bannantine, described the chieftain as he had appeared to them both, admitting, 'the truth is that this monarch must appear in a very contemptible light to persons accustomed to the splendour of the courts of Europe. His Majesty wears no crown, no royal robes, creates no hereditary nobility, has no masters of horse, lord chamberlains or lords of the bedchamber, no guards and, what is still more, no exchequer. The only thing in which he resembles any of the princes of Europe is that his principal amusement, or, rather, occupation, is the chase.'

But the fruits of this initiative were about to be traded away in the bargaining that was to lead to the peace settlement between Britain and France, Spain and the United States of America, which was to be signed at Versailles on 3rd September, 1783. Britain was to recognise the independence of the United States; return French possessions captured in the West Indies, West Africa and East India, and Florida to Spain. Britain, in turn, was to regain lost colonies in the Caribbean and her settlement at Belize in Honduras but, in return for the latter, was to relinquish all rights on the Mosquito Shore, returning the Mosquito Indians to a Spanish rule.

The settlers at Greytown, Black River, Cape Graçias a Dios and the rest were given eighteen months to evacuate their land and most of them drifted to Belize and northward to Yucatan, where the Spanish had also given the British permission to cut logwood. Both Despard and Lawrie argued against the abandonment of the Mosquito Shore and the former went to London to plead against it. He did not succeed, but he did win the trust both of the settlers he represented and of the authorities in Jamaica. Indeed, the displaced settlers, some of whom had known him in Rattan, wrote to both Governor Campbell and to Charles James Fox, the Foreign Secretary, in London, asking that Despard be appointed Superintendent of the new settlements.

So Campbell, who admired Despard as a military engineer, now saw him as a popular and able administrator, and, giving him the local rank of full colonel, appointed him First Commissioner of the new territories in March, 1784. His first task was to reconnoitre the country where logwood and mahogany could be cut, then supervise the settlement of the newcomers from the Mosquito Shore amongst the few settlers, both Spanish and British, who had long been established there. He was a success, his old friends from Rattan and the Shore, writing to Campbell of his 'thirst for knowledge, attention to their true interests and mildness of government, which has, in a very particular manner, endeared him to all who were so fortunate as to be under his command.'

So Despard was confirmed as Superintendent of His Majesty's Affairs in Honduras on 1st December, 1784, at a salary of £500 a year. Much of his time was taken up with diplomacy, for the settlements were on Spanish territory and, although sanctioned by treaty, subject to limitations and inspection. Settlers were permitted to fell timber, but not to cultivate crops, and Spanish officers came regularly to ensure that these regulations were being obeyed. Despard established such happy relations with these inspectors that one spoke of 'the cordial friendship which unites us' and another, who had at first uprooted any vegetable gardens he found, began pretending not to see them. Eventually, thanks to Despard's tact, the settlers were allowed to grow all the fruit and vegetables needed for themselves, and the Spaniards even allowed a British pilot-station to be established on English Key off the coast.

His domestic life was content. Like many British officers and settlers he had taken a Negro mistress, who could be introduced to visitors as housekeeper, or wife, as occasion demanded. 'Mrs. Despard's' name is not recorded but she had a son, whom Despard brought up as his own, although his family were later to say that the father had been another Irish officer she had known previously.

Trouble, however, soon became inevitable when dealing with the settlers themselves. Just as Dalling and Hodgson, and many others, had found, it was almost impossible to maintain tranquillity in these regions when the interests of government and governed diverged. In Honduras and Yucatan, this was caused by disputes between the old settlers and the new. Before the Treaty of Versailles, the area Despard administered had been settled by about seven hundred British; so few that disputes over land and its boundaries had been rare. Now this territory was invaded by nearly three thousand more, including slaves, from the Mosquito Shore and Rattan. Many were old friends of the Superintendent and a few had accompanied him to Nicaragua.

On arrival in Honduras, they quickly found that, although there seemed ample room for all, the best land near the coast and on the rivers was claimed by the original settlers, the 'Baymen'.

When Despard acted as intermediary and arbiter, he was at once accused of favouring the new arrivals and such criticism only stiffened his resolve to continue as he saw fit. One of the magistrates, a Bayman called James Usher, resigned in protest

[202]

Captain Cuthbert Collingwood painted by an unknown
miniaturist when serving in American and West Indian
waters.

Etched by Barlow, from a Sketch taken at his Trial

COL. DESPARD.

Published by Tegg. & Cẹ Febʸ 14ᵗʰ 1803.

Colonel Despard at the time of his trial as drawn by an artist
aware of his public's enjoyment of a national villain.

Nelson as the national hero at the time of the Despard
conspiracy, paintd by Lemuel Abbott.

WONDERFUL MUSEUM.

COL. EDWARD MARCUS DESPARD,
At the place of Execution upon the New Surry Goal just as he appeared when addressing the Spectators, a few minutes before the Platform dropped.

Colonel Despard on the scaffold.

Poster advertising Madame Tussaud's waxwork exhibition with Nelson's name immediately beneath those of the Royal Family and Despard's at the bottom of the bill.

By Permission of the Right Worshipful the Mayor.

LATELY ARRIVED FROM EDINBURGH,

THE GRAND EUROPEAN
Cabinet of Figures,

MODELLED FROM LIFE;—AND NOW

Exhibiting at No. 4, MARKET-PLACE, opposite the REIN-DEER INN:
Where the Curious may be gratified with a View of all the SEVENTY Characters at once.

Madame Tussaud, Artist,

RESPECTFULLY informs the Gentry and Public of HULL and its Vicinity, that her unrivalled Collection has just arrived here.

The full-length PORTRAIT-MODELS of their Most Gracious MAJESTIES

Geo. III. & Queen Charlotte,

THEIR ROYAL HIGHNESSES
THE PRINCE AND PRINCESS CHARLOTTE OF WALES,
Duke of York—Prince Charles Stuart;
LIEUTENANT-GENERAL SIR JOHN MOORE,

Admiral Lord Nelson,
GENERAL WASHINGTON.

Right Hon. Ch. Js. Fox—Right Hon. Wm. PITT,
SIR FRANCIS BURDETT,
Right Hon. H. GRATTAN—Right Hon. J. P. CURRAN,
The Philanthropic Mr. ROSEBERRY, of Dublin,
Mons. TALLEYRAND—L'ABBE SIEYES,
COUNT DE LORGA,
The famous BARON TRENCK—The EMPRESS of FRANCE,
MADAME CATALANI, the celebrated Singer,
A SLEEPING CHILD—The ARTIST and her DAUGHTER.

AN EXACT LIKENESS OF THE BEAUTIFUL BUT UNFORTUNATE

Mary Queen of Scots.
JOHN KNOX, and JOHN WESLEY.

THE CELEBRATED

MRS. CLARKE.

A Coach and a Cannon,

Formed in Gold, Ivory, and Tortoise Shell,—to the Astonishment of the Spectator, is, with great Facility
DRAWN by a FLEA!

The other Subjects composing this UNIQUE EXHIBITION, chiefly consisting of Portrait Characters, in full Dress, as large as Life, correctly executed, may be classed as follows:

I. The late Royal Family of France, viz.
King, Queen, Princess Royal, and Dauphin; with M. de Clerie, Valet de Roi.
Celebrated Characters of the past and present Times, viz.
Henry IV. of France—Duc de Sully—Frederick the Great—M. de Voltaire—Pope Pius—J. J. Rousseau—Dr. Franklin—Buonaparte—Madame Buonaparte—Archduke Charles—General Moreau—General Kleber—Ex-Consul Cambaceres—Elfi Bey, and his Son; with a favourite Georgian Slave, and two most beautiful Circassians.

II. Remarkable Characters:—Subjects, viz.
Madamoiselle Bruiser de Perigord, who foretold the French Revolution.
Princess de Lamballe, who was murdered by the Revolutionary Mob in Paris.
Madame du Barri, the Mistress of Louis XV. who was guillotined in Paris.
Madame St. Amaranthe, guillotined for refusing to be the Mistress of Robespierre.
Charlotte Corde, who suffered by the guillotine for the Assassination of Marat.
Marat in the Agonies of Death, immediately after receiving the fatal Wound.
Heads of Robespierre, Foquilier, de Thionville, Herbert, and Carriere, as they appeared after the guillotine.
A Soldier of the French National Guards, in full Uniform.
An old Coquette, who teased her Husband's Life out.
One of Buonaparte's Mameluke Guards.——Madame St. Clair, the celebrated French Actress.

III. Curious and Interesting Relics, viz.
The SHIRT of HENRY IV. of France, in which he was assassinated by RIVAILLAC; and an accurate Portrait of Rivaillac himself, with various original Documents relating to that Transaction.
A small Model of the original French Guillotine, with all its Apparatus; and two Picturesque Models of the Bastile in Paris;
(In which Count de Lorga was confined Twenty Years:)
One representing that Fortress in an entire State, the other as destroying by the Revolutionists.
A real *EGYPTIAN MUMMY,* 3209 years old, in perfect Preservation.

Colonel Despard.

☞ OPEN EVERY DAY, from ELEVEN in the MORNING till TEN at NIGHT.
※ *Admittance, One Shilling.—Children under Ten Years of Age, Half Price.*
N. B. A Free Ticket, (not Transferable) Price 5s. will admit a Person any Time during the Exhibition.

No. 4, Market-Place, Hull, February 28th, 1812.
ROBERT PECK, PRINTER, PACKET-OFFICE, HULL.

against what he considered autocratic rule, sneering, 'If the smiles of power are to be obtained by no other method than cringing, creeping and fawning, let those court them who will; for, from my own knowledge of the Superintendent's former opinion of his present favourites, I do not hesitate to say that now "the Post of Honour is a private station!" ' Usher was arrested and charged with publishing 'a false, seditious and malicious libel, evidence of a depraved mind and a diabolical disposition.' In court, a jury of Baymen acquitted him and Despard, enraged, abolished the judiciary and ruled by decree, while he brought together a new bench of magistrates composed largely of his old friends, the new arrivals. Some, who watched the development of the confrontation, were reminded of Governor Dalling.

Under British law, trading with the Americans as if they were still the King's subjects was, of course, forbidden. Like Nelson, he discovered quickly that it was unpopular to enforce the Navigation Act and equally unpopular to check the contraband traffic with Spanish settlements that the settlers regarded as a right.

So the old Baymen protested vigorously to Spanish Town and to London, using the wily solicitor, Robert White of Hampstead, in drawing the attention of Whitehall to 'the barbarous commanding officer on the Honduras Coast.' Despard, in turn, rejected 'the most false and frivolous charges.' But the British Government, long weary of Caribbean wranglings, repeatedly shelved all memoranda on the subject, until, irritated into action, the Foreign Secretary, Lord Sydney, put the matter before the King and advised him to support his Superintendent. So, in June, an official letter was sent to Despard, telling him that, 'His Majesty has commanded me to instruct you that the late inhabitants of the Mosquito Shore, who may arrive in the Honduras settlement, are to be accommodated with lands in preference to all other persons whatsoever.'

This eased Despard's position for a time, but the Baymen kept up their protests to London and saw to it that they were brought to the notice of Sydney's successor, Lord Grenville, when he took office in 1789. The new Secretary of State was a conscientious man, yet to be bored into inactivity by petty squabbles in distant outposts, and he read through the Honduras correspondence, coming to the conclusion that something must be badly wrong. It might not be the fault of the Superintendent but, as he was in authority, he must be answerable for the unrest. So Grenville wrote to Despard, telling him that his office was suspended pending an enquiry and giving him the opportunity of remaining until that time in Belize, or returning to London. Assuming that the latter course would be most effective in gaining the support of the new Secretary of State, the colonel decided to return, confident that personal meetings in Whitehall – and, perhaps, presentation at Court – would not only confirm his position in Honduras but even lead to more exalted employment elsewhere.

But the London to which he returned with his West Indian mistress in the early summer of 1790 was not the city he remembered from brief visits as a young officer. The American revolution now belonged to history and attention was fixed on the French revolution; the Caribbean seemed very remote indeed. He had few, if any, friends in the capital, for his family's roots were in Ireland and his regiment, which had come back from Jamaica, had been disbanded.

The 79th, with whom he had proudly paraded in Liverpool thirteen years before, had returned to the city where they had been raised. But most of the eleven hundred, who had marched so jauntily behind their new colours that spring morning, had rotted on the banks of the San Juan river and so few had returned that the War Office had decided to disband the survivors. On 12th February, 1784, the *Liverpool Advertizer* again reported on a parade: 'Monday last, the 79th Regiment, or Royal Liverpool Volunteers, marched to the Exchange and delivered the colours to the Magistrates, who deposited them in the Town Hall. The officers and men were afterwards regaled with plenty of cheer.' It was not as expensive an affair for Liverpool as the former occasion, since there were only eighty-four soldiers to entertain.

So Colonel Despard made his solitary way to Whitehall and presented himself at the Colonial Office, bearing a sheaf of testimonials from his friends in Honduras, and asking for an interview with the Secretary of State. But the minister had more pressing matters to attend to and he was asked to wait. He waited in ante-rooms and was, from time to time, seen by a secretary, or clerk, to whom he had to repeat his story and urge that it be brought to the minister's attention. Sometimes the answers were bland promises; sometimes, a request for more detailed memoranda to add to those already received. But, on each occasion, the outcome was the same. While Despard waited, an official would take down the dusty letter-books from the Honduras shelves, open them and be so appalled at the tedious and self-righteous irrelevancies of the correspondence, that he would close them again and send word that Colonel Despard should return another day. Always he was assured that his case was under consideration and, when he pressed for a full public enquiry into his record since being sent to Rattan nine years before, he was told that that might be the outcome of the present considerations. While he waited, he became a familiar figure in the waiting-rooms of Whitehall and in the nearby coffee-houses and taverns. When the summer ended and the weather became too chill for time-killing walks in St. James's Park, the colonel, muffled in a greatcoat against the unaccustomed cold, and carrying a green umbrella, which was more accustomed to tropical showers than London drizzle, would tour the public houses and tap-rooms in search of warmth, newspapers and conversation.

Seasons, months and then years went slowly by and still he haunted the Colonial Office and wrote memoranda, seemingly to no avail as the events that had brought him to London receded faster into obscurity. Then, after two years, the long wait seemed to have been worth while and he was summoned to hear the decision reached by Lord Grenville. This was, firstly, that there seemed to be no case against him worthy of investigation, so that he was formally absolved of any blame. But, then, when he expressed his intention of returning immediately to Honduras, he was told of the second decision: to abolish the post of King's Superintendent as being no longer necessary. His past services would not be forgotten, he was assured, and would be duly rewarded.

While awaiting details of this recompense, he drew up an

account of his own expenses incurred in Honduras and on his return and submitted them with a request for urgency as his funds were running low. But the interminable waiting began all over again. The reward was never forthcoming, details of his expenses were questioned and, in the event, neither was paid.

As irritation turned to frustration and then to helpless anger, the despairing Despard began to question the value of doing what he had hitherto considered his duty. The well-connected senior officers, who had been responsible for the Nicaraguan catastrophe, seemed to have prospered: promotion to lieutenant-general and promise of a command at Madras for General Dalling; the command at Portsmouth for Admiral Parker; baronetcies for both. But he and Nelson – the two who had emerged with the greatest honour – seemed to have been ignored. While he felt himself invisible in the eyes of his seniors, his friend had only been recalled to sea and given command of the fourth-rate ship of the line *Agamemnon* as war was breaking out with France and almost every healthy naval officer was being given employment.

But, within six months of the beginning of his long wait, an idea had reached him and had grown into a belief that offered an alternative line of duty that could fulfil ambition and restore self-respect. In October, a fellow-Irishman, Wolfe Tone, had founded a new political movement, the United Irishmen, with the aim of banding together Catholic and Protestant for delivery from English rule.

England, as well as Ireland, was rife with dissent at this time and anybody frequenting taverns would hear favourable comment on the revolution in France, which went far beyond the theoretical approval expressed by Whig politicians in opposition. In the Caribbean, most of Despard's friends had supported the American rebels and, when Wolfe Tone went to Paris in the hope of winning practical support for Irish independence, he found that his own political stance had become that of the revolutionary.

Soon afterwards, discontent found wider expression in the birth and growth of the Corresponding Societies, which had developed from the radical debating groups that had spontaneously started in London taverns during the American revolution and had drawn fresh inspiration from the idealistic beginnings of the French. The London Corresponding Society, which set the pattern for others throughout the provincial cities, was essentially a reformist movement drawn from the small traders, artisans and working-men of the capital – including many Irish and some Methodists – with a few radical lawyers, clergy and journalists amongst their leaders.

In the taverns he frequented, Despard found the company of such men stimulating, their ideas heady and their organisations a more practical vehicle for his own discontent than the United Irishmen. He became a member of the London Corresponding Society, joining their debates on the interpretation of Thomas Paine's *The Rights of Man* and the ideas of Rousseau. He was popular – a fellow member describing him as 'a mild, gentlemanly person; a singularly good-hearted man' – and efficient, so that, by 1796, he was not only serving on the committee of the society but had established links with the less-substantial but more subversive United Englishmen, who sought to emulate the United Irishmen. By 1797, the Corresponding Societies were in constant touch with one another and, primarily through this London committee, had established secret links with Paris.

He became a creature of the shadows, his erect figure in the heavy coat, his green umbrella and his glass of brandy, familiar in the taverns where radicals met. Despard's pinched and bitter features could again assume a purposeful and authoritative air. He commanded attention and not only from the eager men who met to talk and argue in the smoke and candlelight of stuffy back-rooms of inns and coffee-houses.

Towards the end of 1797, his standing amongst the revolutionaries was such that he helped found a new radical society, the United Britons, with the active support of a French invasion of England amongst its aims. This necessitated direct contact with Paris and this was made through an Irishman resident in Hamburg named William Duckett, who controlled spies and informers in England for the French.

Yet no tangible evidence against him was produced until the spring of 1798. Then, in March, four suspicious characters were arrested near Margate on the coast of Kent, suspected of trying to escape to France. They proved to be agents of the United Irishmen and United Englishmen and one of them, an Irish priest named O'Coighly, was carrying a memorandum advising the French on political action to be taken after a successful invasion of England. During the priest's interrogation, which was followed by his trial and execution, Despard's name was mentioned. Although O'Coighly refused to divulge details upon which a charge could be based, this was enough to include him in a list of prominent radicals to be detained for questioning.

For the first time, Despard was arrested and confined for several weeks in the Coldbath Fields prison in Clerkenwell, but, after a few weeks, was released for lack of more specific evidence. Then news came from Ireland of the outbreak of armed rebellion and, in alarm, the Prime Minister, William Pitt, suspended the Habeas Corpus Act so that suspected subversives could be interned without trial. Despard was again arrested and sent to the Tothill Fields prison in Westminster.

His imprisonment there, at Coldbath Fields and, for a time, at the House of Correction at Shrewsbury in Shropshire, where he was sent to lessen the risk of his revolutionary infection spreading in the capital, was harsh. In Coldbath Fields, his cell measured only six feet by eight, was furnished only with a table and a bed of two nine-inch oak planks covered with a straw mattress, two blankets and a horse-rug. There was no heating and the barred, unglazed window was only shuttered so that, for exercise, he had to jump between floor, table and bed. For weeks, his diet was bread and water, to which was later added almost inedible scraps of meat and gristle.

Most of the radical leaders were suffering similarly and a campaign for their release, or, at least, for better conditions in prison, was mounted. Despard was helped by his former secretary, James Bannantine, who had followed him to London and wrote a pamphlet in his defence, by his black common-law wife, and by the support of the reforming Member of Parliament, Sir Francis Burdett. Due to their pleading and the consequent publicity, the Government eventually began to consider the possibility of release.

During that year, the Irish rebellion was crushed when a

French attempt to land an army in its support failed. Wolfe Tone was captured and committed suicide before he could be hanged; but amongst his papers was mention of the name Despard. Yet there was still no precise evidence of treason on which he could be brought to trial. Months passed and pleas for his freedom by his mistress and by the faithful Bannantine, failed. So it was not until more than two years had passed that the Government felt confident enough to relax its security precautions and he was released.

During his imprisonment, the world had changed. Revolutionary France had suddenly tried to expand eastward, only to be halted when the young rear-admiral, Horatio Nelson, destroyed their fleet off the Egyptian coast at Aboukir Bay. In prison, Despard had been able to follow his friend's career when his name was prominent in the newspapers after some new, dashing exploit. He had turned the command of his modest fourth-rate to good account in several Mediterranean actions and in the campaign that took Corsica; he had brilliantly saved the day in February, 1797, off Cape St. Vincent, by throwing his ship into the path of the enemy to halt them until Admiral Jervis could come up and win his victory; even in the disastrous raid on Tenerife he had been covered with glory; and blood, since he had lost his right arm. Now he had broken the enemy's dream of eastern conquest. Already a familiar toast in the taverns of London was, "Success to Nelson!"

The frustrated General Napoleon Bonaparte had abandoned his army in Egypt and returned to France to establish himself as its dictator, and the war continued. The French defeated the British in Holland and the Austrians at Marengo and occupied Italy; but their army stranded in the Levant achieved nothing by hollow and bloody victories over the Turks and, when the British took Malta, became even more isolated. In the July of 1799, the British Government banned all political associations and, since the breaking of the Irish rebellion, felt confident that the subversive movements had lost their impetus now that their French ideals were betrayed by the military dictatorship.

The years in prison had further hardened the resentful man. He had had time to brood and plot. Wolfe Tone had shown the way but, where he had failed, a resolute and efficient soldier

[209]

might succeed. From prison, England did not seem the robust and patriotic country portrayed by the political cartoonists. To him, it appeared to seethe with a discontent, which, once given a lead, could not be contained. He had heard stories of the Gordon Riots of 1780, when the capital had been at the mercy of an almost leaderless mob for nearly a week, and of the naval mutinies at the Nore and Spithead in 1797, when the nation's surest shield – the wooden walls and heart of oak, of which it liked to boast – was shown to be flawed. He remembered what he and Nelson might have achieved in Nicaragua, what he himself had done at Black River, and Nelson's subsequent feats of decisive daring at sea. It must have seemed that he need no longer look for a leader in whom to put his trust, for he should be that leader himself.

Towards the end of his imprisonment he had almost abandoned hope of again becoming a leader of the revolutionaries and had gone so far as to apply for voluntary transportation, probably to Australia. But, when he was freed, he visited Ireland and there his faith was rekindled and he returned to London more determined than ever. So, at the beginning of 1801, the man of military bearing – once described as 'mild, gentle and attractive' – strode the streets of London again from his lodgings in Mount Row, Lambeth, with a new sense of purpose.

Both his experience and his inheritance supported him: the years of independent command away from the disciplines of regimental duty; the volatile temper and vaulting imagination of his French and Irish ancestry.

The man in the blue greatcoat with the green umbrella again became familiar in the taverns as he sought old acquaintances with whom to resume his revolutionary duties. But the shadowed world of subversion had changed. The Corresponding Society had been disbanded, its members now simply individual Whigs, or radicals, and, since the executions of 1798, the United Irishmen had remained a very secret society. But he did meet a former member of the latter, a stocky, florid, cheerful Irish carpenter known as 'Mac', who turned out to be named John Macnamara, in his fortieth year, whose hopes coincided with his own. He also met those who promised him the support – financial as well as moral – of people he might never meet but who followed the news from London with the closest interest in Paris.

Macnamara explained that, although political associations were forbidden, a number of 'Free and Easy Clubs' had sprung up in the city's public houses, ostensibly to encourage convivial evenings but also offering opportunities for more serious discussion. So it was that one of these gradually took a more purposeful shape under the name of 'the Constitution Society', which might, of course, mean that it supported the present constitution of Great Britain, or might imply an intention to reform. During the winter of 1801, there were some bread riots in London, a brief mutiny on board British warships in Bantry Bay and the red Cap of Liberty was said to have been displayed in an election disturbance at Nottingham. The moment to do more than talk might be near.

Despard, Macnamara and a cadre of agitators began to recruit in taverns frequented by Irishmen and by soldiers, who were often Irish, too. They avoided those in the heart of the City, or in any of the more prosperous commercial and residential centres of London, visiting those on their fringes: in Soho, off Hatton Garden, in Whitechapel, east of the City boundary, and, above all, south of the river in Southwark, Newington and Lambeth. Those boroughs had an ancient tradition of laxity, if not lawlessness. The Elizabethan theatres had been there, and the bear-baiting and cock-fighting pits; it was a district of taverns and pleasure-gardens, the most famous being at Vauxhall; it was also known for its prisons and asylums. Now terraces of houses for the rising middle class, and for artisans, were pushing south along the roads and among the market-gardens, but it remained an area where men who did not want to attract attention could drop out of sight.

It was soon apparent to Despard that he was unlikely to recruit any men of education, but when two battalions of the Grenadier Guards were posted to London and he heard that one of them – the 3rd. – had been at Chatham, and was thought to have been much infected by the naval mutiny at the Nore, new possibilities became apparent. There had been few educated men on the Mosquito Shore and in Honduras, but he had

[211]

achieved much with only a handful of soldiers and resolute armed men. He might now do as much again.

Introductions were arranged and two guardsmen, John Wood, a lanky, good-looking Derbyshireman of twenty-five, of the 1st Battalion, and John Francis, a tall, handsome Shropshire shoemaker of twenty-three, of the 3rd, agreed to act as recruiting agents. They returned to barracks at the Tower of London and Windsor Castle and set to work. Another guardsman later recalled, Francis telling him, 'There are a great number of independent gentlemen who have united themselves together and are determined to risk their lives and fortunes in establishing a free and independent constitution.'

Francis had then produced a small printed card and asked him to read it. 'Constitution,' it read. 'The independence of Great Britain and Ireland. An equalization of Civil, Political and Religious Rights; an ample provision for the families of Heroes who shall fall in the contest . . . .' Then came the oath, 'In the awful Presence of Almighty God, I . . . . do voluntarily declare that I will endeavour to the utmost of my power to obtain the objects of this Union; namely to recover those rights which the Supreme Being, in his infinite bounty, has given to all men. . . .'

John Francis asked the guardsman to kiss the card; then, telling him that he was now a sworn member of the Constitution Society, taking him off to the Ham and Windmill public house in Windmill Street at the top of the Haymarket for a drink in celebration. Few recruits met Despard, or even heard his name, orders coming from the 'Commander-in-Chief', or 'the Executive', through a chain of command in which 'colonels' commanded divisions of fifty men, or more, and 'captains' cells of ten.

Little seemed to be demanded of the recruits, beyond the secretive, and rather exciting, arrangement of meetings in the upstairs rooms of public houses, where twenty to thirty men would sit drinking, smoking and talking, occasionally proposing a toast such as, 'May the wings of Liberty never lose a feather!' Sometimes the discussion was general and political, although hardly of any weight. One recruit, Guardsman Blades, accompanied John Francis to a meeting at the Black Raven in

Tooley Street, where four of the more prominent members 'and about six or seven Irishmen in a state of intoxication' were deep in discussion, 'the conversation . . . . concerning forms of Government.'

Recruiting went well and soon there were divisions in Southwark, Marylebone, Spitalfields and Blackwall in the East End. Most of the civilian members were tradesmen, artisans and labourers – amongst the most active were a watchmaker and a shoemaker – but the core of the Constitution Society was military: some three hundred guardsmen from the 3rd Battalion, Grenadier Guards, and about forty from the 1st.

Some of the soldiers had joined in the hope of free drinks; some for the excitement; others, billeted in the public houses where meetings were held, for the convivial company; there were also those who shared Macnamara's aim 'to overthrow the Government and have our nation the same as France.' Several of the guardsmen were former non-commissioned officers who had been reduced to the ranks, others had been flogged – one with two hundred lashes for absenting himself from sentry-duty at the King's apartments – and one who had no intention of risking his neck in any conspiracy.

This was Guardsman Thomas Windsor of the 3rd Battalion, who was recruited by Francis, then at once reported the matter to an Army agent named William Bownas. Windsor was told to remain in the conspiracy 'to keep an eye upon these people', remember all he heard and report regularly. His enthusiasm was noticed and soon Francis and Macnamara told him that they hoped to appoint him colonel of a new division in the Borough.

In March, the war ended with the Peace of Amiens and the nation relaxed. Even Nelson, returned from the Baltic and the destruction of the Danish fleet off Copenhagen, and a brief spell commanding in the North Sea and Channel, had retired to his new country house at Merton outside London with his mistress, Lady Hamilton, and her complaisant old husband, Sir William. Even the Constitution Society seemed to lose some of its ardour, Colonel Despard being reported as saying that 'there was nothing to be done, he was expecting news and money from France.'

Then, in August, the word went out that 'there was

something very particular on the carpet'. Despard had decided that the time for action had come and he set about mobilising not only the Constitution Society but its military arm that was now called the 'National Guards'. He walked, he said, twenty miles a day in and around London, being again recognised and remembered by the 'green silk umbrella with a hooked yellow stick — an umbrella that you walk with.'

He strode the dark and muddy night-time streets of London and hovered in the smoky candlelight of its taverns. He was seen at the Bleeding Heart in Hatton Garden and the Tyger on Tower Hill; at The Angel in Cecil's Court, off St. Martin's Lane, and the Black Horse in Oxford Road; at the Coach and Horses in Whitechapel and the Flying Horse at Newington, south of the river.

It was at this last tavern that Despard made his announcement on 12th November, 1802. It was a small meeting of half a dozen trusted conspirators — amongst them Guardsman Windsor — in the back parlour. Before they sat down, a shilling's worth of brandy and water was ordered for the colonel and, when the maid brought it, John Emblin, the Vauxhall watchmaker, flirted with her, saying, 'I'll have a kiss when you come back.'

When the door was shut, Despard said, 'I believe this to be the moment. The people everywhere are ripe and anxious for the moment of attack. The people, particularly in Manchester, in Leeds, in Sheffield, in Birmingham and in every capital town in England are ripe. I can only say, if the people come forward, as I have been given every reason to understand, we have great numbers of the Army, and there are great numbers in all parts of the Kingdom.' Throughout the country, he claimed, forty thousand men were ready to rise.

What he believed them to be ripe for was nothing less than revolution. The plan which he had evolved over the past two years was as grand and daring in concept as Governor Dalling's design to conquer New Spain. It depended upon the resolution of a few men to set in motion a chain of upheavals that would sweep away Monarchy and Government and replace it with a revolutionary republic that would make common cause with France, liberate Ireland and adopt the principles of the United

States of America.

It was to be a *Coup détat*. The King was to be assassinated; the Tower of London, the Bank of England and the Houses of Parliament seized; the capital's communications cut by stopping the mail coaches and smashing the Admiralty's semaphore towers; finally, arms from the Tower and the Bank would be given to the London mob and the city would be in the hands of the Commander-in-Chief, the Executive and the National Guards.

The attempt was to be made on 23rd November, the day when the King was to open Parliament and would therefore be exposed to his assassins on his way by coach from St. James's Palace to Westminster and back. At first it was suggested that conspirators should mingle with the crowd outside the palace, then, as the coach emerged, halt it by shooting two of the horses, and then killing the King. At this, Emblin remarked, 'There are horsemen riding close by the carriage with their horses' heads almost in the window and any person attempting such a thing would be cut to pieces. Who would do it?'

'I would do it with my own hand,' replied Despard. 'I have weighed this matter well and my heart is callous.'

Another, larger meeting was arranged to be held at the Oakley Arms in Lambeth near the south side of Westminster Bridge on 16th November. Meanwhile, Despard busied himself with the details of the *coup* by which the mutineers in the Grenadier Guards would seize the Tower. Having done that, they would march to the East India Company's building in the City, where more muskets were stored, on to the Artillery Ground at Moorfields to collect cannon, and, from there, mount an assault on St. James's Palace. These, and the attacks on the King himself and on the Bank, and the setting up of road-blocks around London, would be coordinated by himself from The Angel tavern in Cecil's Court, keeping in touch with events through a system of mounted couriers.

When Despard arrived at the Oakley Arms on the evening of Tuesday, 16th November, the upstairs club-room was crowded. About thirty men were there, drinking beer, smoking clay pipes and talking; some were in the rough clothes of working-men; others wore the red coats of guardsmen. The

[215]

colonel himself was conspicuous as the only one present with the dress and bearing of a gentleman. Before the business of the evening began. conversation was general but, as soon as Emblin entered and seated himself, one of the conspirators could contain himself no longer and whispered, 'My boy, we have the completest plan in the world, which will do the business without any trouble.'

This plan was a new and bizarre method of killing the King. In discussing official arrangements for the procession to Parliament, John Wood, the 'colonel' of the 1st Battalion's mutineers, reported that his company would be lining the route across the Horse Guards Parade. They would also be mounting guard over a huge Turkish cannon that had been captured by General Abercromby's army in Egypt the year before and was on display there as a trophy of war. It was a formidable weapon with a barrel sixteen feet long and a bore of eight inches, inscribed by its sixteenth-century maker as a 'dragon gun' that would 'roar like thunder'. The ingenious plan was 'to load the great gun . . . . with four balls, or chain-shot, and fire it at the King as he returns from the House – and be damned if that did not send them all to hell.'

In the darkness of the night before the Opening of Parliament, Wood and his accomplices would secretly load the cannon, and mount guard over it next day. Then, when the royal carriage passed its muzzle, he would touch its powder-train with a smouldering slow-match. Emblin was appalled at the possibilities and protested, 'Good God, consider how many people will be in the park that day and how many lives you will take away!' 'Then, damn them, let them get out of the way,' said one of the guardsmen, 'But it will play hell with the houses at the Treasury and round about there.'

Success was to be proclaimed to London by tolling the bell of St. Paul's, and to conspirators in the rest of the country by the stopping of the stage-coaches.

It was nine o'clock and Despard was about to give his instructions for the final dispositions for the day of the attack, when there was a commotion on the stairs, the door burst open and three armed men stood there, one shouting, 'Don't be alarmed! We are police officers with a search warrant.' They pushed into the room and went up to the man of gentlemanly appearance, who rose and stood leaning on his green silk umbrella. Colonel Despard asked to see their search-warrant and, when they refused to read it to him, became angry and tried to prevent them searching him. This, however, was swiftly done but no incriminating papers were discovered; others in the room were found to be carrying the Constitution Society's membership cards.

While the men were being searched, Despard paced up and down, asking why they were being detained. Then he stopped and called out loudly, 'One and all follow me!' and made for the door. He reached the stairs, then saw the room below crowded with police and, when ordered back into the room, quietly obeyed. After a while, the Bow Street officers ordered them all downstairs and into the street, where more constables were waiting. A line of coaches was drawn up outside the door and the prisoners were ordered into them and driven away.

As the clatter and rumble of the coaches on the cobbles died away, a man 'dressed like a bricklayer or plasterer' entered the Oakley Arms and ordered a pint of beer and a clay pipe of tobacco. The Chief Clerk of the Police Office, who was still in the bar-parlour, fell into conversation with him and, as result of what he heard, asked him to attend the magistrates' court at Union Hall as a witness next morning. He then wrote down the man's name, which was Thomas Windsor, whose regular reports had resulted in the decision to make the police raid on the Oakley Arms and take Colonel Despard and his companions into custody.

Although the arrests had been swift and efficient, they had inevitably attracted attention as the officers first crossed the river from Bow Street to Lambeth and, later, as the procession of heavily-guarded coaches returned, taking Despard to prison in Newgate and the rest to Clerkenwell, or Tothill Fields. Next morning, when a series of interrogations began – the first at a Privy Council meeting presided over by the Lord Chancellor – the movement about London of prisoners and escorts, set rumours flying.

Despite the banning of political associations, there had been persistent reports of subversive meetings and clandestine

[217]

political societies throughout the industrial cities of England. Much of such whisperings were drowned by noisy patriotic braggadocio stimulated by fear of renewed war with France, but established society remained haunted by the fear of deep-running revolutionary currents. Rumours of a traitorous colonel and mutinuous guardsmen seemed to confirm the worst apprehensions.

Fearful lest talk of the abortive insurrection cause panic, or even set off riots, the Government managed to keep news of the arrests out of the newspapers. Indeed, there was no mention of them in *The Times* for three days and then it was to deny that the charge against Despard was for high treason, or plotting against the life of the King; it was of 'seducing some of the Guards from their duty and allegiance'. It claimed that the number concerned in the plot was ten, or less. An editorial promised that more details would be reported 'as soon as we consider ourselves at liberty' but that 'at present we conceive, for many reasons, it would be highly improper.'

More accurate news reached men of affairs and amongst them was the newly-active member of the House of Lords, Vice-Admiral Viscount Nelson, who was dividing his time between Merton Place in Surrey and the Hamiltons' house at 23 Piccadilly. His first reaction must have been to wonder whether this was the Despard he had known in Nicaragua and, finding that it was, to ask how such a man could have come to this.

During the past twenty years, he had kept in touch with several of his friends from the San Juan expedition. He had always tried to keep his most valued friendships in good repair, and these meant even more to him now that he had lost two of them with the recent deaths of his father and Captain Locker. The oldest friends were, perhaps, particularly cherished as they recalled his early days of ambition and innocence.

Admiral Parker remained a close friend, and he had been in touch with General Dalling until his death in 1798; his widow had recently asked him to cast a kindly eye on one of their sons serving with the Army at Gibraltar. He also corresponded with Hercules Ross, who was in Scotland, or Bath, when not in Jamaica, and they exchanged gossip about the others.

On returning to London, he had been particularly pleased to

find that Dr. Moseley was now senior physician at the Royal Hospital in Chelsea, caring for the Army pensioners there. He had become something of a celebrity since the publication of his popular work on tropical medicine, in which he described in such lurid detail the horrors of the Nicaraguan venture. They renewed their friendship – and medical consultations – and, on his visits to Chelsea, Nelson heard another echo of the past. The wife of a newly-appointed Staff Officer of the Royal Hospital, a Colonel Matthews, was the former Mary Simpson of Quebec, and it was said that she now spoke rather wistfully of the famous admiral who had once courted her.

Nelson was consulting Moseley about his eyes. He had lost the sight of his right eye when fighting ashore in Corsica, in 1794, and the left, which he took care to shield from bright sunlight with a green shade, had been giving him trouble. He had great faith in the doctor's versatility but a letter from another veteran of Nicaragua warned, 'Do, my good lord, tell me who you consulted besides Moseley, who, though an *excellent physician*, is not, I apprehend, a professional oculist.'

This came from Richard Bulkeley, who had commanded the Liverpool Blues but had retired from the Army and, deciding not to follow his father's successful political career in Nova Scotia, had returned to settle in Shropshire. Of Anglo-Irish stock, Bulkeley was an extrovert but had come close to spoiling the resumption of their friendship, nearly two years previously, by assuming too much intimacy. Nelson had been about to return from Naples with the Hamiltons and face Fanny and the failure of their marriage; it was a time of agonising guilt combined with passionate love. Then a hearty letter had arrived from Bulkeley, saying, 'The fair sex *all* impatiently await your return, each hoping that she may be one of the select few who are to become slaves to your amorous passion. I mention this that you may come back to us determined to gratify your own countrywomen as much as you have, by all accounts, others in your Italian states.'

Despite this, Nelson could not help liking Bulkeley. Back in 1797, when he had been recovering from the amputation of his arm after the Tenerife raid and was being nursed by Fanny in London, the jolly soldier had brought his two young sons to see them at their lodgings in Bond Street. He had shown the boys his sword and told them how he had been using it and one of them, twelve-year-old Dick, had clearly been fascinated. His father had written later to say that nothing but a career in the Navy would now satisfy the boy and, joking that 'as you have *bit* him, you must be his physician', sought his professional patronage, which he had since given.

Now, as news of Despard's arrest spread across the country, Bulkeley wrote from Ludlow to his old friend: 'From everything that the papers related . . . . I had no idea that the detestable conspiracy had gone the lengths you seem to imagine, or involved in it any (poor Despard excepted) but of the lowest orders.'

Nelson's own curiosity was to be satisfied to the full when he heard, during the preparations for the trail of the conspirators, that Despard had asked him to appear as a witness for the defence. It was embarrassing to have to speak on behalf of an intended regicide at a time when the King was openly showing his disapproval of his liaison with Lady Hamilton but, for him, the ties of friendship were always strong, and he agreed.

On 21st January, 1803, the Grand Jury of Surrey sent Despard and twelve of his associates for trial on charges of high treason and this was begun on 7th February at the Sessions House in Horsemonger Lane, Newington, close to the Flying Horse and only a short walk from the Oakley Arms. It was heard before the Lord Chief Justice, Lord Ellenborough, and the prosecution was conducted by the Attorney-General, Spencer Perceval, who, nine years later, was himself to be assassinated in the House of Commons when Prime Minister.

As the prisoners were brought into court from the new prison behind the Sessions House, they were watched with curiosity. Despard was dressed shabbily, with a cotton handkerchief around his neck, and appeared agitated when entering the dock. The others were described as 'vulgar, with much stupidity of face. They seemed of all mankind the most unfit to carry any object whose accomplishment required the least degree of mind or intelligence.' It was in the interests of the Government and Despard's friends to put it about that he was insane; the former, so as to belittle the importance of the plot; the latter, in the hope of leniency. But, as the trial began, the colonel 'displayed a firm, manly deportment.'

All the proprieties were observed, every word of the proceedings being taken down in short-hand. But the outcome seemed a foregone conclusion when Emblin, the watchmaker, and three soldiers, who had been in the plot, were allowed to turn King's evidence and add their damning evidence to that of the informer, Windsor. Witnesses were heard and cross-examined, among them the landlady of the Flying Horse, who remembered leaning on the bar one night and hearing Colonel Despard say loudly in the back room, 'I have weighed everything well within me, and, God may know, my heart is callous.' John Emblin had already said that such words had been spoken in reference to the killing of the King.

Despard himself was thought to have put all his slender hopes on whatever his old friend from Nicaraguan days might say on his behalf. When Nelson entered the witness box and was sworn on the Bible, the two men saw each other for the first time since they had parted, both weak with malaria and dysentery, at the camp below the spectral white shape of the castle of San Juan. Despard, now in his early fifties, was no longer handsome, his hair cropped short, his face ravaged; Nelson now forty-four, wore well-cut civilian clothes, his hair almost white, his famous face – the clouded eye, the prominent nose, the wide, sensual mouth – made so familiar by portraits, settled into the confident cast of one long accustomed to command.

A counsel for the defence asked, 'How long has your Lordship known Colonel Despard?'

'It is twenty-three years since I saw him,' replied the admiral. 'I became acquainted with him in the year 1779 at Jamaica. He was, at that time, lieutenant in what were called the Liverpool Blues. From his abilities as an engineer, I know he was expected to be appointed – '

'I am sorry to be obliged to interrupt your Lordship,' broke in the judge, 'but we cannot hear, what I dare say your Lordship would give with great effect, the history of this gentleman's military life; but you will state what has been his

[221]

general character.'

'We went on the Spanish Main together,' continued Nelson. 'We slept many nights together in our clothes upon the ground; we have measured the height of the enemy's wall together. In all that period of time, no man could have shown more zealous attachment to his Sovereign and his country than Colonel Despard did. I formed the highest opinion of him at that time, as a man and an officer, seeing him so willing in the service of his Sovereign. Having lost sight of him for the last twenty years, if I had been asked my opinion of him, I should certainly have said, "If he is alive, he is certainly one of the brightest ornaments of the British Army" '

Cross-examining for the prosecution, Spencer Perceval, asked, 'What your Lordship has been stating was in the years, 1779 and 1780?'

'Yes.'

'Have you had much intercourse with Colonel Despard since that time?'

'I have never seen him since the 29th of April, 1780.'

'Then, as to his loyalty for the last twenty-three years of his life, your Lordship knows nothing?'

'Nothing.'

Throughout, Despard appeared impassive, occasionally making notes. But Nelson's eulogy could hardly weaken the damning weight of evidence and for this he seemed prepared. On Tuesday, 8th February, he was brought into the dock alone to hear that the jury had found him guilty of high treason, but when the foreman delivered 'the awful verdict', one present noticed that it did not seem to affect him 'in any other way than a common denial to a man in business.' Then, in a gesture towards Nelson's attempt to help his old friend, the foreman continued, 'My Lord, we do most earnestly recommend the prisoner to mercy on account of the high testimonials to his former good character and eminent services.'

Next morning, Macnamara, Francis, Wood and three others – Thomas Broughton, a short, pale, often smiling Lincolnshireman of twenty-five; James Wratten, aged thirty-three, a hungry-looking shoemaker; Arthur Graham, a Westminster slater of 'sottish appearance,' the eldest at fifty-three – were also

pronounced guilty. Then they were joined by Despard to hear
whether, or not, they faced the medieval punishment that had
been traditional for those convicted of high treason.

Lord Ellenborough took his time in delivering the sentence
prescribed by law and, after a lengthy condemnation of the
conspiracy, concluded, 'It only remains for me to pronounce the
sad and painful sentence of the law upon the crime of which you
are convicted. . . .

'That you, the several prisoners at the bar, be severally
taken from hence to the place from whence you came, and from
thence be severally drawn on an hurdle to the place of
execution, and there be severally hanged by the neck, but not
until you are dead, but that you be severally taken down again,
and whilst you are yet alive, your bowels be taken out and
burnt before your faces; and that afterwards your heads be
severed from your bodies, and your bodies be divided each into
four quarters, and your heads and quarters be at the King's
disposal.

'And may God Almighty have mercy on your souls.'

There was an appalled quiet and one who was present wrote,
'The whole of this pathetic address was heard with the most
profound silence and every eye was suffused in tears.' The
condemned prisoners 'conducted themselves with propriety and
decorum' but their womenfolk broke down. Later, in the
condemned cell, Despard was said to 'entertain some slight
hopes of mercy in consequence of . . . . the powerful
mediation of Lord Nelson, but he appeared prepared for either
alternative', while his wife was 'less sanguine and had almost
sunk under the anticipated horror of his fate.'

Nelson was staying at the Hamilton's house in Piccadilly;
his days kept busy with political activity at the House of Lords,
but — as Emma and Sir William were at Merton — his evenings
spent with men friends. Amongst these was the Earl of Minto,
who, as Sir Gilbert Elliot, had governed Corsica after Nelson
had played so prominent a part in taking the island in 1794 as
the principal British base in the Mediterranean. Their conversation alternated between the present and the worsening
relations with France, and the past and Edward Despard.

'We had a great deal of conversation about Despard,' wrote

Minto in a letter to his wife. 'Lord Nelson seems to have been quite right all through and to have behaved with a due mixture of generosity and private feeling with public propriety.'

Then, a few days later, a letter reached 23 Piccadilly from the prison in Horsemonger Lane. Nelson read it with emotion, then forwarded it, without comment, to Henry Addington, who had succeeded William Pitt as Prime Minister. Later he discussed it with Minto, who wrote, 'My dinner at Nelson's was entertaining enough. A great deal of talk about Despard. Nelson read us a letter written to him by Despard . . . . extremely well written and it would have been affecting from any other pen. It spoke in high strain, you may suppose, of his gratitude to Nelson, whose evidence, he says, produced the jury's recommendation. Whether his days were many or few, he said, he would have no other inscription on his tomb than the character given him by Nelson at the trial; he enclosed a petition for pardon, but said hardly anything on the subject.

'Nelson merely sent the letter and petition, just as he had received them, to Mr. Addington, who told Nelson afterwards that he and his family had sat up after supper, weeping over the letter.'

Any hope of a pardon was dashed, when, on Saturday, 19th February, the warrants for the executions were delivered at the prison. There was one small mercy: the King had been 'graciously pleased' to remit part of the sentence, 'viz. the taking out and burning their bowels before their faces' and the quartering of their bodies. Instead they were to be hanged and beheaded after death. On being told, Despard appeared shaken for a moment, then recovered his composure, but his wife was 'extremely affected and during the whole night her grief was overwhelming.'

The executions were to take place together on a large gallows and scaffold erected on the flat roof of the entrance lodge in front of the square, three-storey prison. Meanwhile, the prisoners would be expected to make their peace with God. On Sunday morning, all but two of the condemned men were taken to the grim prison chapel, with its two tiers of barred galleries, where the chaplain 'delivered a very impressive sermon, peculiarly applicable to the fate of the unhappy prisoners.' Macnamara was comforted by a Roman Catholic priest but Despard refused any such solace, explaining that he was an atheist and relying upon his own thoughts and courage. Early that evening, Mrs. Despard was allowed to visit her husband for the last time. 'The colonel betrayed nothing like unbecoming weakness,' it was reported, and when a woman relation, who had accompanied his wife, wept bitterly 'he gently reproached her for thus suffering her feelings to overpower her fortitude.'

When his mistress left, Despard flung himself on his bed and slept briefly. At eight, he woke suddenly and a surprised warder heard him say, 'Me – no never – I'll divulge nothing. No, not for all the treasure the King is worth.' Thinking that he might be talking in his sleep, the warder asked quietly, 'Are you asleep?' 'No,' came the reply. 'Do you know what you have just said?' 'Yes – I said it that you might hear.' But Despard never explained what he meant: whether it was, as it seemed, an affirmation of his resolve not to turn King's evidence, or just a dream from which he had awoken.

Then his solicitor entered the cell to ask where he wished to be buried. He was silent for a moment, then said that he believed Irishmen were often buried at St. Pancras, so it should be there. Again he refused the ministrations of the chaplain, who joined the other prisoners to pass the long night 'in deep and earnest prayer.'

Yet the condemned man's relations with the chaplain were mutually respectful. When the priest had tried to persuade him to read a Bible, Despard pointed to the irons on his leg and said, 'Do not attempt to put shackles on my mind as on my body.' Then, adding that he was always glad to see the chaplain as a friend, suggested that he might care to read a book on logic.

The day of the executions dawned cold and cloudy and, before light, vast crowds began moving towards Horsemonger Lane. In readiness for any disturbance, detachments of the Horse Guards were deployed around the scaffold and the Scots Greys in neighbouring streets, while the Guards at the Tower and Knightsbridge Barracks were under arms 'ready to march at a moment's notice.'

At five o'clock, when the bell of St. George's parish church began to toll, the streets around the prison, and every window and rooftop with a view of the scaffold, was crowded. It was a subdued, murmuring crowd, said to number twenty thousand. At half-past six, the prison bell rang as a signal to unlock the cells and the prisoners were taken back to the chapel for a service lasting three-quarters of an hour, while Despard and Macnamara were brought out into the courtyard for their irons to be knocked off and their arms pionioned. When the two met, Macnamara remarked, 'I am afraid, colonel, we have got into a bad situation.'

'There are many better,' replied Despard, 'and some worse.'

Whereupon he paced to and fro before the chapel door until this opened and the others, having received the Last Sacrament, were led out to be similarly bound. At eight, the procession to the gallows began, led by the Sheriff of Surrey, the chaplain and the executioner with a drawn sword, to join nearly a hundred spectators on the scaffold, where the ropes, the axe, block, a bag of sawdust and the seven coffins were ready.

Now a small cart, from which the wheels had been removed, was drawn by two horses into the courtyard. This was the hurdle, in which the prisoners were to be drawn to their deaths. They went two by two: Macnamara and Graham; Broughton and Wratten; then Wood and Francis; Despard, last. Arrived at the scaffold, Macnamara climbed the steps first and as the noose was fastened round his neck, he prayed, 'Lord Jesus, have mercy upon me!' Graham looked pale, Wratten resolute, and Broughton smiled as he ran up the steps, to turn pale as the noose was made fast. Then Francis – 'tall, handsome and well made' – and Wood followed, dressed in their soldiers' red coats.

Despard went up last, 'with great firmness', dressed in a brown greatcoat and boots, his hair unpowdered, and took his place next to Francis. When the noose was slipped over his head, he himself adjusted the knot to beneath his left ear – in the hope of instant death – and a hood was then placed on his head like a stocking-cap. The chaplain spoke a few words to each, Despard thanked him with a little bow and then all was ready.

[226]

Now Despard spoke to the Sheriff and asked if he might address the crowd. This was allowed, with the warning that if he said anything 'inflammatory or improper', the platform would instantly be dropped. So, stepping as close to the edge of the scaffold as the halter would allow, he began, 'Fellow citizens, I am come here as you see, after having served my country faithfully, honourably and, I trust, usefully, for thirty years to suffer death upon a scaffold for a crime, which I am no more guilty of than any man who is now looking at me.'

The platform was not dropped perhaps because the Sheriff took this to be a simple plea of innocence and not a declaration that Despard, as an Irishman, did not recognise the jurisdiction of the King, nor, therefore, his own conviction of high treason.

'I do solemnly declare that I am no more guilty of it than any of you who may be now listening to me. But though His Majesty's ministers know I am not guilty, they avail themselves of the opportunity, which they have of destroying a man, because they think he is a friend to the poor and the oppressed. But, fellow citizens, I hope and trust that, notwithstanding my fate, and, perhaps, the fate of many others, who may follow me, that still the principles of liberty, justice and humanity will triumph over falsehood, despotism and delusion and everything else hostile to the interests of the human race. And now, having said this, I have nothing more to add but to wish you all that health, that happiness and that freedom, which I have made it my endeavour, as far as lay in my power, to procure for every one of you and for mankind in general.'

That was the version published in *The Times* next day, but another, circulated in the taverns where the Constitution Society had met, added the words, 'I know that, from having been inimical to the bloody, cruel, coercive and uncon-stitutional measures of Ministers, they have determined to sacrifice me under what they are pleased to term a legal pretext . . . . Although I shall not live to experience the blessings of the godlike change, be assured, Citizens, that the period will come, and that *speedily*, when the glorious cause of Liberty shall effectually triumph.'

There was a scatter of applause around the scaffold from 'Friends of the Cause', but otherwise his words were heard in awestruck silence. As Despard stepped back into line, he turned to Francis, standing next to him, and remarked, 'What an amazing crowd!'

All on the scaffold – excepting Despard – now joined in the Lord's Prayer.

Then the chaplain began to move down the line again, shaking hands with each. Despard looked at the sky and said to Francis, ' 'Tis very cold. I think we shall have some rain.' Then the hoods were pulled down over their faces, the chaplain stood back and the executioner descended to attend to the mechanism of the drop beneath the scaffold.

'The last and most dreadful part of the ceremony was now about to be performed,' said one who was present. 'The most awful silence prevailed and the thousands present all, with one accord, stood uncovered. At seven minutes before nine o'clock, the signal was given, the platform dropped and they were all launched into eternity.'

Despard died instantly, his hands twice convulsively clenching. Macnamara, Wood, Graham and Wratten struggled briefly, but Francis and Broughton writhed and the executioner pulled at their legs to hasten the end. After hanging for half an hour, the seven dead men were cut down and their bodies taken to the back of the scaffold for decapitation. A moment later, the executioner stepped to the front of the scaffold, held up something that caused a gasp of horror and shouted, 'Behold the head of a traitor – Edward Marcus Despard!'

EPILOGUE

The black plumes and black horses of a hearse, followed by three mourning coaches, waited outside the undertakers' parlour in Lambeth on the morning of Tuesday, 1st March, while crowds gathered to watch the funeral procession of the late, notorious Colonel Despard. But few can have noticed the arrival there of a small, middle-aged, bird-like woman, carrying a bag containing the tools and materials of her trade. However, next morning, *The Times* reported that, 'An artist, it is said, took a cast of Mr. Despard's face a few minutes before the lid of the coffin was screwed down.'

The name of the artist was Marie Tussaud and her task that morning seemed, to her, no more than a commercial opportunity and certainly not ghoulish. In Paris, during the French Revolution, she had often made death-masks from the severed heads of celebrities executed by guillotine and, once initial scruples had been overcome, it was simple for there was no need to insert quills into the nostrils to allow breathing. In this case, the face of Colonel Despard would surely prove a sensational addition to her travelling exhibition of wax figures, particularly if lit by a ghastly blue light.

When she had completed her work, the procession moved away, reaching Blackfriars Bridge as the bells of the city churches chimed at mid-day. More than a hundred constables accompanied the hearse but the vast crowds were silent and orderly. Crossing the Thames, the sound of the horses and wheels could be heard in the silence as they reached the corner of Fleet Street and turned right for the gentle ascent of Ludgate Hill towards St. Paul's Cathedral.

Something of a sensation had been caused by the news that the traitor was not, after all, to be buried among the Irish at St. Pancras, but in the shadow of Sir Christopher Wren's great domed church that dominated London. When the King had

[229]

given sanction for the body to be returned to his widow, it had been realised that he was eligible for burial in the churchyard of St. Faith, a long-vanished medieval church that had stood near St. Paul's, its burial-ground now within the cathedral's bounds. With the support of Sir Francis Burdett, who had pressed for his release from prison two years before, permission was granted.

The ceremony had been delayed a few days so that Despard's supposed son could return from France for the occasion. He had joined the Army and held the rank of ensign at the time of his father's arrest. He then left for Paris but, on his return, resolved to return to Jamaica and is thought to have held a commission in the West Indies Regiment.

Watched from crowded windows, the procession passed round the cathedral and entered St. Paul's churchyard by the north gate. The grave, fourteen and a half feet deep, had been dug close to the north door; there the brief committal ceremony was conducted and completed before the great bell of the cathedral struck one o'clock.

While Despard's memory was kept gruesomely alive by the exhibition of his blue-lit features in Madame Tussaud's Grand European Cabinet of Figures, his widow was not forgotten by her husband's most illustrious friend. Although Nelson had been shocked by the defiance implicit in Despard's final denial of his guilt, he was moved by the widow's distress and spoke of it to Lord Minto, who wrote, 'Mrs. Despard, he says, was violently in love with her husband, which makes the last scene of the tragedy affecting indeed. Lord Nelson solicited a pension, or some provision for her, and the Government was well disposed to grant it; but the last act on the scaffold may have defeated any chance of indulgence to any member of his family.'

In the event, it was Sir Francis Burdett who saw to her welfare, so impressed had he, too, been by 'her fidelity in every situation to the last.' He arranged her passage to Ireland, where he maintained her until her death. Her son, however, was not regarded by Despard's relations as a member of the family and was later dismissed as a gambler and rake.

The trial and death of Despard coincided with the end of more than two years of peace and tranquillity in Nelson's life.

Increasingly, life at 'Paradise Merton' had become less idyllic as Sir William Hamilton, now aged seventy-two, at last became irritated by his wife's pre-occupation with her lover and his friend, and he was visibly ailing. He returned to his house in Piccadilly, where, comforted by both Emma and Nelson, he died on 6th April.

The prospect of continued peace in Europe was again in the balance and Nelson was preparing himself for a return to active service. After visiting Lord Minto, the latter wrote, 'He told me in strict confidence that for some time back there have been great doubts between peace and war and that still Government is under the greatest uncertainty whether they shall be forced to some hostile measure or not. One of those in contemplation has been to send him to the Mediterranean, by way of watching the armament and being ready if wanted. He says he is thought fitter for that delicate service, as on the one hand he wishes the continuance of peace, and therefore is not likely to precipitate matters; and, on the other, Bonaparte knows that if he hoists his flag it will not be a joke.'

In the event, the Admiralty announced his appointment to command in the Mediterranean two days before France declared war and, two days later, he hoisted his flag in the great first-rate *Victory* at Portsmouth. There was to be no immediate cataclysmic confrontation at sea, but the weary months of blockading the French fleet in Toulon, that prevented Bonaparte from fulfilling his ambition to invade England. For nearly two years, Nelson never set foot ashore.

Early in 1805, the French twice escaped from Toulon: the first time, to be driven back by bad weather; the second, in April, to escape through the Straits of Gibraltar into the Atlantic. The instructions to the French admiral, the Comte de Villeneuve, was to make for the West Indies and, after devastating the British islands there, join with other squadrons and sweep back across the Atlantic to take control of the English Channel and enable an invasion army to cross. Following in Villeneuve's wake, Nelson soon realised that, once again, he was bound for 'The Grand Theatre of Actions.'

Again he sailed the deep, blue waters of the Caribbean and scanned the hard line of its horizon for enemy sails. Again, he

[231]

anchored in Carlisle Bay at Barbados and recognised again the once-familiar shapes of the Leeward Islands. He searched from Tobago to Antigua but the French remained ahead. Between poring over charts and assessing the latest reports of sightings from frigates, or merchantmen, he entertained his young officers to dinner in the great cabin, and to one of them he could talk with particular feeling of these seas and of the great adventure that he and the boy's father had shared; for Midshipman Richard Bulkeley was now serving in the flagship.

Nelson followed Villeneuve back across the Atlantic to find that he had been able to take refuge in Cadiz, where the Spanish fleet also lay. So he returned, disappointed, to England, to find that he still had the trust – and, indeed, love – of his compatriots. There was, waiting for him, a letter from Hercules Ross, written from his castle in Scotland.

'My dear Lord,' he had written, 'I have both by night and day accompanied your Lordship across the Atlantic and as far to the westward as the scene of our earlier days, and imagination has often carried me aloft to look for the flying enemy.

'Though disappointed, thank God my noble friend has returned in health, but that there remains some great action to be achieved by him worthy of his fame.'

That great action was to be fought off Cape Trafalgar on 21st October that year.

Nelson had made his farewells with Emma Hamilton and their daughter, Horatia, at Merton, and returned to the sea. Again he was in the *Victory* but now blockading the combined fleets of France and Spain in Cadiz. Once again he was with Cuthbert Collingwood; now a vice-admiral and his second-in-command. On the day after the enemy had broken out of harbour and thirty-three of their ships of the line were being brought to battle by Nelson's twenty-seven, bearing down in two divisions upon the enemy's line, one led by himself, the other by his old friend, he exclaimed, 'See how that fine fellow Collingwood carries his ship into action!'

At the height of the battle then beginning, Nelson, pacing his quarterdeck and shielded from enemy fire only by gunsmoke, was shot by a sniper and carried below. As he lay dying amongst the wounded, while the great ship jarred and shuddered with each broadside fired or received, he spoke his last words and pleaded for the future welfare of Emma and Horatia. Before he sank into unconsciousness, a midshipman came down with a message for his flag-captain, Hardy, who was with him. Nelson asked who the messenger was and was told it was Midshipman Bulkeley. 'It is his voice,' said the dying man; then, to the son of his comrade of those distant days in Nicaragua: 'Remember me to your father.'

The death of Nelson and his victory at Trafalgar threw the British people into the mingled anguish and ecstacy that was expressed in the vast display of public emotion on the day of his funeral. On the cold, raw morning of 9th January, 1806, the streets of London filled with crowds of a size not then remembered; the largest, certainly, since those that had watched the killing of Colonel Despard three years before.

To the throb of muffled drums, the head of the funeral procession had reached St. Paul's Cathedral, where the dead hero was to lie, before his body had left the Admiralty in Whitehall. It was a massive congress of his friends: those who had known him as a private man – including Admiral of the Fleet Sir Peter Parker, now aged eighty-five and following the coffin as chief mourner, with his memories of Port Royal and Spanish Town; and Alexander Davison, who had kept him to his duty at Quebec – and those who had never spoken with him, but held him as a friend.

Nelson was laid in a marble sarcophagus in the crypt, directly beneath the golden cross at the summit of the dome that shines over London in the sun. Five years later, when Cuthbert Collingwood died, his body was brought home from the sea and also taken to the crypt of the cathedral. There they lie today: Nelson in his glory, with the faithful Collingwood ten paces to his left. Some seventy paces to his right, though there is no monument in commemoration, was, and is, Edward Despard, two centuries after they shared a tent on the banks of a river in the jungle.

Notes on Manuscript Sources

The bulk of the hitherto unpublished material relating to the San Juan expedition is in the Public Record Office, mostly in volumes 76 to 82 of the 137 series of Colonial Office papers. More is in the Admiralty letter-books of the period, captains' logs and ships' muster-books. The official reports on the Despard conspiracy and trial are in the 11th series of the Treasury Solicitor's papers, items 121 and 332.

Further unpublished, and unfamiliar material is in the Manuscript Department of the British Library, where documents relevant to the West Indies and North America are also to be found; in the Nelson Papers at the National Maritime Museum, Greenwich; and the Nelson Papers in the Nelson Collection at the Monmouth Museum, Gwent. Some of the Despard family papers – including a memoir by Elizabeth Despard (1770 – 1866), Colonel Despard's niece–are in the possession of Mr. M.H. Despard. Those of Hercules Ross of Jamaica are in the possession of Mr. Hercules Ross and in the Royal Naval Museum, Portsmouth.

SELECT BIBLIOGRAPHY

Bannantine, James. *Memoirs of Colonel Despard* (1799).

Bennett, Geoffrey. *Nelson the Commander* (1972).

Brett, Thomas. *A Naturalist in Nicaragua* (1874).

Clarke, J. and McArthur, J. *The Life and Services of Horatio, Viscount Nelson* (1809).

Dancer, Dr. Thomas. *A Brief History of the Late Expedition against Fort San Juan* (1781).

Feurtado, W.A. *Official and Other Personages of Jamaica* (1896).

Fortescue, Sir John. *The History of the British Army* (1903).

Gurney, Joseph and William. *The Trial of Edward Marcus Despard* (1803).

LeMoine, Sir James. *Quebec Past and Present* (1876).

LeMoine, Sir James. *Picturesque Quebec* (1882).

Lloyd, Christopher and J. L. S. Coulter. *Medicine in the Navy: 1714 – 1815* (1961).

Matcham, George. *Notes on the Character of Lord Nelson* (1861).

Matcham, M. Eyre. *The Nelsons of Burnham Thorpe* (1911).

Metcalf, George. *Royal Government and Political Conflict in Jamaica: 1729 – 1783* (1965).

Meyer, Harvey K. *Historical Dictionary of Nicaragua* (1972).

Minto, Countess of. *The Life and Letters of Sir Gilbert Elliot* (1874).

Moreton, J. B. *West India Customs and Manners* (1793).

Moseley, Benjamin. *Treatise on Tropical Diseases* (1795 and 1804).

Naish, G. P. B. *Nelson's Letters to his Wife* (1958).

Nicolas, Sir Harris. *The Letters and Dispatches of Lord Nelson* (1844–46).

Nugent, Maria, Lady. *Lady Nugent's Journal* (1907).

Oman, Carola. *Nelson* (1947).

Oman, Sir Charles. *The Unfortunate Colonel Despard and Other Essays* (1922).

Rawson, Geoffrey (ed.) *Nelson's Letters from the Leeward Islands* (1953).

Roberts, Orlando W. *A Narrative of Voyages and Excursions on the East Coast and in the Interior of Central America* (1827).

Spinney, David. *Rodney* (1969).

Squier, E. G. *Nicaragua: Its People, Scenery and Monuments* (1860).

Thompson, E. P. *The Making of the English Working Class* (1963).

Valentine, Alan. *Lord George Germain* (1962).

Warner, Oliver. *A Portrait of Lord Nelson* (1965).

Warner, Oliver. *The Life and Letters of Vice-Admiral Lord Collingwood* (1969).

Wilkie, Colonel Fletcher. *The Military History of Jamaica* (United Service Journal, 1842).

Dictionary of National Biography.
Navy List.
Army List.
West Indies Pilot.
Bath Chronicle.
Bath Journal.
Gentleman's Magazine.
Jamaica Gazette.
Liverpool Advertiser.
London Gazette.
The Mariner's Mirror.
Quebec Gazette.
The Times.

INDEX

INDEX

INDEX